NEW DIRECTIONS IN
Biblical
Archaeology

NEW DIRECTIONS IN

Biblical Archaeology

EDITED BY

DAVID NOEL FREEDMAN AND

JONAS C. GREENFIELD

GARDEN CITY, NEW YORK

DOUBLEDAY & COMPANY, INC.

1969

Thanks are due to *McCormick Quarterly*, which first published the following articles: *The Early History of the Qumran Community*, Frank Moore Cross; *Twenty Years of Discovery*, Robert G. Boling; *The Scrolls and the Old Testament Text*, Patrick W. Skehan; *Cave 11 Surprises and the Question of Canon*, James A. Sanders; *The Old Testament at Qumran*, David Noel Freedman; *The Dead Sea Scrolls and the New Testament*, Floyd V. Filson; *A Qumran Bibliography*, Edward F. Campbell, Jr., and Robert G. Boling.

Grateful acknowledgment is made to *The Biblical Archaeologist* for permission to reprint "The Temple Scroll" by Yigael Yadin, appearing in *The Biblical Archaeologist* issue of December 1967. Copyright 1967 by American Schools of Oriental Research.

Contents

Preface

On March 14–16, 1966, a Symposium on Biblical Archaeology was held in the San Francisco Bay Area under the joint sponsorship of the Department of Near Eastern Languages of the University of California at Berkeley and the biblical studies faculties of the Graduate Theological Union of Berkeley and San Francisco Theological Seminary of San Anselmo. The purpose of the conference was to gather outstanding leaders in this field and have them present the results of their most recent research and reflections. The principal speakers were Professor William F. Albright (John Hopkins University), Dr. Yohanan Aharoni (Hebrew University), Professor Frank M. Cross, Jr. (Harvard University), Dr. Moshe Dothan (Israel Department of Antiquities and Museums), Dr. Trude Dothan (Hebrew University), and Professor G. Ernest Wright (Harvard University).

The Israeli scholars were currently involved in excavations and related archaeological research: Aharoni as director at Arad, and the Dothans at Ashdod, and particularly with the Philistines. Their papers inevitably reflected the excitement of recent discovery and exhibited the first efforts at interpretation and synthesis of the data.

The Americans all have long been associated with archaeological activity in the Holy Land. As the dean of Palestinian excavators and mentor, directly or indirectly, of most of those presently active in this field, Albright was the logical choice to initiate the discussion. He provided a survey of the present state of the discipline, an evaluation of recent discoveries, and a prognosis for the future. Cross, a leading authority on Hebrew and Aramaic epigraphy, had just been assigned the newly discovered Dâliyeh papyri and seals for scholarly study and ultimate publication. He presented a preliminary report on these extraordinary materials. Wright's career as archaeologist, biblical scholar, and theologian has spanned three decades. During that time he has maintained an abiding interest in the relationship between archaeological research and the articulation of biblical religion. His paper treated freshly that difficult and much debated issue.

The sponsors planned that the papers would be discussed in open meetings attended by the other speakers. It was also their hope that these discussions would prove reciprocally stimulating to the speakers, and edifying to the audience. In this expectation none was disappointed; and many of the insights offered and comments made have found their way into the revised drafts that are published in this volume.

A word of explanation about the time lapse between the Symposium and the Symposium volume is doubtless in order. Original plans for immediate publication were shelved in favor of a more leisurely yet equally demanding schedule. It seemed wiser to allow the participants time to absorb the effects of the critical confrontation at the Symposium, and also to incorporate new data (which are constantly being brought to light) into the published versions of their papers. As a result the articles have the substance of 1966, but the overtones of 1969. The discoveries are no longer new, but they are not less important. At the same time the analyses and projections put forward on a provisional basis three years ago have a different look. Some have been withdrawn prudently, others have been altered significantly, still others have advanced to the status of prevailing view or accepted hypothesis, buttressed by much evidence and compelling arguments.

Much has happened in the meantime. New finds, new names, and new places are mentioned in these reports. One of the more exciting discoveries of the past year was the Temple Scroll, the latest, longest, and possibly the most important of the famous Dead Sea scrolls. A preliminary report on its contents by the scholar now preparing it for publication, Yigael Yadin, is included here. Since its acquisition was publicly announced just twenty years after the first Dead Sea scrolls were found, it seemed fitting to add a group of articles on the Dead Sea scrolls, assembled in the *McCormick Quarterly* for March 1968. In this way we have been able to provide here a comprehensive survey of the work being done in a major area of biblical archaeology and research that was necessarily by-passed in the Berkeley Symposium of 1966. The six articles in the colloquy cover the principal topics of interest, placing the manuscripts in the setting of the Qumran community, and describing their relationship to the biblical literature of both Old and New Testaments.

The New Directions of 1966–69 remain the directions, the concerns and the objectives of biblical archaeologists, both the professionals who write and the amateurs who read.

DAVID NOEL FREEDMAN
JONAS C. GREENFIELD

May 1969

CHRONOLOGICAL TABLE

ACCORDING TO

W. F. ALBRIGHT (OCTOBER 1968)

	B.C.E.
Lower Paleolithic (Challean, etc.) ends before	60,000
Middle Paleolithic (Mousterian, etc.) ends before	30,000
Upper Paleolithic (Aurignacian, etc.) ends before	10,000
Lower Mesolithic (Kebaran) ends after	11,000
End of Lisan Pluvial Age	ca. 9000
Upper Mesolithic (Natufian) begins after	9000
Pre-pottery Neolithic, begins after	7000
Pottery Neolithic, begins after	5500
Chalcolithic, begins after	4000
Early Bronze I	ca. 3100–2800
Early Bronze II	ca. 2800–2500
Early Bronze III A	ca. 2500–2400
Early Bronze III B	ca. 2400–2300
Early Bronze III C	ca. 2300–2200
Early Bronze IV (First Intermediate)	ca. 2200–2000
Middle Bronze I (XIIth Dynasty)	ca. 2000–1800
Middle Bronze II A (XIIIth Dynasty)	ca. 1800–1725
Middle Bronze II B (Early Hyksos)	ca. 1725–1600
Middle Bronze II C (Late Hyksos)	ca. 1600–1525
Late Bronze I (Early XVIIIth Dynasty)	ca. 1525–1400
Late Bronze II (Late XVIIIth & XIXth Dynasties)	ca. 1400–1225
Amarna Age	ca. 1375–1350
Exodus	early 13th Century
Israelite Conquest of Palestine	between 1275 and 1225
Philistine Occupation of the Coast	between 1225 and 1175
Philistine Conquest of Western Palestine	between 1050 and 1025

Accession of David	ca. 1000
Division of Monarchy	ca. 922
Assyrian Destruction of Samaria	early 721
Babylonian Destruction of Jerusalem	ca. 587
Persian Conquest of Palestine	539
Macedonian Conquest of Palestine	ca. 330
Antiochus IV Ephiphanes	175–164
Jewish Revolt, raised by Mattathias and his sons, helped by the Asideans (*Hasidim*)	167
Judas Maccabaeus	166–160
Demetrius I Soter	162–150
Jonathan	160–142
Jonathan named High Priest by Alexander	152
Alexander Balas	150–145
Exodus of Essenes to Qumrân, led by the Teacher of Righteousness (QT)	ca. 150
Demetrius II	145–138
Antiochus VI	145–142
Tryphon executes Jonathan	142
Simon appointed by Demetrius High Priest and Ethnarch of the Jews	143–134
Simon and his sons appointed High Priests forever, by popular vote	141
Antiochus VII Sidetes	138–129
John Hyrcanus I, High Priest and Ethnarch	134–104
Demetrius II (bis)	129–125
Enlarging of Qumrân buildings (Phase Ib)	ca. 110
Aristobulus I High Priest and King	104–103
Alexander Jannaeus	103–76
Demetrius III Eukairos	95–78
[*Dm*]*trys* fails to take Jerusalem (QT) "Lion of Wrath" crucifies many of his enemies (QT)	88
Alexandra (*Šalamsiyón*) Queen, Hyrcanus II High Priest	76–67
Aristobulus II High Priest and King	67–63
Pompey in the East	66–62
Pompey captures Jerusalem	63
Hyrcanus II High Priest	63–40
Antigonus High Priest and King	40–37
Herod the Great King	37–34
(Jos.) Earthquake damages Qumrân	31

Gap in occupation of Qumrân	?–ca. 4
Archelaus Ethnarch of Judea and Samaria	4 B.C.E.–C.E. 6
Essene reconstruction of Qumrân	ca. 4
Nero	54–68
First Jewish Revolt	66–70
Destruction of Qumrân	68

List of Illustrations

Abbreviations

BA	*The Biblical Archaeologist*
BANE	*The Bible and the Ancient Near East: Essays in Honor of William Foxwell Albright,* ed. G. Ernest Wright (New York: Doubleday, 1961)
BASOR	*Bulletin of the American Schools of Oriental Research*
BJRL	*Bulletin of the John Rylands Library*
CBQ	*Catholic Biblical Quarterly*
DJD	*Discoveries in the Judaean Desert*
HDSB	*Harvard Divinity School Bulletin*
HTR	*Harvard Theological Review*
HUCA	*Hebrew Union College Annual*
IEJ	*Israel Exploration Journal*
JBL	*Journal of Biblical Literature and Exegesis*
JNES	*Journal of Near Eastern Studies*
JSS	*Journal of Semitic Studies*
JTS	*Journal of Theological Studies*
NTS	*New Testament Studies*
OTS	*Oudtestamentische Studien*
RB	*Revue biblique*
RQ	*Revue de Qumran*
RSO	*Rivista degli studi orientali*
TLZ	*Theologische Literaturzeitung*
VT	*Vetus Testamentum*
VTS	*Vetus Testamentum Supplements*
ZAW	*Zeitschrift für die alttestamentliche Wissenschaft*

NEW DIRECTIONS IN
Biblical
Archaeology

The Impact of Archaeology on Biblical Research—1966

W. F. ALBRIGHT

The title of my lecture has three terms which I must define: archaeology, biblical research—and 1966.

First, what is archaeology? A good many things can be said about it. Already it is the favorite avocation of a host of Anglo-Saxons and Israelis—and now the Japanese are actively competing with the West, not only in science and mathematics, but even in archaeology. The University of Tokyo has brought out six massive volumes on the archaeology of western Asia and many more are in preparation, including several on the results of work in Israel. Since the director of the expedition in Israel is a Buddhist, the Japanese consider themselves quite independent of any Jewish or Christian bias. If they follow strictly scientific methods, their results will agree with those obtained by good Jewish and Christian scholars. It must even be confessed that the West can seldom afford any longer to publish such sumptuous volumes on archaeological stratigraphy as the Japanese are bringing out!

Let us first define biblical archaeology in time. In my usage it extends from about 9000 B.C.E. to about 700 C.E., a few generations after the Arab conquest. Of course this does not mean that remains of earlier or later date are without significance, only that in such ancient and modern times we soon reach periods of diminishing returns for biblical research.

Then we must delimit the geographical space that is covered by biblical archaeology. It is true that Palestine is the homeland of both the Old and New Testaments. But in order to study biblical archaeology properly, one should know as much as practicable about the archaeology of all ancient lands from the Atlantic to India. All these countries are mentioned in the Old Testament—from the Phoenician colonies in northwest Africa and Spain to the Indus Valley. Phoenician and Hebrew were sister dialects, both descended from South Canaanite; they were virtually identical in Galilee and close to one another in Samaria. Even in Judah the difference was slight. In fact, Hebrew was called "the language of Canaan (Phoenicia)" down to the time of Isaiah. A distance of over four thousand miles from west to east and of more than two thousand miles from north to south about covers the geographical range of biblical archaeology. Palestine is especially significant, but the Hebrews of the Bible came from Mesopotamia and part of them lived for centuries in Egypt. The more we learn about the civilization of ancient Israel, the more important do its principal components become.

In many ways the Phoenicians, who shared a common border with Israel for about half of its total western and northern boundary, also shared a common culture. The Phoenicians, at least as early as the ninth and probably by the tenth century B.C.E., were extending their activities as far as western Spain. Hardly any Phoenician remains have been found in eastern Spain, but the earliest Phoenician trade routes ran from Cádiz up the valley of the Guadalquivir and to northwestern Spain, past the frontiers of Portugal, by Aliseda (Cáceres). The minerals of northwestern Spain were brought south over this route to be exchanged for trade goods from the eastern Mediterranean. It was unsafe to use the Atlantic route because of winter storms and summer piracy.

In short, the phrase "Bible Lands" covers an area far larger than the forty-eight states of the continental United States, a rough ellipse of over five million square miles, all of which has some meaning for biblical archaeology.

In the third place we must consider the kinds of material with which one deals in biblical archaeology. Here we have not only unwritten documents—in other words, artifacts made by human hands, including cities, fortress walls, public buildings, houses and tombs, down to household objects of all kinds; but also all ancient written objects found in exploring and excavating. Since the Bible is a collection of writings, we shall naturally learn more about it from written sources than from unwritten. Yet we must remember that writing without artifacts is like flesh without a skeleton, and artifacts without writing are a skeleton without flesh.

Methodologically considered, archaeology includes stratigraphy and typology, that is to say, the analysis of superimposed layers of remains, and the classification and comparative study of objects. The upper strata of a site are nearly always later than the lower ones, though there is generally some confusion caused by earlier debris being washed down over later debris or by ancient pits being dug into or through older strata, which often reverse normal stratification or confuse it. Turning to artifacts, one must study them as classes and as smaller groups, much as Linnaeus classified plants and animals over two centuries ago. The typological classification of artifacts is in principle very much like that of living beings, along the lines of genus and species taxonomy sketched by Aristotle over 2,300 years ago.

The evolutionary principles involved are curiously similar, even though phylogeny is the result of genetic processes, and the development of artifacts is the result of imitation. The distinguished vertebrate paleontologist of Harvard University, George G. Simpson, has long insisted that it makes little difference in the mathematical theory of evolution whether one is dealing with imitation or with genetic processes; evolution follows very much the same basic principles in both. (By this I mean, of course, mathematical and not "biological" principles.) This was pointed out originally by Simpson's teacher, Bashford Dean, curator of medieval armor in the Metropolitan Museum of Art as well as of fossil fish in the American Museum of Natural History in New York. Dean had found, in the course of his work in these superficially so divergent disciplines, that the evolution of medieval armor and of fossil fish had a great deal in common.

Having defined "archaeology," one must fix the meaning of "biblical research." For my purpose it may be defined as the systematic analysis or synthesis of any phase of biblical scholarship which can be clarified by archaeological discovery.

Our approach must be historical in the broadest sense. Every biblical unit is either historical in content or reflects a given stage of history. No matter how little history a biblical book may seem to contain, it originated in a historical situation and reflects a definite stage in the history of religion, the history of ideas, the history of institutions, and the history of the Hebrew language. Naturally, every historical approach has its limitations. We can never tell by the use of approved historical methods what the innermost thoughts of David were, any more than we can reconstruct the mind of Woodrow Wilson or John F. Kennedy. No matter how intensively we study documents and memoirs, we can seldom know what any great man may have intended at a given moment. Nor can we know what happened privately in ancient times. Events must be matters of public knowledge and phenomena must be attested by scientific methods in order to enable the historian to be sure of them. The historian who claims too much for history will find himself in the position of the late R. G. Collingwood, who doubled as archaeologist and philosopher in order to clothe the bare bones of his excavations with the aid of metaphysics. His book on Roman Britain was long a classic. But Collingwood was not satisfied; he wanted to give archaeological remains meaning by resorting to the neo-Hegelianism of Croce and the historical relativism of Dilthey, who carried on the tradition of Schleiermacher. Collingwood wrote delightful essays, but was never able to produce a magic key to historical consciousness, whether dead or living.

In trying to understand the past there are important facts to be borne in mind. Man attained his present taxonomic status as *Homo sapiens* at least 150,000 years ago, probably before the beginning of the Abbevillian culture of Western Europe. (I follow the Emiliani correlation.[1]) By that time he must have possessed language and religion, as well as remarkable skill in making tools. At least 70,000 years ago, people were already living in stone "villages" in southeastern France. Some 40,000 years ago Middle Stone Age men in central Russia were buried in romper-like fur garments covering the entire body below the waist, with small fur jackets above. Some 20,000 years later the prehistoric Moravians were making animal figurines of baked clay and their neighbors in France and Spain were at work on the cave paintings of Altamira and Les Eyzies.

Until very recently it was thought by many scholars who accepted the late Vere Gordon Childe's hypothesis of a "Neolithic Revolution" that most of the innovations which distinguished pre-Neolithic primitives from modern man were introduced into the Middle East suddenly, about the fifth millennium B.C.E. We now know that planting and reaping grain, together with incipient village life, began immediately after the end of the last Ice Age (the last Pluvial of Palestine), about 9000 B.C.E. We know that irrigation began soon afterwards, that the oldest fortified towns were built centuries before 6000 B.C.E., that pottery was invented a millennium later, and

[1] See Glossary (Ed.).

that literate urban life was flourishing well before the end of the fourth millennium B.C.E.

When the Sumerian empire of Erech (Warka) was founded in the late fourth millennium B.C.E., and Egypt was unified a little later, a very large number of different tools, kinds of material, processes, and gadgets were already being used in scores of different arts and crafts. Their languages were complex and logical, and bilingualism was about to begin its three-thousand-year career in Babylonia.

Just as manual tools were reaching a level of development not really surpassed until the Hellenistic Age, so vocal tools of communication were being refined to a remarkably high point. We think with vocal tools just as surely as we work with manual tools, and there is no proof that the mind has changed substantially in many thousands of years.

The earliest known Egyptian literature, the Pyramid Texts, were composed in a language already archaic by the middle of the third millennium. They were no doubt handed down orally for centuries before being put into hieroglyphs. In the same way, the archaic literary Sumerian in which the Maxims of Shuruppak were being copied about 2500 B.C.E. presumably goes back several centuries earlier, to the empire of Erech. Both Egyptian and Sumerian, though languages of totally different structure, were flexible and quite capable of expressing abstract ideas and generalized qualities such as "goodness, kingship" as well as causative relationship.

Philosophy itself has not changed materially since Plato and Aristotle in the fourth century B.C.E. As the late Alfred North Whitehead used to say, "All philosophy since Plato consists chiefly of footnotes to him." Though that may sound like an exaggeration, in principle it remains correct. Neither Christianity nor Judaism has changed in essentials (except sometimes for the worse) to any extent in the past two thousand years. We are really not so different from our ancestors as we sometimes think. Our capacity for evil and for good is as great as theirs, but no greater, except as our tools become more powerful.

We all, of course, have presuppositions of a philosophical order. I must admit that I try to be rational and empirical in my approach. I am not a member of the school of rational empiricists, nor am I a logical empiricist (logical positivist), but I firmly believe in the primacy of logical reasoning and the value of systematic collection of factual data. Since our whole modern science is built on this approach, my position should not be novel, especially since I am really a frustrated scientist at heart. (The biggest surprise of my life came when I was elected to the National Academy of Sciences in 1955.)

We now come to the question of defining "1966." By this seemingly otiose "definition" I want to emphasize the necessity of trying to keep up to date. This does not mean that anyone can actually be fully abreast of the state of knowledge in any field at a given moment, much less that such knowledge is always accurate. It does mean that one must try to follow the progress of research and publication as fully as possible in a field which is developing with the rapidity of biblical archaeology in the wide sense that we have outlined. I have a friend who continues to send me clippings from the London *Times* and other British and American journals which carry reliable news reports of the latest developments in archaeology. Without these clippings I should be months behind the times. And yet it is no crime to be "out of date" if one does one's best to keep up in the area or period in which one is most at home, and then studies pertinent scholarly publications in related fields. (It is unfortunately true that if one accepts the latest reports uncritically, one is bound to make serious mistakes.)

The danger of chasing after scholarly fads instead of building on logically and empirically sound foundations is even greater. The intellectual fads of today are even more short-lived than those of the Greeks and Romans. For instance, many developments in philosophical theology today are every whit as absurd as the speculations of the Gnostics were in their time. Søren Kierkegaard, who founded modern existentialist theology in the mid-nineteenth century, was already on the verge of Simonian and Marcionite rejection of the Old Testament and the Old Testament God. Rudolf Bultmann has created a much more Gnosticizing "theology," which turns biblical theology upside down. Paul Tillich went even further in mixing Gnostic (chiefly Jungian) and Neo-Platonic concepts in a veritable witches' broth of metaphysical speculation. Such fads have totally demoralized biblical research, substituting a *réchauffage* of old hierarchies of abstraction for the concrete facts of historical human experience. But, however much one may dislike their futility, just as early Christianity developed through conflict with Gnostic and other heresies, so today Christianity cannot attain its goal without fighting its way through existentialist jungles.

What is true of existentialism in philosophical theology is also true of the now declining attempts to reinterpret ancient myths and religious institutions by psychoanalysis (Freud) or "analytical psychology" (Jung). The vogue now being enjoyed by the structuralism of Lévi-Strauss is likely to be even more short-lived.

When one considers the amount of time wasted in defending and promulgating dubious, or even impossible hypotheses, one may feel discouraged. At this point one may profitably think of all the eggs which a fish must lay in order to keep the aquatic population stable! Then the tremendous amount of apparently waste effort in every intellectual discipline may seem less ominous; in fact, it seems to be necessary in order to keep the intellectual population more or less stable, as well as to ensure that worth-while output will continue.

But one can usually diagnose a fad by a few simple tests. If a new theoretical model or hypothesis is only a passing fad, it probably will not exhibit any new regularities that can be classified systematically and supported by consistent empirical data. For instance, in serious scholarly research one soon learns to laugh at the chase after ciphers supposed to be imbedded in ancient literature. That does not mean that no cryptograms were written in antiquity, but that their use was very limited and quite predictable. Ancient authors were just as eager as modern writers to be understood. Cryptograms were used only by those who wanted to keep their esoteric knowledge for themselves and for their pupils. The search for cryptograms cannot be any more successful in the Greek tragic poets than in Shakespeare, nor are they more likely to occur in the Hebrew Bible than in the works of St. Thomas.

I have perhaps overemphasized basic attitudes and approaches at the expense of concrete details. In this age of specialization it is necessary to keep faith with a general audience of educated people, without taking refuge behind a barrage of technicalities. But there must be constant improvement in the quality of our research tools and methods. In excavating ancient sites we now have more powerful stratigraphic methods, developed by Sir Mortimer Wheeler and Kathleen Kenyon—the analysis of stratified deposits of debris as well as of building remains still *in situ*. This analysis is an extremely valuable tool in the hands of an expert, but it may be very misleading indeed in the hands of a tyro or even of a trained archaeologist who, like the late G. Welter Mauve, was skeptical about the value of Palestinian pottery chronology. In spite of the notable triumphs of Miss Kenyon and her ablest pupils, pottery chronology has suffered some serious setbacks in the hands of archaeologists without adequate training in it. A new American school is now rising, which combines the methods of G. A. Reisner and Wheeler, with close attention to pottery; it is headed by G. Ernest Wright and his pupil Paul W. Lapp.

Because of the almost universal tendency to suspect new methods and approaches—whether in natural science or in historical studies —such new disciplines as stratigraphic archaeology, pottery chronology, and paleography have had difficulty winning recognition. The successful decipherment of Egyptian and cuneiform was rejected by some of the foremost Orientalists of the nineteenth century, and few ranking biblical scholars paid any attention to either until after this century had begun (see below). The work of Schliemann at Troy nearly a century ago was ridiculed by leading classical scholars, and the discovery that pottery was an indispensable chronological tool of the serious historian was summarily rejected by many academic experts between 1890 and 1910.

We are today almost at the end—one hopes—of a period of widespread skepticism among philologians as to the value of archaeological context and typological analysis of the evolution of form. Unfortunately, the legion of skeptics has until recently included most biblical scholars, both Christian and Jewish. This negative approach has led to wholesale rejection of archaeological evidence bearing on biblical history. Striking examples are the refusal of many to accept clear-cut evidence for the date and character of the Israelite conquest of Canaan in the thirteenth century B.C.E. as well as of the Chaldean conquest of Judah in the sixth century. Even more irresponsible is the refusal to accept the Dead Sea scrolls as authentic manuscripts of the Hellenistic and early Roman periods (see below). Some scholars throw out the baby with the bath, rejecting the conclusions of epigraphists and paleographers who treat the evolution of scripts just as archaeologists deal with the chronology of other artifacts. Even now some refuse to believe in the Dead Sea scrolls, declaring that they are very late, or that they are hoaxes! The founder of the hoax theory of the Dead Sea scrolls sat in my office in Baltimore in the autumn of 1948, a few months after John Trever and E. L. Sukenik had first publicly recognized the antiquity of the scrolls. I tried to show the enlargements of some Leica prints which Trever had sent me, but he refused even to look at them, dismissing them with a wave of his hand as "hoaxes": "I don't need to look at them. I know they're hoaxes." Since then I have often met New Testament scholars who have told me, "Oh, I don't believe a word of what you say. I think it's all nonsense. I was a student of so-and-so at such-and-such a university (the American equivalent of 'Oxbridge')." I soon learned to reply, "What have you read on the subject?" Back came the expected crusher, "I don't waste any time on such stuff!" Judging from the stated opinions of some scholars, there has been a strange conspiracy in which Ta'amireh Bedouin, antiquity dealers, and distinguished specialists of different nationalities and religious confessions plotted together how best to deceive the world. One theory was that a consortium of antiquity dealers from Jordan and impecunious students from Israel planned a gigantic hoax, following in the wake of Shapira nearly a century ago. If one believes the conspiracy motivation of international archaeology, one can believe anything, including flying saucers from outer space.

If we turn to decipherment and interpretation of written documents, we find similar improvement in research tools. Today we are learning how to preserve excavated documents, how to decipher unknown or little-known scripts, how to work out grammars and dictionaries of recently deciphered languages by a complex but rigorous alternation of induction and deduction. After grammars, dictionaries, and handbooks are published, containing available material, systematically classified, consistent and self-corroborating, confirmed by a host of transcriptions from one system of writing to another, identical texts in two or more languages, as well as parallel accounts of the same events in different ancient languages, we may be certain that our results are correct in principle. The methods used are those of modern comparative and historical linguists.

We are at last able to date biblical compositions by language and style as well as by content. Thanks to the extraordinary recent increase in the quantity of Northwest-Semitic literature in dialects closely related to Hebrew, we can begin to explain Hebrew poetic texts which have not been understood for more than 2,000 years. Most of these passages were not even understood by the Jewish scholars who translated the Old Testament into Greek between 2,250 and 2,100 years ago! This is the time to which many radical scholars attributed the original composition of most of the Psalms up to within the past few years—and some still do! Yet the Jews who were supposed to have put the Psalms into Greek no later than about 100 B.C.E. failed to understand a great many passages which can now be explained on the basis of Canaanite literature. To explain briefly, we are now able to distinguish some 15,000 words in Accadian (Semitic, Assyrian and Babylonian) and almost as many in Egyptian; this vocabulary covers some 2,500 years in the former and 3,500 years in the latter case. In the Hebrew Bible we probably have some three to four thousand different words which have been distinguished by Jewish tradition, as against several times that number which were in fairly common use through the long history of Northwest Semitic and its various dialects. Besides, these dialects were much closer linguistically to one another than even such languages as Portuguese, Castilian, and Catalan, or northern French and Provençal, or than the Scandinavian languages, whose speakers understand each other if they travel to any extent or have any education.

Father Mitchell Dahood, S.J., has done brilliant work in recovering the lost meaning of obscure verses in the Psalter, as well as in Proverbs and Job. Born in Montana of Lebanese parents, he is now professor at the Pontifical Biblical Institute in Rome, where he applies the methods which he learned from me and from Professors Cross and Freedman with great skill and industry. But most biblical scholars still criticize our methodology and, like a distinguished American biblical scholar of the past generation, they insist that "Ugarit has no more to do with the Bible than Aztec has to do with the Plains Indians!" Actually much early Hebrew verse dates from the second millennium, and was composed in a poetic dialect closely related to the generalized epic dialect of Canaan in which Ugaritic verse was composed. Today we can say with Galileo, *eppur si muove,* the world moves anyhow! I have no hesitation in saying that, even if Dahood is substantially correct only a third of the time, he has personally recovered more of the original meaning of the Psalter than all other scholars together during the past two thousand years!

Finally, I want to call attention to the use of historical analogy in reconstructing biblical history. (I have devoted a small volume of Rockwell Lectures—given at Rice University in 1962 and published in 1966—to the theme *Archaeology, Historical Analogy, and Early Biblical Tradition.*[2])

[2] Louisiana State University Press.

I want to emphasize the fact that historical models are indispensable, but that one must be very sure of analogies before using them in historical research. Kantian philosophers have been very skeptical about historical analogy. Hegelians have welcomed it with open arms but have employed very inadequate procedures in setting it up and checking data. Today the term "model" has often replaced "analogy," but with curious oscillations. The use of models started with physicists—e.g. Nils Bohr's famous model of the atom. But in the latest scientific publications by physicists the word "model" will hardly be found at all. The reason is simple. The use of stochastic and probabilistic models has been taken over by social scientists, as well as by educators, philosophers, and theologians to such an extent that the word has lost its original meaning, and often means nothing but a vague analogy without mathematical content, until the specialists in the exact sciences are afraid to use it any more, and often return to the use of "analogy." I want to emphasize the fact that one must have a whole series of independent analogies, all leading to a consistent model, before one can use this method with safety. The danger of having a pattern radically altered by a few facts is so great that it is extremely dangerous to generalize models unless one has convergent evidence along quite independent lines. One illustration must do. In a recent book (the Jordan Lectures, given in London in 1965, and appearing in 1968 as *Yahweh and the Gods of Canaan*[3]) I deal with the question of early Hebrew poetry and the development of verse forms in Canaanite and Hebrew literature. The earliest Hebrew verse from late pre-Mosaic and Mosaic times was closely related in style to the verse of Ugarit. We find in both similar grammatical phenomena, similar vocabulary, similar stylistic peculiarities. If one sets up a stylistic sequence-dating and takes account of the changes between ca. 1300 and ca. 900 B.C.E. one can easily arrange them along a curve that agrees beautifully with the succession of historical allusions. The analogies involved are so close that it is hard to escape the force of their impact. The forms of repetitive parallelism characteristic of the song of Miriam from the early thirteenth century can be duplicated in the Canaanite epics copied at Ugarit in the preceding century. By the late tenth century we have a completely transformed style, without repetition and with maximal variation in vocabulary. In other words, the chronological shift in poetic style is pegged at beginning and end,

[3] New York: Doubleday.

and directly conforms to the evidence of content. This means that our analogies do indeed enable us to construct a model.

It was no less a scholar than Julius Wellhausen, to whose Hegelian presuppositions we owe the still dominant theory of Israelite religious evolution—which I have opposed throughout my life— who was largely responsible for dating the poetry of the Bible so late. He was the first to insist on the Hellenistic date of the Psalms, and to oppose the early dating of much Hebrew poetry by men like Heinrich Ewald and Franz Delitzsch. As a result the followers of Wellhausen vied with one another in lowering the date of biblical verse, until finally most Hebrew poetry was actually dated after most Hebrew prose!

Now contrast with this critical view, the fact (which may easily be verified all over the Old World) that in almost every culture it can be shown that the oldest literary prose is *later* than the oldest verse. There is nothing surprising about this fact since verse forms are much easier to remember than prose. Since verse was always composed either to be sung or to be chanted to the accompaniment of musical instruments, it stands to reason that it would be fixed in form both for mnemonic reasons and for use with already known melodies. In other words, if most biblical scholars are right, Hebrew poetry would be the one outstanding exception in the Old World. Needless to say, this proposition is so absurd that it offers no obstacle to our contrary view, but rather provides additional, quite independent confirmation. If we use historical evidence properly and examine all possible analogies, we emerge with whole series of congruent analogies, which together yield a consistent model.

I shall give another example of what happens to a great scholar who is unaware of the weak points in reasoning from analogy. Julius Wellhausen was one of the greatest Semitists of his day, eminent in both Arabic and Hebrew studies. He tried to reconstruct early Israelite life on the basis of pre-Islamic Arabic poetry, which described the life of Arabian camel-nomads in the fifth–seventh centuries C.E. But Wellhausen refused to believe that Egyptian hieroglyphs or Assyro-Babylonian cuneiform had been deciphered. I have among my reprints one of a paper published by Wellhausen in 1876, which he gave my teacher Paul Haupt at the beginning of the latter's career as an Assyriologist. In it Wellhausen insisted that almost the entire decipherment of Babylonian cuneiform was wrong. All through his life he scarcely ever used cuneiform or Egyptian sources, and he downgraded their significance at every opportunity. Instead he drew all his parallels from pre-Islamic Arabia.

Today, of course, we know that the lands of the ancient Orient were united by innumerable ties. Together with hundreds of thousands of texts and inscriptions in many languages and scripts, there is a vast treasure of other archaeological data, nearly all dated and interpreted within narrow limits of uncertainty. All this material has direct and indirect bearing on the historical, aesthetic and religious interpretation of the Old Testament, the intertestamental literature, and the New Testament. As historians in the broadest sense, we cannot understand the origin and development of Judaism or its offshoot Christianity without drawing on the wealth of now available material of archaeological origin.

One of the most important contributions to the history of biblical religion is G. E. Mendenhall's discovery of the close analogy between the structure of the early Hebrew covenant between God and Israel and that of Hittite suzerainty treaties from the third quarter of the second millennium B.C.E. While the covenant model which he has demonstrated, has been rejected by some scholars, it is for wholly unsatisfactory reasons.

Let us turn back to the Dead Sea scrolls. Until their discovery, and publication (in part) since 1947, the date of most Apocrypha and Pseudepigrapha[4] was very uncertain. Since the first discoveries at Qumran, they have been nearly all dated to within half a century or so by the convergence of paleography with historical facts, archaeological context (coins, pottery, etc.), radiocarbon counts, and internal evidence. Any doubts about the validity of paleographic dating (to those who have a good eye and memory for form) have been removed by the excavations at Wadi Dâliyeh (see the essay in this volume by F. M. Cross), the finds of Bar Cochba's time in Wadi Murabba'at and elsewhere, and the excavation of Masada by Yigael Yadin. It is, accordingly, quite certain that the Qumran manuscripts begin about 300 B.C.E. or a little later and extend down to no later than 68 C.E.

The new material from the Dead Sea finds makes it possible to fill yawning gaps in the history of Hebrew and Aramaic. We can now tie the earliest Hebrew prose of the Qumran sectarians to the corresponding prose of Daniel, and can date the latest biblical Hebrew poetry well before Ben Sira (ca. 200 B.C.E.) and the *Hodayot*

---

[4] See Glossary and Professor Skehan's essay below (Ed.).

of Qumran. We can date such books as Esther and Tobit in the late Persian period, and can fix approximate dates for many other previously known and unknown Jewish religious works in Hebrew and Aramaic. What this means for the history of religious ideas in the hitherto obscure age between the fifth century B.C.E. and the Christian era is hard to exaggerate, especially when one recalls the uncertainty of our knowledge twenty years ago!

In evaluating the contribution of this rich new evidence for New Testament research, we must always remember that we are looking for data of *public* significance. Most of the events described in the Gospels were private or were witnessed by comparatively few persons, most of whom had died before the written record began. On the other hand, the teachings of Jesus were collected and transmitted with fidelity, in part precisely because they fitted so well into Jewish religious life in the last century of the Second Temple.

Ashdod of the Philistines

MOSHE DOTHAN

Tel Ashdod[1], near the remains of the village of Isdud, was always identified with the ancient biblical Philistine Ashdod, later called Azotus. It is situated about three miles from the coast, on the edge of the sand dunes which border the sea in this area. It encompasses an acropolis of about seventeen acres and a lower city covering a much larger area. The summit of the tel is about fifty meters above sea level and rises about twenty-two meters above the surrounding area. The first settlement was built on a natural, isolated hill, mainly sandstone covered by a thin coat of soil. It is not yet possible to determine the exact extent of the city because of the centuries-long accumulation of sand dunes on the west and the cultivation of the fields, both in ancient times and at present. But our survey leads us to believe that the city, at the time of its greatest extent, was at least ninety acres in area. During the last few centuries the villagers of nearby Isdud dug into the rich soil of the mound in order to fertilize their lands and to make adobe bricks for their dwellings. While this destruction of a part of the site proved a great loss for the expedition, it also revealed some important phases of the stratification even before the excavation proper.

The primary aim of the first three seasons of excavation was to establish the duration of the Ashdod settlement and its stratification

[1] The excavations of Tel Ashdod are part of the Ashdod project sponsored by a joint Israeli-American expedition. The participating institutions in the first three seasons were the Pittsburgh Carnegie Museum, the Pittsburgh Theological Seminary, and the Israel Department of Antiquities. David Noel Freedman and James L. Swauger served as directors of the project—Freedman the first two seasons and Swauger the third—and I served as the archaeological director. The work was undertaken in 1962, 1963, and 1965, each season lasting approximately two months.

both on the acropolis and in the lower city. For this purpose three main areas were chosen and excavated in the first two seasons—A, B, and D. Area G was excavated during the last two seasons and Areas H and K were excavated during the third season only. It has been possible to make a provisional correlation among the local stratigraphies of the various areas. Altogether there are twenty strata of settlement, some of which are represented in certain areas only: Stratum 20 is Early Bronze II; Stratum 19 is Middle Bronze II; Stratum 18, Late Bronze I; Strata 17–14, Late Bronze II; Strata 13–10, Iron I (of which at least three are Philistine strata); Strata 9–6, Iron II; Stratum 5, Persian; Stratum 4, Hellenistic; Stratum 3, Maccabean; Stratum 2, Herodian and Early Roman; and Stratum I, Late Roman and Byzantine. Obviously these divisions are not yet final. Further analysis of some strata has shown that they should be split further into additional phases. But we have here, I believe, a general scheme from which there will not be any serious deviations.

Let us now turn to some of the literary sources for the history of Ashdod. Until recently the earliest non-biblical source concerning ancient Ashdod dated back no further than the eleventh century B.C.E. This is the Egyptian Onomasticon of Amenope. But documents discovered at Ugarit now indicate the important role played by Ashdod in the fourteenth and thirteenth centuries B.C.E. The contents of some of the documents were published recently. They show that Ashdod, a Canaanite name as demonstrated lately by Cross and Freedman,[2] was one of the three Canaanite cities in Palestine that had commercial relations with Ugarit, the other two being Akko (Acre) and Ashkelon. It seems that by the fourteenth century Ugarit imported quantities of textiles from Ashdod. The gentilic "Ashdodite" appears in the texts, and indeed so many times in one tablet that it seems to represent a distinct section or enclave of the population of Ugarit: perhaps emigrants or refugees from Ashdod, immigrants to Ugarit. On the other hand, the term "Ashdodite" may also have represented a kind of professional guild, for instance, makers of purple dye. In this connection it may be noted that we found installations for making purple (*purpura*) from shells (*murex brandaris* and *murex truncatus*) in nearby Tel

[2] F. M. Cross and D. N. Freedman, "The Name of Ashdod," *BASOR* 175 (1964), 48–50.

Mor, excavated a few years ago, which probably served as the ancient harbor of Ashdod.

The Bible furnishes considerable information about Ashdod. We know from Joshua that it was apportioned to the tribe of Judah,[3] but the conquest of Ashdod is not mentioned at all. Ashdod always appears as one of the chief cities of the Philistine pentapolis.[4] According to I Samuel, the Ark of the Covenant was brought to the temple of Dagon in Ashdod and remained there until the inhabitants were stricken by a great plague.[5] Ashdod is not mentioned in the Bible again until the time of Uzziah (783–742 B.C.E.) "who broke down the wall of Ashdod and built cities about Ashdod and among the Philistines."[6]

From the Assyrian sources we know that in 713–712 B.C.E., Sargon II of Assyria sent a military expedition headed by the Tartan, the field marshal of the Assyrian army, against Ashdod because the city refused to pay tribute. This is mentioned in Isaiah 20:1. "In the year that the commander in chief who was sent by Sargon the king of Assyria came to Ashdod and fought against it and took it. . . ." When the rebellion was crushed, the entire kingdom of Ashdod was annexed by Sargon and became an Assyrian province. Its inhabitants were exiled and others were settled in their stead. The full account of the conquest appears in the annals of Sargon in the king's palace in his capital, Dur-Sharrukin. The fate of the people of Ashdod up to the Babylonian conquest is mentioned by several of the prophets, e.g. Jeremiah, Zephaniah, and Zechariah.[7] Eventually Ashdod became a Babylonian and later a Persian province.

After the return of the Jews from the Babylonian Exile, Ashdod is reported to have been in opposition to Judah. At the same time there appears to have been considerable intermarriage between Jews and Ashdodite women; their descendants spoke the Ashdod dialect, as we learn from Nehemiah.[8] This is the last reference to Ashdod in the Hebrew Bible. The history of the Hellenistic-Roman city of Ashdod (Azotus), known mainly from the books of Maccabees, Josephus, and the New Testament, is outside the scope of this essay.

[3] Josh. 15:45–47.
[4] Cf. Josh. 13:3; Judg. 1:18 (LXX); Amos 1:7–8.
[5] I Sam. 5:1–8.
[6] II Chron. 26:6.
[7] Jer. 25:20; Zeph. 2:4; Zech. 9:5–6.
[8] Neh. 13:23–24.

I shall concentrate on the Ashdodite period from the end of Late Bronze II until the Babylonian conquest. During this era the city may rightly be called Ashdod of the Philistines.

Tel Ashdod (see plan—Fig. 1) is situated close to the Via Maris, the ancient coastal road which connected Egypt with Mesopotamia. The new town of Ashdod and the ancient port of Ashdod, Tel Mor, are to the northwest. To the south is Ashkelon. This area is about forty to forty-five kilometers south of Tel Aviv-Yafo.

The destruction of the tel wrought by the local villagers (as mentioned above) shows quite clearly in Figure 3 as a vertical section between Areas A and B. The period represented in Area B is Late Bronze Age, while six meters higher in Area A is our Hellenistic stratum.

Figure 2 shows the topographical features of the tel. Areas A and B are situated on the acropolis, Area C is southeast of them. About 250 meters southwest of it is the excavated part of the lower city, Area D. Area G is on the northern edge of the city, while Areas H and K, which were excavated in the third season, are at the western edge of the acropolis. In all, approximately one acre has been excavated, that is about one-ninetieth of the tel.

The Late Bronze II strata of the fourteenth century are illustrated by Figure 4. It shows a house (probably a public building) with courtyard and a few small rooms surrounding it. The floor plan is very similar to that of one of the public houses at Megiddo, Stratum 8. The next figure shows two silos of the last Late Bronze stratum (Fig. 5). This was the city under the Egyptian suzerainty of Rameses II (Fig. 6).

The local pottery, contemporary with the fourteenth–thirteenth century building, is shown in Figure 7. To the same period belongs a large pilgrim flask (not illustrated) found last season. Figure 8 shows the Cypriote pottery of the thirteenth century, including some sherds of "milk bowls" while some of the many Mycenean pieces found on two of the floors of the Late Bronze strata are illustrated in Figure 9. A figurine in the Canaanite tradition (Fig. 10) also belongs to the Late Canaanite strata.

We now come to the Philistine settlement of Ashdod. There is no final stratigraphical evidence to suggest that the Philistines were the people who destroyed the Late Bronze Age town of Ashdod. In Area A, above the Late Bronze destruction level and above an as yet unclarified level, we found part of a fortress (Fig. 11). The walls, constructed of sun-dried bricks, are 1.6 meters wide and are preserved to a height of 2 meters. It seems improbable that this was the main fortress, but was more likely a small citadel attached to the southern part of the main city wall. Pottery dating suggests that it was erected at the beginning of the Philistine settlement of Ashdod, i.e. approximately 1170–1160 B.C.E.

At least three Philistine strata were uncovered in Areas A and H. If we bear in mind that Philistine levels were also uncovered in Area G, it would seem that from its very beginning the Philistine settlement spread over a large area, probably the whole acropolis. In Area H part of an apsidal circular structure was uncovered, connected with a square building, which is rather unusual since no other apsidal Philistine buildings are known. It was not a silo, for none of the characteristic silo materials was found there.

In the northern part of the city (Area G), we found part of an enormous wall in our last season of excavation. Above it and connected with it there was a smaller and parallel wall belonging to Iron II. This means that part of this wall was probably no longer in use by the eighth and seventh centuries but in the twelfth, eleventh, and tenth centuries we believe that this wall was the main fortification of the acropolis. The wall, more than 6 meters thick, is built of well-made bricks. In this area two distinctive strata of Philistine settlement were found.

Philistine pottery, with its characteristic ornamentation recalling that of Mycenean pottery, is shown in Figure 12. It contrasts very distinctly with that of the Late Bronze Age, as is evident when one compares the representations of birds, the former Philistine (Fig. 13) and the latter Late Bronze (Fig. 14). We also found many figurines of birds which are very similar to those painted on the Philistine vessels (Fig. 15). Even more interesting perhaps were the finds from a Philistine floor, which included a Twentieth Dynasty scarab, a cylinder seal portraying a deer or gazelle and a gold ring, which we call the ring of Delilah. We found "Astarte" figurines, of a type popular in the Late Bronze Age. Figure 16 shows one lacking a head, but she is supporting her breasts with her hands in a typical pose.

In a Philistine pit in Area C we found a figurine (Fig. 17). This is a schematic representation of a head with a beak nose and two appliquéd eyes, set on a long neck. It was impossible to know if this represented a male or female but from the complete figurine

(Fig. 18) which was found during the last season, we know now that it must have been female. Figure 18 is a seated female figurine with the lower part of her body made in the form of a four-legged table or couch. As we shall see in the later Philistine temple of the ninth and eighth centuries (Area D), the same features occur on figurines which must have formed the upper parts of couches, chairs or offering tables (Fig. 19). The early Philistines who settled in Ashdod seem to have worshiped a goddess. She is similar to a Mycenean mother goddess, a schematic representation of a woman seated on a chair. Our goddess seems to be a Philistine rendering of her. We did not find any male figurines of this period. I would therefore suggest, though the evidence at the moment is insufficient, that the Semitic god Dagon was introduced later into Philistine Ashdod.

Part of a seal, found in the Philistine stratum of Area G, shows, on the back, the hindquarters of a lion. Engraved on the obverse (flat side) is a silhouette of a man seated on a chair and playing a lyre which stands on a table next to him. His head with its schematic nose is attached to a long neck and is similar to the previously shown figurines. His headdress may be a representation of the feather headdress of the Philistines. This type of elongated figure is quite typical of the Philistine figurines at Ashdod (see Figs. 17, 18).

We now move to Area D, the lower city. Not enough remains of the tenth century were found to give a consistent picture of the city at that time. However, by the ninth century there appears to have been a population explosion at Ashdod. The relatively small acropolis was then joined by a large lower city, of which only a part was excavated. A small temple or sanctuary was uncovered, with a peculiar, whitewashed block altar (Fig. 20), in which we found many votive vessels and much pottery characteristic of the late ninth and eighth centuries.

Among the cult vessels were many *kernoi,* hollow pottery rings with attachments. Liquid was poured inside through the cups and then poured out through the mouths of the animal heads. A whole vessel of this type was not found, but enough was preserved to show that a *kernos* usually consisted of a ring with four attachments, three probably being animal heads and the fourth a cup (Fig. 21).

The next figures show the usual type of "Astarte" figurine common to the ninth and eighth centuries, holding her breasts either with both hands or with one hand holding her breast and the other along her body (Fig. 22). During the survey of Area D, a mold from which some "Astarte" figurines were made was found (Fig. 23).

Representations of men include a figurine which was probably part of a cup as the head is completely hollow (Fig. 24). The figurine in Figure 25 may be a woman.

The miniature couches or tables of the ninth and eighth centuries mentioned above, sometimes with hands and arms depicted on them, continued the Philistine tradition for over three hundred years. We are uncertain, however, if a figurine was attached to the table as in the Philistine period since no whole examples have been found. Because of the representations of hands and arms on the couches it is, however, probable. The figurines in Figures 26 and 27 may have been of this type. The figurine of a lyre player is shown in Figure 28. One of the hands is broken but the lyre can be seen. Thus, in the eighth century the early Philistine tradition of men playing the lyre was still maintained.

On an eighth-century potsherd[9] we found our first inscription, incised before firing (Fig. 29). It reads in Hebrew characters, *phr* and is probably to be read *happōḥēr*, "the potter." Originally, the inscription may also have included the name of the artisan. The word *pōḥēr* is problematic as words with root *phr* appear only in late Aramaic and in Arabic. Brief as it is, the inscription shows that by the eighth century B.C.E., if not earlier, the Ashdodites shared a common script and language with their neighbors, the Phoenicians, and with the people of Israel and Judah.

The city, to which belonged the sanctuary mentioned above, was most probably destroyed at the end of the eighth century. About thirty skeletons were found in a small room. The way in which they were thrown together suggests a very quick, hurried burial (Fig. 30). The pottery which was buried with the skeletons can be dated to the eighth century. Therefore, the city's destruction may well be attributed to Sargon II, king of Assyria.

Three fragments of a basalt stele of Sargon II were found at Ashdod (Fig. 31). The fragments are inscribed in cuneiform script typical of the Assyrian monuments of the eighth century B.C.E. Unfortunately, little has survived of the stele. One fragment, however, can be reconstructed; as in his inscriptions found in Khorsabad and Cyprus, Sargon described here the conquest of several countries

[9] See Glossary (Ed.).

during his campaigns. The lost parts of the stele may well have mentioned the conquest of Ashdod (712 B.C.E.). The significance of this stele (published by Prof. Hayim Tadmor) lies in the fact that archaeological evidence found *in situ* verifies the written sources about Ashdod, i.e. the Bible and the Assyrian annals.

Another feature of Area D was the pottery kilns. At least ten were found in a small area, some of them superimposed one above the other. One kiln was found with the pottery *in situ* (Fig. 32) and has been dated to the beginning of the seventh century or perhaps a little later. It was in the stratum above the destruction level of Sargon. One of the kilns was reused as a grave after it had fallen into disuse (Fig. 33). The pottery found with the skeleton can be dated to the seventh–early sixth centuries. We attribute it to the period of the destruction by Nebuchadnezzar, who conquered Ashdod at the beginning of the sixth century.

In the third season of excavation we uncovered buildings of the Persian period. This explained the enormous quantity of "Persian" material, and early Attic ware, found in the two previous seasons. According to Herodotus and other sources, Ashdod was an important city at this time; in 1968 we enlarged the area in order to uncover more of this very large Persian public building.

Another important find of this period is an ostracon with the characteristic script of the late fifth or early fourth century B.C.E. The inscription is in Hebrew or what may be called "Ashdodite" and reads *kerem Zebadiah* (Zebadiah's vineyard). The occurrence of the theophoric name "Zebadiah" is interesting in the light of what we know from the Book of Nehemiah about the relations between the people of Jerusalem and the Ashdodites.

With the conquest of Ashdod by the Maccabees, the heyday of the city's importance passed and Azotus *Paralius,* Azotus of the coast, three miles to the west, replaced it as the principal city of the area.

This brief outline was intended to show some of the results of the excavations of Philistine Ashdod. Though in three seasons we barely scratched the surface of the tel which covers the remains of a great city, the results are of considerable archaeological and historical significance. Let us hope that the seasons following will bring more valuable material to elucidate the history of Ashdod.

In 1968, a fourth season of excavations was undertaken and we here summarize the results that bear on the previous work.

The most significant is the stratigraphy and changes in the fortifications of Area G. The earliest fortified structures, probably a tower or tower gate, belong to the LB II period (strata 17–14). In stratum 13, the outer part of the tower was destroyed and a double wall connected with the settlement of the Sea Peoples was in use. In the main Philistine stratum (12) a casemate wall was the main feature of the fortifications in this area. In the last Philistine stratum (11), the fortifications were weakened and finally in stratum 10 (late 11th–early 10th century) this fortification was changed into a massive wall, probably with buttresses.

In Area H, four strata of the Early Iron Age were found among them three Philistine. Above the last LB II stratum a settlement of Sea Peoples was established partly on a layer of ashes and destruction and partly directly upon the structures of the preceding period. Together with the usual Philistine vessels, a group of interesting sherds was found in the lowest Philistine stratum. They differ from the usual Philistine ware in the color of clay after firing. Their decoration bears a striking resemblance to Mycenean IIICl ware, especially from Cyprus. It is possible that this pottery was brought by the first settlers of the Sea Peoples. If the assumption is correct that there is a connection between this ware and Mycenean IIICl ware, important chronological and physical evidence is provided concerning the origins and the dating of the first wave of the Sea Peoples in Ashdod.

BIBLIOGRAPHY

Dothan, M., "Ashdod: A City of the Philistine Pentapolis", *Archaeology* 20 (1967), 178–86. Preliminary reports have appeared in *IEJ* and *RB*.

Dothan, M., and Freedman, D. N., "The First Season of Excavations, 1962", *Atiqot* English Series Vol. VII (Jerusalem, 1967).

Dothan, M., et al., "The Second and Third Seasons of Excavations", *Atiqot* English Series, in press.

Tadmor, H., "Fragments of a Stele of Sargon of Assyria" *Eretz Israel*
8 (1967), 241–45.

In June–August 1968 there was a fourth season of excavations
of Ashdod under the direction of M. Dothan and J. Swauger. A
preliminary report will appear in *IEJ,* 1969.

The Israelite Sanctuary
at Arad

YOHANAN AHARONI

I am very delighted to give this brief general account of the main results of our excavations at Arad. This symposium is a rare opportunity to bring the material before such eminent scholars, teachers and colleagues of mine as Professors Albright, Wright, and Cross and have their comment. In this lecture I may put to you more questions than answers. This is an excellent example of biblical archaeology solving one or two problems and opening many new ones.

Where is Arad and what was its importance in antiquity? Arad is a biblical town, well known from the Bible—about twenty miles east–northeast of Beersheba, the capital of the Negev in the south of Israel. It was situated on the border of the country guarding the approaches from the desert in a region which is today virtually unsettled. It has now become one of the main areas of the nomad population of Israel. Our excavation at Arad was made possible to a large extent by the foundation and construction of a new city, modern Arad, fortunately not on the ancient hill, but a short distance from it. It is fortunate for archaeology in Israel that modern town planners are interested in learning something about the ancient city which they are rebuilding and are ready to provide us with some means for excavation. Arad is one of the prominent mounds of the eastern Negev, guarding the boundary of Judaea and dominating one of the most important roads leading down from Judaea to the Dead Sea, to the Arabah and to Ezion-Geber and Elath, the famous port and trading center with which we are so familiar from the Bible. The excavations revealed different periods of occupation. One part of the excavation, which my colleague Ruth Amiran supervises, is the Early Bronze Age city, belonging to the first centuries of the third millennium B.C.E. This is a very interesting discovery, but I won't discuss it on this occasion. The reasons for the foundation of a large city in such an early period in this desert-like area, and for its complete abandonment, still remain a riddle.

Settlement was renewed only in a part of the ancient city early in the Iron Age, about the eleventh century B.C.E.—in the later phase of the period of the judges, not long before or at the very beginning of the monarchy. It started as an open settlement, but was quickly converted into a fortress. This citadel mound is relatively small, different from most known Palestinian city mounds. It has an area of only about 50×50 meters (Fig. 40). It is a rather small citadel, no city, but very strongly fortified and surrounded by a kind of open settlement. Our excavation was limited mainly to this citadel mound. It is built up, as usual, of many strata, one upon the other. The later ones are from Persian, Hellenistic, Roman, even early Arab times. Fortunately most of these later fortresses did not penetrate too deeply into the earlier strata. Six citadels preceded by another stratum belong to the Iron Age. From the tenth century B.C.E., to about the destruction of the First Temple, i.e. during a period of about 350 years, we found six citadels built, destroyed, and built again and destroyed again. Such a large number of destruction levels fulfills the dream of any archaeologist. We were able to open room after room full of vessels, most of course broken, but some intact, buried under debris of the fallen roofs and burned levels of all six strata. It is hardly astonishing that a fortress guarding the border was always one of the first places to suffer in any period of political or military weakness of the kingdom. Thus it is not our doing that these six clearly defined strata, with hundreds and hundreds of complete vessels (after their reconstruction) provide a dependable stratification. We can't be very inaccurate in dating these various strata between the period of Solomon in the middle of the tenth century B.C.E. and about the end of the First Temple period, a little after 600 B.C.E.

The two most exciting finds in this citadel were unquestionably the many ostraca[1], and the sanctuary. It is impossible to describe the ostraca in detail and I shall limit myself to a few examples in order to give you a glimpse of their contents. We have about

[1] See Glossary (Ed.).

two hundred ostraca, about half of them in Aramaic from the Persian period (about 400 B.C.E.) and half of them in Hebrew from the First Temple period. I am happy to report that we have not only pottery evidence for the chronology but also epigraphic evidence for almost every one of our strata. The importance of the ostraca is not only in their number, which almost doubles the inscriptional material from this period which has been found so far in Palestine, but that for the first time we have part of a royal archive. These do not belong to one stratum only. Indeed, our main find belongs to the latest stratum, that is from about the same date as the Lachish letters. But we have earlier ostraca, some of them almost entirely legible. Even fragmentary pieces are of great importance from a paleographic point of view. The ostraca contain most of the letters of the alphabet from five out of our six strata. It is only from the first stratum of the tenth century that we possess only one ostracon with a few letters. Most of the ostraca were found in rooms near or inside the southern wall, where the dwellings of the citadel were situated.

Before discussing the temple at Arad I would like to offer some highlights of the inscriptional material. First of all one must mention the so-called "Arad bowl." On a pottery bowl found in the third citadel we have the letters *'ayin-rēš-dālet* in ancient Hebrew letters inscribed several times, strangely enough always written backwards or in reverse order (i.e. mirror writing; Fig. 43). I have no certain explanation for this strange way of inscribing the name of the city several times on the same bowl. May be it was done by someone unfamiliar with writing, who just copied the name of the city and scratched it very crudely on the bowl. (I remember that my own children, when they started to learn to write during their first school year, wrote in either direction, without seeing any difference.) In any case we were quite happy with this inscription because it brought further confirmation of the identification of the place.

It is my duty to extend a warning to you who intend to participate as volunteers at Arad or at any of our excavations. Some volunteers sit for hours just doing what we call "pottery dipping." In the field it is almost impossible to recognize inscribed potsherds, because they are dirty and blackened with ashes. Putting them into water and brushing them can easily cleanse them of all remnants of script. We therefore invented this method of dipping. Out of every basket (after it is numbered and taken down to the camp), every sherd is dipped into water and examined on both sides. Do not think that we found an inscription on every other sherd. Usually thousands and thousands of sherds must be examined until one or two letters are found. However, some of our "dippers" were more fortunate. In one of the rooms of the southern casemate wall seventeen ostraca were found in one heap belonging to the period of the last citadel. Nine of them are almost complete and in an excellent state of preservation.

Most documents are addressed to the same person called Eliashib. One of the best preserved contained the following inscription translated into English (Fig. 44):

> To Eliashib: and now, give to the Kittites[2] three measures of wine,[3] and write the name of the day.[4] And from the rest[5] of the first flour take [or mix] one measure[6] of flour in order to make bread for them. From the wine of the large bowls[7] give.

The contents of most of the ostraca are similar, concerned mainly with the delivery of wine, flour, or bread and oil to certain persons. One of them is addressed not to Eliashib, but to another person called Nahum:

> To Nahum[8]: and now go to the house of Eliashib, son of Eshyahu,[9] and take from him one measure [or jar] of oil. And send it quickly and seal it with your seal.

On the other side of this same ostracon a note is added in another handwriting, containing a date: "On the twenty-fourth of the month Nahum gave oil by the hand of the Kitti, one." The number is written with hieratic numerals, a most interesting phenomenon in Hebrew epigraphy. It is obvious that the oil was sent duly sealed and the ostracon was kept as a kind of a receipt in the archive of Eliashib.

---

[2] $k\ t\ y\ m;$ I believe they were Greek mercenaries.
[3] $b(att\bar{\imath}m)$ 3; from $bat,$ a measure.
[4] Note that "day," $ym,$ is spelled without the waw (ywm) as in other contemporary documents.
[5] $'wd,$ written with the expected $waw.$
[6] $'\bar{e}p\bar{a}h$ "ephah" (?).
[7] $'agg\bar{a}n\bar{o}t,$ large vessels of a distinctive type, probably indicating like the "first flour," a special kind of wine.
[8] $n\ \d{h}\ m.$
[9] This explains how the letter ended up in Eliashib's archive. It is the only letter containing his patronymic: Eshyahu.

In a room beside the ostraca room, we had another striking surprise. Together with some other ostraca three ancient Hebrew seals were found. They were made of hard semiprecious stone, showing good workmanship, and inscribed with ancient Hebrew names (Fig. 45). They come from the stratum before that of the Eliashib ostraca, which means they belong to our fifth citadel while the ostraca belonged to our sixth and last citadel. All three have the identical inscription, one in an abbreviated form: "[belonging] to Eliashib son of Eshyahu." These then are the seals with which Eliashib conducted his royal business! For the first time seals of this type have been found *in situ* and with clear indication of their use. They are so-called "private seals" lacking any indication of the owner's title or office. In this case, however, we know that Eliashib was not a private citizen, but an official functionary in charge of the royal stores and perhaps the whole administration at the citadel of Arad. This is a new fact which must now be taken into consideration in the scholarly study of the Hebrew seals and seal impressions. The appearance of the identical name in the Citadel 6 ostraca and the Citadel 5 seals is also surprising. As we may hardly doubt that this was the same functionary who returned to his duties with the rebuilding of the fortress, the dates of the two destruction levels cannot be far apart. One ostracon is written by an inferior of our Eliashib and starts with a formal greeting, in contrast to the usual short opening (Figs. 46–47):

To my lord Eliashib: May Yahweh[10] seek your welfare. And now, give Shemaryahu————,[11] and to the Kerosi give ————.[12] And regarding the matter about which you commanded me, *Shalom.*[13] In the house of Yahweh he is dwelling [*or* sitting].

Is it possible that the temple of Arad is meant here? This is highly improbable for two reasons: First, as we will see, the sanctuary was already destroyed in the period of the sixth citadel; secondly, the temple mentioned was evidently located at the place from which the letter was sent, rather than Arad where Eliashib was, since it conveys information of which the latter was presumably unaware. It is very plausible that the Jerusalem temple is meant. It should

10 *yhwh,* the ancient tetragrammaton.
11 Indicated only by a sign.
12 Another sign.
13 I.e. "it is all right," or "it has been carried out."

be remembered that the letter is from the very end of the First Temple period, after the reforms of Josiah and the abolition of worship outside Jerusalem. The suggestion is strengthened by the fact that one of the two men who delivered the letter is called the Kerosite (*Kērōsī*). The sons of Keros are mentioned in the Bible as a family of the Nethinim, who served in the Jerusalem temple (Ezra 2:44; Neh. 7:47). Since it is a rather unusual name we must suppose that "the Kerosite" is a member of the Jerusalem Nethinim family. It seems clear that our Eliashib had some connection with the temple. Should we assume that some functions of the priestly administration continued at Arad even after the abolition of the sanctuary?

Undoubtedly our greatest surprise at Arad was the discovery of the Israelite sanctuary. As usual in archaeology, you may calculate in advance where the most important structures are likely to be, but the actual finds are always surprising. Had I been asked before going to Arad what I was looking for, the last thought in my mind would have been an Israelite sanctuary. For those unacquainted with Palestinian archaeology, we should stress that this is the first Israelite temple which has been discovered by archaeology. Before returning to the question of how to explain its existence in Arad, let us describe it.

The general structure and arrangements of the Iron Age citadel remained the same: only its fortifications changed through the centuries of occupation. In earlier periods the citadel was surrounded by a broad, solid wall with small indentations, strengthened by a second wall beneath the slope. This huge fortification appears almost grotesque in comparison with the area of the small citadel. This wall was built in the ninth century in our second citadel (for simplicity I shall not use here the numbers of our strata but call the various citadels 1–6, counting the earliest citadel number 1). It continued in use up to the fifth citadel though in various strata it was further strengthened through the addition of casemate-like inner walls. However, it was not the earliest wall. Beneath it we found clear traces of another casemate wall[14], built in the tenth century (Citadel 1). There is an interesting change of the type of fortification from a casemate wall in the tenth century to a solid wall in the ninth century and again to a casemate wall

[14] See Glossary (Ed.).

in the eighth century (Fig. 41). This is in agreement with the general picture in Palestine as revealed by other excavations.

The solid ninth-century wall is preserved to a height of five meters and more: beneath it we found a rock-hewn water channel (Fig. 42). Water supply was always one of the main problems at Arad, as there is no spring or well in the vicinity. The channel was constructed solely for the transfer of rain water collected in cisterns outside the citadel. It brought the water into deep plastered cisterns hewn in the rocks which are beneath the sanctuary in part. Unfortunately, one corner of the sanctuary collapsed later, when the roof of one of these cisterns caved in.

This brings us finally to the temple itself. The Holy of Holies was found on the very last day of the second season of excavation. (Last-minute discoveries of this sort are not uncommon in excavations.) Three steps led up to it. On the second step we found two small, beautifully carved altars, carefully laid on their sides. On both altars there were still traces of burned matter, evidently the last offerings. On the floor was a stone pillar (*maṣṣēbāh*) which had fallen down. This is the first absolutely certain example of an Israelite *maṣṣēbāh,* mentioned so frequently by the prophets and so much debated among scholars (Fig. 48).

The general plan of the sanctuary shows some striking similarities and some dissimilarities to the Jerusalem temple (Fig. 49). The courtyard is relatively large, covering almost half the space of the sanctuary. From it we enter two adjoining units with central doors. The courtyard was divided into a larger outer and smaller inner part. The latter possibly fulfilled the function of the biblical porch (*'ūlām*). A striking similarity is its orientation: the entrance is on the east and the Holy of Holies points exactly to the west; this is also the case with the Jerusalem temple and with the desert sanctuary. At the entrance to the main room we found two bases of stone pillars which evidently must be compared with the biblical Jachin and Boaz, the two free-standing pillars flanking the entrance of the temple. The large altar of burnt offerings stood in the corner of the courtyard (Fig. 50). It was crowned by a large flint slab, surrounded by two plastered gutters, probably for the blood of the animal sacrifices. The altar is built of small unhewn stones, in contrast to the wall behind which has many dressed stones. We are immediately reminded of the biblical law that the stones of the altar should not be dressed (i.e. touched by iron, Exod. 20:25). The altar, like the rest of the sanctuary, was destroyed and repaired several times. However, the first altar was about one foot shorter than the later altars, though they were always built at the same spot and in later levels maintained exactly the same size.

The small finds were few and simple. Outstanding is a small bronze figurine of a lion couchant, found near the altar (Fig. 51). In the Holy of Holies we found a seal with its ring, unfortunately of iron and therefore badly corroded. Cult objects include two offering tables of stone and a fragmentary incense burner of a type known from other places in this period (Fig. 52). Beside the altar of the second citadel several large, rounded offering bowls were discovered, and some small, shallow ring-burnished dishes. On a pair of them two similar signs are scratched. The first is an ancient Hebrew *qōf;* the second is written with variations and is perhaps a symbol. Since the signs are repeated these must be connected with their function as offering bowls.

We also have some ostraca from the temple, found in one of its side rooms. Though small, they are complete ostraca, with the name of one person written on each of them. Interestingly enough, two ostraca contain names of priestly families well known from the Bible: "Meremoth" (*m r m w t,* written with a *waw,* Fig. 54), and *Pashḥur* (*p š ḥ r,* Fig. 53). Do we have here the earliest instance of the priestly lot for rotation of service in the sanctuary?

One of the most interesting problems is the stratigraphy of the temple: When was it built and when was it finally destroyed? Fortunately both questions have clear-cut answers. Beneath the large, solid ninth-century wall the tenth-century Solomonic casemate wall protrudes. The Holy of Holies of the sanctuary that was never changed was built against the tenth-century fortification, together with the construction of the first citadel. On the other hand the total destruction of the temple is vividly illuminated by the casemate wall of the sixth citadel, which cuts straight through the temple. It stands right in the middle of the main room of the sanctuary, the *hēkāl;* this undoubtedly signifies the complete destruction of the temple. It is very probable that this final destruction of our temple is to be attributed to the famous reform of Josiah, so well known from the Bible (II Kings 22–23).

Finally we offer some particulars of the sanctuary which are of interest for its interpretation. The *hēkāl* is a very distinct broad room, not symmetrical in relation to the general axis of the building. The opening is off-center, the northern side being about one and a half yards longer than the southern. Digging down, we finally uncovered a wall which belonged to the first, tenth-century sanctuary. It stood nearer to the center and the room was therefore symmetrical in its original phase. Another remarkable fact was that the altar was used for the last time in temple number four. As we saw, the temple existed down to the fifth citadel and was totally destroyed only with the sixth citadel. What does that mean? A temple without an altar? We shall return to this question.

Mention should be made of a very unusual discovery. In one of the rooms of the third citadel we found a large seal of relatively crude design. It had no inscription, only strange lines (Fig. 55). Comparing the drawing with the general plan of our citadel, it became apparent that the citadel is represented in schematic form. Among other items of interest, the seal provides a contemporary sketch of the sanctuary, indicated by a distinct rounded structure. It also shows an entrance to a long corridor, which made it possible for the visitor to go directly to the stores in the temple precinct without entering the inner part of the citadel. Two rows of rooms and dwellings were on the south and southwestern side. The only dissimilarity appears to be the shape of the courtyard, which is small and rectangular in the seal. But this is probably our fault, not the mistake of the artist. The area of the courtyard was destroyed completely by the great Hellenistic tower. It seems that the ancient craftsman has helped fulfill the dream of every archaeologist before his excavation: to be provided with a general plan of the ancient structures.

We may summarize our provisional findings, perhaps more in the form of questions than answers. The first question: Is this really an Israelite sanctuary, dedicated to Yahweh, the God of Israel? I believe we have enough evidence to establish this basic fact. It seems obvious not only from its general plan and contents, e.g. the ostraca of the priestly families, but also from the fact that the sanctuary was an integral part of the royal citadel. It was built together with the new Israelite citadel, not in an earlier city where perhaps an earlier pagan temple could have been converted to this use. (It was an important part of the royal administrative center illuminated by the ostraca.)

The second question concerns the relation of the Arad sanctuary to the Jerusalem temple and to the tabernacle, the desert sanctuary described in the Book of Exodus. Mention has been made of the westerly orientation which is exactly the same as that of the Jerusalem temple and of the tabernacle. Then there are the four basic components of the temple: the courtyard, the inner court (vestibule, *'ūlām?*), sanctuary (*hēkāl*), and Holy of Holies (*d^ebīr*). The altar is a square of five cubits.[15] These were the measurements not of the Jerusalem temple but precisely those of the altar of the tabernacle: "You shall make the altar five cubits long and five cubits broad and the height of it shall be three cubits" (Exod. 27:1). It was also made according to the biblical law: "If you shall make an altar of stone you shall not make it of hewn stone" (Exod. 20:25, etc.).

As for the two pillars, I do not claim that they supply a solution to the question of what Jachin and Boaz stood for. But I think that we must consider the physical relation of the pillars to the Solomonic temple in Jerusalem. What was their exact location? In almost every reconstruction of the Jerusalem temple, these two free-standing pillars are placed in the courtyard, at the entrance of the *'ūlām*. In Arad that was not the case. They stood at the entrance to the main room, the *hēkāl*. Similar pillars appear also in Canaanite or Phoenician prototypes of the Jerusalem temple, for instance at Hazor in the fourteenth–thirteen centuries B.C.E. They are also inside the first room at the entrance to the second room. The same is the case at Alalakh (Tell el-Atchana), and at Tell Tainat, a Phoenician example of a later period. I am not aware of a single instance of a temple of this kind with two pillars which stand in the courtyard, outside the porch. Two passages in the Bible describe their situation: In I Kings 7:21 we read that Solomon set up the pillars at "the porch of the holy place" (*l^e'ūlām hahēkāl*). This passage is ambiguous; but in II Chronicles 3:17 we find a clear statement: "And he set up the pillars before the holy place" (*'al p^enē hahēkāl*). Of course in most commentaries *hēkāl* is deleted and replaced by *'ūlām,* in order to remove the assumed difficulty. Actually there is not a single compelling argument for placing these pillars in the courtyard rather than in the porch, neither in the Bible nor in any prototypes or analogous buildings. The position of these two large free-standing columns not before the first room but inside it

[15] See Glossary (Ed.).

demands quite distinct alterations in the commonly accepted plan of the restoration of the Jerusalem temple.

Briefly, let us consider another technical question: the size of the sanctuary. At first glance the temple at Arad looks very different from the plan of the Jerusalem temple in proportions and size, in spite of the common features that have been mentioned. In the Jerusalem temple the main room (the *hēkāl*) is a *long room,* twenty cubits broad and forty cubits long, with the entrance on its narrow side. In contrast, the main room at Arad is a distinctly broad room with the entrance in the long side. Just how long and wide was this room? The exact standard of the Hebrew cubit in the period of the monarchy is unknown. It is usually compared with the well-known contemporary Egyptian measures. In Egypt we find cubits of two sizes: the so-called common cubit which is about one and a half feet long (45 cm.) and the so-called royal cubit (or long cubit) which is about three inches longer (52.5 cm.). By measuring the length of the main room at the Arad sanctuary an interesting fact emerges: at the beginning this room was nine meters long, that means exactly twenty short, common Egyptian cubits. We have noted the fact that in the second citadel it was made about five feet longer. This is again exactly twenty cubits, but of the longer royal type. The same difference in measurements appears also in other features of the sanctuary, for example, with respect to the altar. The difference between five common and five royal Egyptian cubits is a little more than one foot: this is exactly the difference between the earlier and later altars! It has become completely clear that between the first and second sanctuary at Arad (that is, between the tenth and the ninth centuries) the measurements of the temple were deliberately changed from the short cubit to the royal or long cubit. If we turn once again to the Books of Chronicles (which I think all of us increasingly value as a treasure book of ancient information) we read in II Chronicles 3:3: "Now these are the foundations which Solomon laid for the building of the house of the God: the length by cubit *after the first measure* (*bammiddāh hārī'šōnāh*) was sixty cubits, and the breadth, twenty cubits." Thereby two remarkable facts emerge: (a) the north-south measurement at Arad is exactly the same as the Solomonic temple in Jerusalem, i.e. twenty cubits, and (b) the Jerusalem temple was built according to the first, the early measure. This enigmatic passage is now confirmed at Arad. It seems that the standard of the cubit was changed between the tenth and ninth centuries, a matter hinted at also by Ezekiel. After the change, the measurements of the Jerusalem temple were not in accord with the current standard but in accord with the "first measure" which was no longer in use. This change, probably due to Egyptian influence, raises interesting questions and points again to the valuable information contained in the Books of Chronicles.

Finally, we come to the most important question: How can we explain the establishment of the sanctuary at Arad; why, of all places and cities, was Arad chosen? I am aware of two possible answers which do not exclude one another completely; each may be partly true. One is proposed by my teacher, Professor Benjamin Mazar, and has been published in a recent issue of the *Journal of Near Eastern Studies*, dealing with the Kenites and the sanctuary at Arad. Mazar connects the Arad sanctuary with the information preserved in the first chapter of Judges, verse 16, where we hear that the children of Hobab the Kenite (according to the Septuagint version) Moses' brother-in-law (or father-in-law), went up out of the city of Palm-trees into the wilderness of Judah which is in the Negev (the south) of Arad. Beside the stories about Hobab (Reuel and Jethro) leading the children of Israel in the desert, the only other passage dealing with the family of Hobab is in the story of Deborah (Judg. 4). Jael was the wife of Heber the Kenite, who separated himself from the family of Hobab, the brother-in-law of Moses, and set his tents up in Galilee at a place called *'ēlōn b^eṣa-'^anannīm* ("the oak of Zaanannim"). All other place names in the Bible compounded with the term *'allōn/'ēlōn* "terebinth", "oak", "holy tree" like *'allōn bākut, 'ēlōn mōrēh, 'ēlōn m^{e'}on^enīm,* etc. are all holy places with an altar and sometimes a sanctuary. This sheds an interesting light on the figure of Jael, who evidently belonged to a clan dedicated to priestly duties. It is hardly coincidence that we find members of the family of Hobab, whose relationship to Moses is widely attested, in two places connected with worship: in Galilee near a holy tree and at Arad where we found the sanctuary.

However, a basic question remains: What was the reason for the location of the sanctuary? Was it just because of the Kenite tradition at the place? We are reminded of the vast literature of the last century and the beginning of our century about Yahweh the God of the Kenites. Do we have at Arad evidence for their overwhelming importance in ancient Israelite worship? Was this the reason for the foundation of the sanctuary, one of the few sanctuaries outside Jerusalem in the period of the monarchy?

I am more inclined toward another solution, one that still requires much study and research. In the Bible we have allusions to altars and sanctuaries at many places all over the country; several are connected with the patriarchs, the family of Moses, and other priestly families. But few places of this kind offer any hints of the building of a temple during the period of the monarchy. Is it not possible that there was some special reason for the building of the royal sanctuary at Arad, as a result of which the tradition of the family of Hobab was kept alive in the Bible? What is our information about other sanctuaries outside Jerusalem? The two famous sanctuaries of Dan and Bethel were built in Northern Israel after the division of the kingdom. Where are these places? Both are on the borders of the northern kingdom: Dan on the north, Bethel on the south. Both also have early traditions of priestly families. Most illuminating is the tradition of Dan in Judges 18:30: "Jonathan the son of Gershom the son of Moses and his sons were priests of the tribe of Dan until the day of the captivity of the land." The sanctuary of Dan achieved importance at the time of Jeroboam I. The tradition of an important priestly family was there before, but the establishment of the important temple at the place is attributed by the Bible to Jeroboam I, after the division of the kingdom.

The prophet Amos alludes to other sanctuaries of the same type. In Amos 5:5 we read "But seek not Bethel, nor enter into Gilgal and pass not to Beersheba." And in 8:14 we have, "They that swear by the sin of Samaria and say, 'As your god, O Dan, lives,' and 'As the way of Beersheba lives.'" He obviously compares four places of worship and perhaps a fifth, Samaria. All four (Dan, Bethel, Gilgal, and Beersheba) were on the borders of the two kingdoms, at remote places such as Arad. They were royal sanctuaries, as we know from Amos 7:13 in the speech of Amaziah the priest of Bethel: "But prophesy not again any more in Bethel, for it is the king's sanctuary, and it is a royal house." Is this just coincidence or does it accord with an ancient law predating the concentration of worship in Jerusalem? Do we not have here a phenomenon of temples at different places of the kingdom: in the capital (Jerusalem and Samaria) and at the borders? In reality they are not exactly on the border, but in royal citadels dominating the border which served also as administrative centers of the border territories, similar to Dan and Beersheba. And is this not the meaning of the familiar expression describing the borders of the Israelite settlement in the country?

We may have a hint of this state of affairs in a strange passage in Isaiah 19. After denouncing Egypt, the prophet concludes with a messianic prophecy that the Egyptians shall adopt the true worship of Yahweh, the God of Israel. How is this thought expressed? On that day "there shall be an altar to the Lord in the midst of the land of Egypt, and a pillar (*maṣṣēbāh*) at the border thereof, to the Lord," Isaiah 19:19. This passage raises many difficulties and is explained differently in the various commentaries. Isaiah himself points to a solution in verse 21: "And the Egyptians shall know the Lord in that day. And they shall worship with sacrifice and oblation [at the altar!] and shall vow a vow unto the Lord [at the *maṣṣēbāh,* at the border!]. . . ."

We must bear in mind that Isaiah does not describe an actual situation but a utopian picture of Egypt, accepting the true worship of Yahweh as established in his days in Judah. This vision depicts an altar in the midst of the country, i.e. in the capital, and a *maṣṣēbāh* at its border. Though speaking of Egypt does he not describe the prevailing situation in Judah? This may fit the biblical description of the concentration of worship in two main stages during the days of Hezekiah and Josiah. The first stage in the days of Hezekiah concentrates sacrifices in Jerusalem, so vividly expressed in the words of Rab-shakeh before the walls of Jerusalem: "Is it not he whose high places and whose altars Hezekiah has taken away and has said to Judah and to Jerusalem, 'Ye shall worship before this altar in Jerusalem'?" (II Kings 18:22). In this connection we note the strange fact mentioned earlier that the temple at Arad was rebuilt through five strata, but the altar through only four. On top of the altar, about half a meter higher, we found clear traces of the fifth citadel floor with intact vessels. Thereby it became clear that no altar stood in the temple of the fifth citadel, in spite of the fact that this was the sanctified place of the altar during the four earlier strata. Only the second stage— that of Josiah—brought the complete destruction of all sanctuaries and temples outside Jerusalem.

I am well aware that I have raised more questions than I have answered. However, the many problems unfolded by the Arad excavations will doubtless be most stimulating for biblical research and for the study of the ancient history of Israel and its worship.

BIBLIOGRAPHY

Aharoni, Y., and Amiran, R., "Arad—A Biblical City in Southern Palestine", *Archaeology* 17 (1964), 43–53
————, "Excavations at Tel Arad—Preliminary Report of the First Season", *IEJ* 14 (1964), 131–47
Aharoni, Y., "Arad: Its Inscriptions and Temple", *BA* 31 (Feb. 1968), 2–32
————, "Excavations at Tel Arad—Preliminary Report of the Second Season", *IEJ* 17 (1967), 233–49
————, "Hebrew Ostraca from Tel Arad", *IEJ* 16 (1966), 1–7
————, "Three Hebrew Ostraca from Arad", *EI* 9 (1969), 10–21
Mazar, B., "The Sanctuary of Arad and the Family of Hobab the Kenite", *JNES* 24 (1965), 297–303
Yeivin, S., "A Hieratic Ostracon from Tel Arad", *IEJ* 16 (1966), 153–59

Papyri of the Fourth Century B.C. from Dâliyeh

A Preliminary Report on Their Discovery and Significance[1]

FRANK MOORE CROSS

I

In the early spring of 1962, Ta'âmireh Bedouin discovered ancient documents buried together with scores of skeletons in a cave of the Wadi Dâliyeh, a desolate canyon north of Jericho on the rim of the Jordan rift. Western scholars were alerted to the new finds in April 1962, when papyrus fragments were brought for sale to the Palestine Archaeological Museum. Père Roland de Vaux of the École Biblique et Archéologique Française received them, and, recognizing immediately their antiquity and importance, transmitted news of the discovery to heads of the other archaeological institutes in Jerusalem, seeking means to acquire them for the Palestine Museum.

First word of the papyri came to the writer from Professor Paul W. Lapp, then Director of the American Schools of Oriental Research in Jerusalem. Père de Vaux had left a fragment of one document with Professor Lapp for study overnight. Professor Lapp wrote that the papyrus, judging from an evening's study of its script, could

[1] This paper is an expansion of the lecture given at the Symposium on Biblical Archaeology held in Berkeley and San Anselmo, March 16, 1966. The latter was published under the title "Aspects of Samaritan and Jewish History in Late Persian and Hellenistic Times," *HTR* 59 (1966), 201–11. Cf. also, "The Discovery of the Samaria Papyri," *BA* 26 (1963), 110–21.

be dated about 375 B.C.E., contained a reference to Samaria, and might be an official document.[2]

In mid-October 1962, I was able to write to Père de Vaux and Professor Lapp that the American Schools of Oriental Research was prepared to enter into negotiations for purchase of the documents, thanks to the establishment of a fund in the Schools by Elizabeth Hay Bechtel.[3] On November 19, after complex negotiations, the primary lot of the Dâliyeh papyri and associated artifacts (sealings, coins, seal rings) were acquired by the American Schools for presentation to the Palestine Archaeological Museum. Publication rights were reserved for the writer by the American Schools, and Professor Lapp agreed to undertake the excavation of the cave site of the discovery in the Schools' behalf.

Our preliminary examination of the lot of papyri and sealings (made on November 17, prior to purchase) gave rise to mixed feelings. On the one hand the papyri were in an advanced state of decay, worm eaten, and, for the most part, in small fragments. The best-preserved papyrus (No. 1), bearing seven seals intact, appeared to be complete. Two or three others were extensively preserved. We were to find later that even Papyrus 1 was incomplete, and, contrary to our expectations, the several boxes of small fragments rarely joined to the larger pieces of papyri. We were in possession of the last remnants of a very large corpus of documents. On the other hand, one of the first items to come to our attention was a sealing affixed to the remnants of a papyrus (No. 5; see Figs. 34–35) inscribed in a clear Palaeo-Hebrew script (not the Aramaic hand of the papyri). It read:

> [   ] *yhw bn* [*sn'*]
> *blṭ pḥt šmr*[*n*]

". . . yahū, son of [San]ballaṭ, governor of Samaria."

[2] This dating proved to be accurate within the limits set by relative typology. The papyrus in question (No. 15), now extensively reconstructed from several fragments, appears to date from the early reign of Artaxerxes III 358–338 B.C.E.).

[3] The "Dead Sea Scrolls Fund" of the American Schools of Oriental Research has been responsible for the purchase of a series of manuscript discoveries, from Cave 4, Qumran, the large Psalms Scroll of Cave 11, Qumran, and most recently the Dâliyeh papyri. The latter two purchases have been made possible by benefactions of Mrs. Bechtel.

The first name, on the basis of later study, probably is to be read [*lyš' ?*]*yhw*, [Belonging *to Yĕša'*]*yahū*.[4]

It was evident that the governor of Samaria had affixed his seal to this papyrus, and that he possessed the familiar family name of the governor of Samaria in the days of Nehemiah: Sanballat (*Sin'uballiṭ*).[5] There could be no doubt that, however fragmentary, the new find of papyri was of extraordinary importance.

Another fragment which came to hand in the first viewing of the lot from Dâliyeh proved to be the piece studied by Professor and Mrs. Lapp. The last line on the reverse read [*b*]*šmryn šṭr' znh* [*k*]*tyb*, "this document was written in Samaria." Above, on the preceding line, partly broken, appeared the names of the officials before whom the document was executed: [*yš*]*w' br sn'blṭ ḥnn sgn'*, "[before Yeš]ūa' son of Sanballaṭ (and) Ḥanan the prefect."

Immediately upon purchase, the largest and best preserved of the papyri was prepared for opening. After photographs of the intact papyrus roll were taken, the cords of its seven seals were slit, and the exacting task of unrolling begun. Papyrus 1 proved to contain twelve lines of bold Aramaic script (see Fig. 36b). Contrary to our expectation, the papyrus was poorly preserved. A substantial part of the left side of the document was missing, probably because it was unprotected by sealings or the tough fiber strings binding the rolled papyrus in its sealings. The papyrus records the sale of the slave Yehōḥanan son of Še'īlah to a certain Yehōnūr, a man who figures several times in the papyri, by Hananiah for the price of

---

[4] The following pertinent readings are found in the Dâliyeh papyri or their sealings:

    (1) [*yš*]*w' (or* [*yd*]*w') br sn'blṭ wḥnn sgn'* . . . (Papyrus 14)

    (2) *qdm* [*Ḥ*]*nnyh pḥt šmryn* . . . (Papyrus 8)

    (3) [*yš'?*] *yhw bn* [*sn'*]
        blṭ pḥt šmr [*n*]

    (4) *ly*[*š/dw*]*'*

The last two readings are in Palaeo-Hebrew on sealings. They are the only inscribed seals in the lot of more than 125 impressions and seal rings. Evidently, in Persian fashion, only officials had inscribed seals. Ḥanan the prefect probably must be equated with the governor Hananiah, suggesting that he succeeded an older brother Yešū'/Yeša'yahū in the governorship. The alternation of caritatives (Ḥanan, Yešū') and formal names (Ḥananyah, Yĕša'yahū) is not unexpected in this period.

[5] Cf. Neh. 2:10, 19; 3:33; 4:1; 6:1, 2, 5, 12, 14; 13:28 (snblṭ); Elephantine Papyrus 30:29; Dâliyeh Papyrus 14 (sn'blṭ).

thirty-five pieces of silver (shekels). It is of note that all three principals bear Yahwistic names.

The most important datum in Papyrus 1 is its double date formula. The first line of the papyrus begins *b20 l'dr šnt 2 r'š mlkwt [d]ryhwš mlk' bšmry[n mdynt'* . . .] "on the twentieth day of Adar, year 2 (the same being) the accession year of Darius the king, in the province of Samaria . . ." Only one Achaemenid king died in the second year of his reign, Arses, who was slain by the infamous eunuch Bagoas and succeeded by Darius III (Codomannus). Thus the papyrus was written on March 19, 335 B.C.E.[6]

As other documents were opened, new date formulae appeared. Several documents are from the early reign of Artaxerxes III (Ochus, 358–338 B.C.E.) including Papyrus 8 written on March 4, 354, "before [Ha]naniah governor of Samaria." The earliest dated piece belongs between the thirtieth and fortieth year of Artaxerxes II (Mnemon), that is, between 375 and 365 B.C.E.[7] Thus the range of dates extends from about 375 down to 335 B.C.E. or slightly later, some forty years. The range covers one of the darkest eras in the history of Palestine.

In the negotiations for the papyri, we had made one of the stipulations of purchase the agreement of the Bedouin to lead us to the cave site where the find had been made. However, it was not until December 2 that the Ta'âmireh made good the bargain. Mr. Yusuf Sa'ad, at that time curator of the Palestine Archaeological Museum, was led to the cave, and in turn Mr. Sa'ad led de Vaux and the Lapps to the site on December 11.

The site of the discovery proved to be the Muġâret Abū Šinjeh, a cave of the Wadi Dâliyeh lying some 14 kilometers north of ancient Jericho, 4 kilometers southwest of Kh. Fasâyil.[8] The closest point accessible to a four-wheel-drive vehicle is located about a kilometer southwest of Fasâyil. From there the cave is at a distance of one hour and a half by foot up into the hills, a climb broken

---

[6] Apparently this document is the first contemporary witness to the two-year reign of Arses, or for that matter, to the accession year of Darius III. Cf. R. A. Parker and W. H. Dubberstein, *Babylonian Chronology, 626 B.C.E.–C.E. 75* (Brown University Press, 1956), pp. 19, 35 f.

[7] This is Papyrus 21. It is very fragmentary, but preserves the symbols 20+10; only units could have followed; and the reign must be that of Artaxerxes II.

[8] The site on the 1:100,000 map series is at coordinates 1890×1557; on the 1:20,000 at 1889×1556.

by precipitous ravines to a height of roughly 450 meters above the Jordan.

II

The expedition of the American Schools of Oriental Research led by Professor Lapp carried out two seasons of excavations in the Wadi Dâliyeh, the first in January 1963, the second in February 1964.

The Cave of the Papyri, labeled Cave 1 by the excavator, and a number of adjacent caves in the canyon walls were explored. Cave 1 penetrates some sixty-five meters into the cliff side. The site of the manuscript finds was at the far end of the main cave shaft. A side shaft led upwards to a gallery named by the excavators the Bat Dome. Its roof swarmed with layers of bats. From this gallery several passages branched off, one of them leading some twenty meters to a room called the Hot Room. Like the site of the manuscript find, it contained pottery of the third quarter of the fourth century B.C.E. and human skeletons—and little oxygen.

When I first viewed the site, it appeared to me that an expedition could not be installed and supplied in the Wadi Dâliyeh without helicopters. However, the Bedouin found a long, circuitous route which could be traversed by donkeys. The tents of the expedition were pitched in the precipitous sides of the Wadi bed, in cave entrances, or on terraces built out on ledges, with the full knowledge that a flash flood, if it came, would wipe out the camp. By necessity the expedition was carried out in the winter, the season of rains in the hill country. Summer heat which climbs regularly above 100 degrees forbade digging in a safer season. The digging in the cave itself presented formidable obstacles. The cave floor contained millennial deposits of powdery bat guano. Any digging or sifting produced clouds of foul dust which blinded and choked the toughest digger, and routed the more fastidious of the excavators. Veteran Ta'âmireh laborers were put back to work in their diggings. Among these was Muḥammad ed-Dîb Ḥassan who as a shepherd boy in 1947 made the first of the manuscript discoveries in Qumran. Work parties dug a trench from the entrance of the cave down to the find area, and put down soundings in other recesses of the cave. In several undisturbed places in the extremities of the cave, including a small area adjacent to the disturbed levels where the papyri were found, homogeneous deposits of fourth-century pottery together with skeletal remains were found immediately beneath a shallow surface layer accumulated in later times.

The number of skeletons in the cave was staggering; many were dug out and scattered by Bedouin. Perhaps two hundred men, women, and children lost their lives at Dâliyeh. A few fragments of papyrus had escaped the clandestine excavation of the Ta'âmireh. Four small fragments (two of which joined) were discovered in the first season. A large fragment was found in the second campaign. While none of these joined to the papyri purchased, they were of the same date and left no doubt that the original provenience of the main lot had been found. The excavation was rich also in other finds: two clay bullae, a "Philisto-Arabian" coin, bits of linen, personal jewelry, remains of food stores, and large quantities of pottery of the third quarter of the fourth century.

III

The first systematic examination of the contents of the Dâliyeh documents was undertaken on my return to Jerusalem at the end of July 1963. In the interval, however, a papyrologist was able to begin work on the fragments. Thanks to the aid of the British Academy, the Rev. J. W. B. Barns came to Jerusalem to use his great skills in putting together the dilapidated lot. While unacquainted with the script and language of the papyri, he accomplished miracles in reconstruction by analysis of fiber patterns and by study of destruction patterns.

On August 7, 1963, a new, small lot of fragments and sealings was purchased from the middleman of the Ta'âmireh tribesmen. It is by no means certain how many papyri were left in the cave by the fugitives who died in the cave of the Wadi Dâliyeh. Perhaps twenty pieces are worthy of being numbered as "papyri." There remain literally hundreds of small fragments, few of which can be joined to each other or to the larger papyri. The original deposit may have been in excess of a hundred documents. The primary destructive agent seems to have been worms rather than rot. Many of the rolled documents were devoured through, leaving patterns like paper dolls when the papyri were opened. One is forced to the grisly speculation that the worms which multiplied in the heaped corpses of the dead also attacked the papyri.

One hundred and twenty-eight clay seal impressions (bullae) have been recovered from all sources including excavation. In addition, there are two gold signet rings both in good condition. About seventy of the bullae are in a good state of preservation, unbroken and unblurred. Two of the seals, one the governor's seal, were inscribed, both in Palaeo-Hebrew. Usually, the seals contain either Attic motifs in the contemporary Greek style or Persian mythic and royal motifs. (see Figures 37, 38, and 39). A very few belong to the so-called Greco-Persian style. The sealings in the Greek style impress one with the vivacity of Greek influences of Samaria in the era before the coming of Alexander.

The content of all the papyri is legal or administrative. Wherever opening or closing date formulae are preserved we are told that the document was written in the province and/or the city of Samaria, often executed before the governor or prefect. Some of the documents are linked by the persons who were parties to the contract. A certain Yehōnūr appears in three documents, Neṭīra' son of Yehōpadanī in four. The names which appear in the papyri are most often Yahwistic when they contain a theophoric element, but there is also a sizable number of foreign names reflecting the mixture of the Samaritan population. Among the latter are names with the divine element: *Qôs* (Edomite), *Kemoš* (Moabite), *Ba'l* (Canaanite), *Nabū* (Babylonian), and *Šahar* (Aramaic). There are an unusually high number of slave documents suggesting that their owners were men of means. There are also the more usual contracts having to do with loans, sales of property, and marriage.

IV

The finds in the Wadi Dâliyeh provide a wealth of data with which to date the deposit of the papyri. By combining information to be found in the papyri themselves, in the associated artifacts, especially the coins, and from Josephus and the Greek historians, we are enabled to reconstruct with a high degree of probability the actual history of the papyri and their owners, whose bones were intermingled with the papyri.

We have written above that the papyri contain date formulae covering the middle third of the fourth century B.C.E. They are a homogeneous corpus, deposited when some two hundred men, women and children were massacred in the cave. The papyri also show that the owners of the papyri were men of substance, patricians of Samaria.

The artifacts from the excavations of the manuscript area of the cave (by both Bedouin and scholar) point in the same direction. The exquisite seal rings, the jewelry, and remnants of fine linen all point to their affluence.

Of particular importance for the date of the deposit are the coins recovered from the site. While all but two of these came from Bedouin excavation, there is no doubt whatever as to their provenience.[9] All date from immediately before the conquest by Alexander in 332 B.C.E.

One of the coins is an Attic tetradrachmon of a developed type attributed to the time of Philip II, father of Alexander the Great. Another is a silver stater of Persic standard minted by Mazday (Mazaeus), late in his tenure as satrap of Cilicia, no later than the reign of Darius III (336–331 B.C.E.). Two small silver coins were found by Professor Lapp in his second season of excavation. Both were sixteenth of a shekel pieces (trihemiobole-Phoenician). One was a coin of the class "Philisto-Arabian," a rather unfortunate designation which includes the fourth-century coinage of Judah; it is a coin minted in Palestine imitative of Attic coinage: a head of Athena on the obverse, an owl and inscription $A\theta E$ on the reverse. It dates from the middle third of the fourth century. The second coin belongs to the type issued in Sidon in the fourth century. It is either a coin of Straton II (343/2–332) or a Palestinian imitation of the Sidonian coin in question; it is well known that in fourth-century Palestine many coins were struck patterned after the Sidonian coinage.

A fifth coin, of which there were a number of identical exam-

[9] Virtually everything offered for sale as coming from the Wadi Dâliyeh in fact did come from the cave. There were two notable exceptions, some Greek and Hebrew inscriptions on ribbed Roman ware obviously pilfered from the excavations at Herodium, and a cigarette box of tiny fragments of papyri in Greek and cursive Aramaic, almost certainly left over from Ta'âmireh digs in the Wadi Murabba'ât. However, the latter was designated as a separate lot by the representative of the Bedouin from the beginning, and later, on being sharply questioned, admitted that its provenience was uncertain. The only alternate possibility is that these few fragments from Jews of the Second Revolt against Rome were recovered from Cave 2 in the Wadi Dâliyeh where the Bedouin also dug, and which when excavated by Professor Lapp's expedition yielded magnificent Middle Bronze Age I pottery, but also an important occupation dating to the Second Jewish Revolt. No remains of documents turned up (with the exception of grafitti on jars).

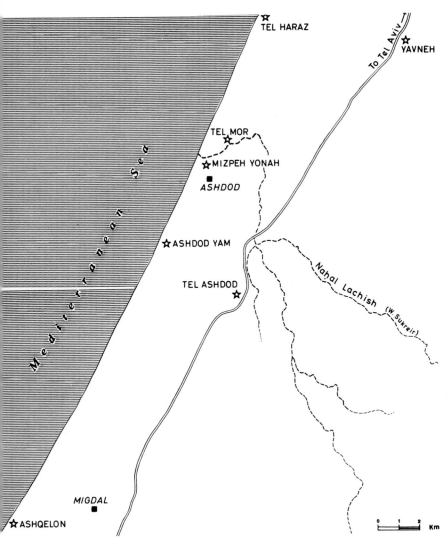

1. Map of Tel Ashdod and vicinity.

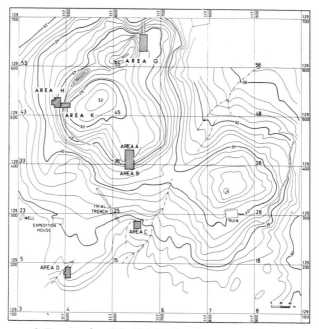

2. Topography of the Tel showing the excavated areas.

3. Areas A and B and the vertical section between them.

4. Late Bronze II strata in Area B—part of fourteenth-century house.

5. Two silos of the latest Late Bronze stratum.

 6. Unstratified scarab belonging to the period of the destruction of the last Late Bronze II occupation. It is of Rameses II, reputedly the Pharaoh of the Exodus.

7. Local pottery of fourteenth and thirteenth centuries.

8. Imported Cypriote pottery of the thirteenth century.

9. Mycenean sherds found in
Late Bronze strata.

10. Canaanite female figurine.

11. Section of brick wall of Philistine
fortress.

12. Area C—Philistine sherds.

13. Philistine pottery—representations of birds.

14. Late Bronze representation of birds.

15. Philistine bird figurine.

16. "Astarte" figurine.

17. Head and neck of Philistine figurine.

18. Figurine of a Philistine goddess.

19. A miniature offering table of ninth-eighth centuries. The upper part—a figurine— is missing.

20. Area D-ninth-and eighth-century temple with whitewashed altar (between the two horizontal meter rods.)

21. Kernos ring and animal head.

22. "Astarte" figurine of ninth-eighth centuries.

23. "Astarte" figurine mold.

24. Hollow head—probably part of a cup.

ples,[10] is a well-known Tyrian didrachmon whose date in the past has been disputed. On the obverse is a divinity (Herakles-Milqart) astride a hippocamp above a double line of stylized waves, beneath which swims a dolphin. On the reverse is an Athenian owl, and representation of Egyptian royal symbols, the crook and flail. On the right of the owl is the Phoenician letter 'ayin and the number "15."

As late as 1957 Henri Seyrig, the distinguished French numismatist, still argued that these Tyrian coins were post-Alexandrine.[11] The chief argument was the fact that the coin was minted on the Attic standard rather than on the Phoenician standard, and the shift of standard reflected the coming of Alexander. It is true that in other Phoenician cities, notably Aradus and Sidon, shifts were made from the Persic or Phoenician standard to the Attic with the conquest of Alexander. However, the analogy between the shifts of standard is not perfect. The coins of Aradus and Sidon of Attic standard were Alexandrine coins, not independent issues of royal mints. With Alexander's coming the latter became excessively rare in Phoenicia, Syria, Palestine, and Cyprus. From this point of view, coins of our type, belonging to independent royal issues, are strange[12] and quite puzzling after Alexander's destruction of the city.

It is a well-known fact that the Attic standard was not first introduced into the Levant by Alexander. It was the prevailing standard at Gaza and Judah in the fifth and fourth centuries and seems to have been known also in Syria and Phoenicia before Alexander.[13]

---

[10] I have seen five specimens from Dâliyeh only one of which we acquired for the Palestine Archaeological Museum with the lot of papyri. Reports of the middleman, Khalil Iskander Shaḥin, indicate that a large hoard was found in the cave. The hoard was broken up, however, and sold to private collectors.

[11] "Antiquités syriennes: sur une prétendue ère tyrienne," Syria 34 (1957), 93–98.

[12] The closest analogy I know is the shift in Mazaeus' coinage from Persic to Attic standard which took place presumably when he moved from his satrapy in Cilicia to Mesopotamia, and from the suzerainty of Darius to that of Alexander.

[13] An example is the 'Abd-Hadad coinage of Hieropolis (Bambyce); cf. E. Babelon, Catalogue des monnaies grecques . . . Les perses achéménides, etc. (Paris, 1893), p. 45. See also George F. Hill, Catalogue of the Greek Coins of Phoenicia (London: Oxford University Press, 1910), p. xxiii, who discusses a unique coin of Aradus which appears to be of Attic standard.

There is no a priori reason why Tyre could not have shifted to the Attic standard before Alexander.

Henri Seyrig has, I believe, made one important contribution to the discussion of this Tyrian coinage. He argues conclusively that this coin and others of similar series bear the abbreviation of the king's name and his year number. This has precise analogies in pre-Alexandrine coinage of Phoenicia as well as in Alexander's coinage from Phoenicia. He rejects attempts to date the series by a putative era of Tyre as well as the notion that these coins were issued contemporaneously with Alexandrine types which probably began about 306 B.C.E. at Tyre. Rather he refers the coins to the period 332 to 307 B.C.E., immediately after the fall of Tyre to Alexander. But from all we know of Alexander's relations with Tyre, it is the last city we should expect to be granted immediate permission to issue an independent royal coinage. Tyre alone of the Phoenician cities opposed Alexander. The siege of Tyre which lasted from January to July/August 332 was notorious for the atrocities committed by the Tyrians against Macedonian prisoners, and for the fierce vengeance exacted by Alexander when the city fell. A reported eight thousand were killed, thirty thousand sold into slavery. Tyre was then reconstructed as a Macedonian fortress.[14] There is a notice also that Philotos was made military governor of Tyre.[15] While the king of Tyre was spared when he took refuge in the Milqart (Herakles) temple, there is no evidence which can stand scrutiny that the monarchy was shortly restored by Alexander.[16]

There are very good reasons for shifting these Tyrian coins to the period immediately before Alexander. The context in which they were found at Dâliyeh is sufficient evidence. However, there is more. At Tell Abū Hawâm a large hoard of Tyrian coins was found. There is a sequence of about 109 coins including the owl series of Phoenician standard, and the series of Attic standard. But despite its proximity to the great Alexandrine mint of 'Akko no Alexandrine

---

[14] Cf. W. W. Tarn, *Alexander the Great* (Cambridge University Press, 1948), I, 40.

[15] Q. Curtius Rufus *Hist. Alex*. iv. 5. 9 (ed. E. Hedicke).

[16] Two passages have been cited in this connection, Diodorus Siculus xvii. 47. 1 (ed. Dindorf) and Justin *Epit . . . Trogi* xviii. 3. 18–19 (ed. O. Seel). Both confuse kings of Sidon with Tyre, notably Straton. Cf. Hill's terse refutation of the argument that the monarchy survived in Tyre, *Catalogue . . . of Phoenicia*, p. cxxiv, n. 3. On the questionable character of Justin as a source, see Tarn, *Alexander the Great*, II, 122–33.

coins were found with the hoard. A second hoard from Tell Fukhar has been published since the Dâliyeh discoveries which shows the same pattern: Tyrian owls of Attic standard found only in pre-Alexandrine contexts.[17] There seems to be every reason to attribute them to Azemilkos,[18] the last king of Tyre before Alexander, whose Semitic name begins precisely with *'ayin,* the abbreviation of the king's name on the Tyrian pieces. Azemilkos ruled seventeen years, if these coins were his, and the Dâliyeh hoard belongs to the fifteenth year, 334 B.C.E.

In view of the evidence accumulated above, one must look to the coming of Alexander as the terminus *ad quem* for the massacre of Samaritan patricians and the abandonment of the series of late, pre-Alexandrine documents and artifacts in the Dâliyeh cave. A precise occasion for the dread event easily suggests itself. If Josephus is to be believed, the Samaritans initially ingratiated themselves with Alexander.[19] Later while Alexander was in Egypt, Curtius reports[20] that the Samaritans burned alive Andromachus, Alexander's prefect in Syria. The crime was not only heinous, it was the first sign of revolt in Syria-Palestine, and Alexander returned in all haste to Samaria, and according to Curtius took vengeance on the murderers who were "delivered up to him." According to Syncellus, and one passage in the *Chronicon* of Eusebius, Alexander destroyed the city and settled a Macedonian colony on the site; according to another passage in Eusebius, and Jerome, Perdiccas settled the city with Macedonians.[21] While it is highly likely that Alexander destroyed the city, it is probable that he hurried on to Mesopotamia, and that

[17] See A. Kindler, "The Mint of Tyre—the Major Source of Silver Coins in Ancient Israel" [in Hebrew], *Eretz-Israel,* viii [the E. L. Sukenik volume] (Jerusalem: Israel Exploration Society, 1967), 318–25, Pl. 1A. Kindler has come to the same conclusion, that these coins must be raised in date to the period before Alexander. Somehow, however, he has missed my discussion of the Dâliyeh coins (*BA* 26 [1963], 116–18). He argues the case primarily on the basis of the Tell Abū Hawâm and Tell Fukhar hoards. He also records a point which escaped me, namely that M. Narkiss as early as 1939 argued for a pre-Alexandrine date for this Tyrian owl series.

[18] Arrian *Anab. Alex.* ii. 24. 5; ii. 15. 6.

[19] *Antiq.* xi. 297–345 (The Loeb Classical Library *Josephus,* Vol. VI, ed. Ralph Marcus). On the special historical problems of this section, see Marcus' discussion and references in Appendix B, pp. 498–511, and Appendix C, pp. 513–532.

[20] Q. Curtius Rufus *Hist. Alex.* iv. 8. 9–10.

[21] For references and a critical discussion of the problems of the texts, see Marcus, *Josephus,* VI, Appendix C.

Perdiccas during Alexander's lifetime was designated to found the Macedonian city.[22]

This construction of the events now has some support in archaeological data. G. Ernest Wright[23] has recently argued that two circumstances, the rebuilding of Shechem after a long abandonment in the late fourth century and the contemporary appearance of Hellenistic towers at Samaria constructed in Greek rather than Palestinian design, are most easily explained if Samaria were resettled by Macedonians in the time of Alexander, and if the Samaritans at the same time returned to Shechem to found their new capital.

The following sketch of events, I believe, most easily satisfies all of our data. The leaders in Samaria who were implicated in the rebellious acts that led to the prefect's death fled Samaria on learning of Alexander's rapid march on the city. Presumably they followed the main road down the Wadi Fâr'ah into the wilderness, and found temporary refuge in the Wadi Dâliyeh cave. A great number fled, whole families, fairly well supplied with food. Their origin and status are well attested by their seals and their legal documents. They were discovered in their hiding place by the Macedonians, either by assiduous search or, more likely, through betrayal by their fellows who remained in Samaria,[24] and mercilessly slaughtered to a man.[25]

[22] This is the solution in essential form already suggested by Wilrich and Schürer, and most recently supported by V. Tscherikower, *Hellenistic Civilization and the Jews* (Philadelphia, 1959), pp. 47 f., and 103 f. Elias Bickerman writes, "It often happened that when a Greek colony was established, native villages under its control formed a union around an ancestral sanctuary. Following the same pattern, the countryside of (now Macedonian) Samaria constituted an organization, in Greek style, the Sidonians of Shechem, for the purpose of serving the god of Israel. Shechem, the most ancient capital and the most sacred site of Israel, became the natural center of the confederation" (*From Ezra to the Last of the Maccabees* [New York: Schocken, 1962], pp. 43 f.).

[23] "The Samaritans of Shechem," *HTR* 55 (1962), 366–77; on the date of the temple on Mount Gerizim, see R. J. Bull and G. Ernest Wright, "Newly Discovered Temples on Mount Gerizim in Jordan," *HTR* 58 (1965), 234–37.

[24] Curtius' words, cited above, could easily be so construed.

[25] Professor Lapp has suggested that a great fire was built in the opening into the cave, suffocating the Samaritans cowering in the extremities of the cave. This is a plausible suggestion. A parallel is to be found in a modern conflict not dissimilar. In June 1845, at Dahra in Algeria, the French commanded by Aimable Jean Jacques Pélissier burned the mouth of a cave where, according to Pélissier, one thousand insurgents, men, women, and children, had taken refuge. See A. Bernard, *L'Algérie*, p. 239.

V

The significance of the discoveries in the Wadi Dâliyeh despite the banal contents of the papyri is considerable. Any light shed on the fourth century B.C.E. in Palestine is highly welcome; one doubts that there is a century less known in the entire first millennium.

For the science of palaeography, it is difficult to exaggerate the importance of these papyri. A few short inscriptions from Judaea, written in lapidary Aramaic or in Palaeo-Hebrew script, exist, but the new papyri cover much of the century, and establish the first set of absolute dates for the fourth-century Aramaic cursive. This has immediate implications for the chronology of the third-century biblical manuscripts from Qumran: the dating proposed by the writer for the archaic Samuel manuscript (ca. 225 B.C.E.) now appears to be minimal. The chronology of the Archaic Period (pre-Hasmonean) may prove too low by a generation; the archaic Samuel then would date from 275–225 B.C.E. It is clear also that the so-called Hasmonean hands of Qumran cannot be reduced in date, but are now fixed.[26]

The new papyri will provide important new material for the description of social institutions in Persian Palestine, for studies in the history of law, and for the description of the linguistic and orthographic evolution of Aramaic in the West. But discussion of these topics must await another occasion.

Tatters of historical data will be dredged from the papyri. The appearance of a Sanballat who flourished in Samaria in the first half of the fourth century gives an unexpected answer to a question debated for generations by students of the history of the Jews and Samaritans in the post-exilic era. Sanballat of Beth Horon is well known as the devious and malicious enemy of Nehemiah, mentioned frequently in the memoirs of Nehemiah, and once in a papyrus from the Jewish Colony at Elephantine in Upper Egypt.[27] He was governor of the province of Samaria in 455 B.C.E., when Nehemiah arrived in Zion, and by 410 was an aged man, whose son Delaiah acted in his name. Sanballat gained notoriety in the Bible for his opposition to the restoration of the walls of Jerusalem, and for con-

---

[26] F. M. Cross, "The Development of the Jewish Scripts," in *BANE*, pp. 133–202.

[27] The gentilic "Horonite" is best explained as derived from Bêt Hôrôn.

spiring against the life of Nehemiah, in league with Tobiah, the Jewish governor of Ammon, and Gashmu, king of the Qedarite league, whose territory extended from northern Arabia into southern Palestine.

Nehemiah prevailed, of course, proving as wily as he was pious. He fortified the city, increased its population, and completed his first tour of duty as governor in 433 B.C.E. After a sojourn of indeterminate length, he returned to the Holy City. At the close of his memoirs, recounting the details of his reforms in Judah, he relates a last episode in which Sanballat plays a role. Nehemiah discovered that the son of Joiada the Zadokite high priest and the daughter of Sanballat the Horonite had been joined in a diplomatic marriage uniting the two great families of Judah and Samaria.[28] Nehemiah in righteous indignation chased the young man out of Jerusalem. Unhappily, we do not know his name. According to Josephus, however, after Johanan, son of Joiada, became high priest, he killed his brother Jesus in the Temple. So dreadful was the event that Bagoas, the Persian governor of Judah, a successor to Nehemiah, entered the Temple by force, defiling it, and imposed a heavy tribute on the Jews for seven years.[29] Jesus evidently had been laying claim to the high priesthood with the aid of Bagoas. It would not be surprising if Jesus were the elder brother, son-in-law of Sanballat, who had proper claims to the diadem.[30]

In the *Antiquities,* Josephus tells a similar story with similar names, but the plot is played out in the era of Darius III and Alexander the Great. Sanballat, appointed governor of Samaria by Darius III, arranged a marriage between his daughter Nikaso and a certain Manasseh identified as the brother of Johanan the high priest. Manasseh was expelled from the altar, and retired to Samaria. This was the occasion, according to Josephus, for the building of the Samaritan temple on Mount Gerizim. Sanballat set up his son-in-law in business, so to speak, providing him with his own temple. According to the tradition received by Josephus, Alexander the Great

[28] Neh. 13:28.
[29] *Antiq.* xi. 297–301. This event probably must be dated before 404, since according to Neh. 12:22 Jaddua I (see below) came to the throne during the reign of Darius (II). Josephus identifies Bagoas as the *stratēgos* of Artaxerxes, presumably confusing him with the notorious eunuch of Artaxerxes III.
[30] Cf. N. H. Snaith, *Studies in the Psalter* (London: Epworth Press, 1934), pp. 13–14; H. H. Rowley, "Sanballat and the Samaritan Temple," *BJRL* 38 (1955), 184 f.

himself commissioned its building on his arrival in Palestine in 332.[31]

In the past, scholars viewing these two similar accounts were incredulous. Cowley's sentiment was typical: "The view that there were two Sanballats, each governor of Samaria, and each with a daughter who married a brother of a High Priest at Jerusalem is a solution too desperate to be entertained."[32] Many historical constructions were attempted to provide a solution. Most saw the account of Josephus as a secondary reflex of biblical Sanballat and the intermarriage of the fifth century. A few gave credence to an Alexandrine date for the founding of the Samaritan temple. In a bizarre attempt to salvage Josephus' reputation as a historian, C. C. Torrey moved Nehemiah down into the fourth century, claiming that the Sanballat of Samaria mentioned in the Elephantine Papyri was grandfather of Sanballat the Horonite, enemy of Nehemiah and father of two (!) marriageable daughters.[33] Some scholars even moved the building of the temple on Gerizim back into the fifth century, despite the silence of the Chronicler on the question of a separate Samaritan cultus.[34]

If I mistake not, no scholar has proposed the existence of a Sanballat who flourished in the first half of the fourth century, after Sanballat the Horonite was dead, before the day of the Sanballat of Josephus' account, laid in the reign of Darius III (335–330 B.C.E.). However, once the existence of a second Sanballat, father of governors of Samaria, is firmly established, paradoxically it becomes far easier to accept a third Sanballat in the age of Alexander. That is to say, with the appearance of Sanballat II in the Dâliyeh Papyri, most if not all objections to a Sanballat III melt away. The point is this. We know well that it was a regular practice in the Achaemenid empire for high offices, that of satrap or governor, to become hereditary. It is evident that the Sanballatids held the governorship of Samaria for several generations, as did the Tobiads of Ammon. Moreover, we know that the practice of papponymy (naming a child for its grandfather) was much in vogue among the Jews and sur-

[31] *Antiq.* xi. 302–12, 321–25.

[32] A. Cowley, *Aramaic Papyri of the Fifth Century B.C.* (Oxford University Press, 1923), p. 110 (quoted by Rowley, *BJRL* 38 [1955], 173, n. 1).

[33] See, for example, his discussion in *The Second Isaiah* (New York: Scribner, 1928), pp. 456–60, and references.

[34] For detailed bibliographical references, see Rowley, *BJRL* 38 (1955), *passim*.

rounding nations precisely in this era.[35] One may refer to the Tobiads where papponymy is documented for about nine generations.[36] The high priests of Judah in the Hellenistic era present almost as striking a picture. The Oniads alternate the names Onias and Simon over five generations.

We can reconstruct with some plausibility, therefore, the sequence of governors of Samaria in the fifth and fourth centuries. Sanballat the Horonite is evidently the founder of the line, to judge by the fact that he bears a gentilic, not a patronymic. He was a Yahwist, giving good Yahwistic names to his sons Delaiah and Shelemiah. Sanballat I must have been a mature man to gain the governorship, and in 445, when Nehemiah arrived, no doubt was already in his middle years. His son Delaiah acted for his aged father as early as 410. The grandson of Sanballat, Sanballat II, evidently inherited the governorship early in the fourth century, to be succeeded by an elder son (Yeshūaʻ?), and later by another son, Hananiah. Hananiah was governor by 354 B.C.E., and his son, or his brother's son, Sanballat III, succeeded to the governorship in the time of Darius III and Alexander the Great.[37]

Josephus is not wholly vindicated. It is clear that he identified biblical Sanballat and Sanballat III, jumping from the fifth to the late fourth century. Moreover, it is highly likely that a similar haplography occurred in Josephus' sources for the sequence of Zadokite high priests. From the Elephantine letters we know that Bagoas had become governor and that Johanan, son of Joiada, had taken the high priestly office no later than 410. Nehemiah furnishes us with the name of his son Jaddua, a caritative form of his grandfather's name, Joiada. Unless the name of Darius in Nehemiah 12:10, 22 is added by a late editor, we must suppose that Jaddua took priestly office before 404 B.C.E.[38] It is hardly conceivable therefore that he exercised the priestly office until 332, much less had a brother of marriageable age in 332, as we should have to affirm if biblical Jad-

---

[35] Cf. W. F. Albright, "Dedan" in *Geschichte und Altes Testament,* ed. G. Ebeling (Albrecht Alt Festschrift) (Tübingen, 1953), p. 6, n. 3.

[36] On papponymy in the Tobiad family, see B. Mazar, "The Tobiads," *IEJ* 7 (1957), 137–45, 229–38, and, especially, p. 235 and n. 73.

[37] This is not counter to probabilities. Sanballat I no doubt died ripe in years, his eldest already advanced in age. This construction is, of course, hypothetical. Our evidence is tantalizingly limited.

[38] See n. 30, above; see also W. F. Albright, *The Biblical Period* (Pittsburgh: The Biblical Colloquium, 1950), p. 54.

dua is identified with Jaddua the high priest whose brother married Nikaso, daughter of Sanballat III. It seems highly probable that we must insert a Johanan (?) and a Jaddua III in the series of high priests.[39]

What, then, are we to say about the marriage of the son of Joiada to a daughter of Sanballat I, and the marriage of the brother of Jaddua to the daughter of Sanballat III? Certainly we can no longer look at the episode with the same historical skepticism. After all, the names and relationships are by no means identical. It appears that the noble houses of Samaria and Jerusalem were willing to intermarry despite the ire of certain strict Jews, presumably the progeny of the reforms of Nehemiah and Ezra.

In the past it has been difficult to reckon with the possibility of repeated intermarriage between the aristocracy of Samaria and the theocratic family of Jerusalem. We are inclined to read back into the era of Nehemiah and Ezra the extreme alienation, indeed the hatred, which marked the relationship of Jews and Samaritans in Roman times, and to attribute to Ezra the developed legal tradition related to the Kūtîm in Rabbinic sources. There has been mounting evidence, however, that the schism which separated the Samaritans finally, and irreversibly, from their Jewish coreligionists came much later, long after the end of Persian rule. For one thing, it is evident that the religion of Samaria derived from Judaism. Its feasts and law, conservatism toward Torah, and theological development show few survivals from the old Israelite religion as distinct from Judaean religion, and no real evidence of religious syncretism. Even the late Jewish apocalyptic has left a firm imprint on Samaritanism.[40] For this and other reasons, scholars have increasingly been inclined to lower the Samaritan schism into the last half of the fourth century, and some would discover the occasion of the radical break of Jews and Samaritans as falling precisely in the era of Alexander the Great.

There can be little doubt that the erection of the temple of Gerizim as a rival to Zerubbabel's temple in Jerusalem further aggravated the traditional bad relations between Samaritan and Jew. It

[39] Counting Joiada as I. Cf. Paul W. Lapp, "Ptolemaic Stamped Handles from Judah," *BASOR* 172 (1963), 33, No. 54.

[40] See Bickerman, *From Ezra to . . . Maccabees,* pp. 42–43, who observes that the conflicts of the Persian period between Samaria and Jerusalem were largely political, rather than religious.

need not, however, be regarded as the final event leading to total estrangement. Curious to say, the Hellenistic era added at least three, perhaps four, rival cults to that of Jerusalem. In the second century B.C.E. Onias IV, pretender to the Zadokite high priesthood, built a temple in Leontopolis in Egypt.[41] At the beginning of the second century, Hyrcanus of the Tobiad family built a temple in 'Arâq el-'Emîr in Trans-Jordan.[42] If Josephus is correct, the Essenes conducted a sacrificial cultus by the Dead Sea.[43]

It is difficult to speak of the Samaritans as a fully separated sect, so long as direct Jewish influence shaped their doctrine and practice, so long as the biblical text which they used was held in common with the Jews, so long as Jew and Samaritan used a common national style of script. In other terms, when do Samaritan and Jewish theology and discipline begin separate, increasingly diverging lines of development? When does the textual tradition of the Samaritan Pentateuch branch apart from the textual tradition established in Jerusalem? When does the Samaritan script begin to evolve in its distinctive path?

In 1940, W. F. Albright wrote as follows: "If we compare the oldest lapidary examples of Samaritan writing with the coins of the Hasmoneans . . . , dated between 135 and 37 B.C.E., a relatively late date for the origin of the Samaritan script as such seems highly probable. Moreover, since Shechem and Samaria were conquered by the Jews between 129 and 110 B.C.E., and were lost to the Romans in 63 B.C.E., it would only be natural to date the final schism between the sects somewhere in the early first century B.C.E."[44]

With the discovery of the Qumran scrolls, especially the hundred or more biblical rolls from Cave 4 Qumran, Albright's position was confirmed in principle. The writer drew on a number of new lines of evidence which appear to establish firmly that the Samaritan Pentateuch, its textual type, orthographic style, Palaeo-Hebrew script, and linguistic usage, all developed in the Maccabean and

[41] Josephus *War* i. 31, 33; vii. 422–35.
[42] See Paul W. Lapp, "The Second and Third Campaigns at 'Arâq el-'Emîr," and "The Qaṣr el-'Abd: A Proposed Reconstruction," *BASOR* 171 (1963), 8–38 and 39–45.
[43] On a possible sacrificial cult at Qumran, see F. M. Cross, *The Ancient Library of Qumran*, rev. ed. (New York: Doubleday Anchor, 1961), pp. 100–6.
[44] *From the Stone Age to Christianity* (Johns Hopkins Press, 1940, 2d ed., Doubleday Anchor, 1946), p. 336, n. 12. Cf. *BASOR* 140 (1955), 33, n. 29, and *BASOR* 81 (1941), 51.

early Hasmonean periods.[45] Recently two of my students have developed in detail these and other positions relating to the Samaritan Pentateuch in Harvard dissertations: Bruce K. Waltke, "Prolegomena to the Samaritan Pentateuch" (1965); and James D. Purvis, *The Samaritan Pentateuch and the Origin of the Samaritan Sect,* published in 1968 in the series Harvard Semitic Monographs.

We can now place the Samaritan Pentateuch in the history of the Hebrew biblical text.[46] It stems from an old Palestinian tradition which had begun to develop distinctive traits as early as the time of the Chronicler, and which can be traced in Jewish works and in the manuscripts of Qumran as late as the first century of the Christian era. This tradition was set aside in the course of the first century in Jerusalem in favor of a tradition of wholly different origin (presumably from Babylon), which provided the base of the Massoretic recension. The Samaritan Pentateuchal tradition breaks off very late in the development of the Palestinian text. Early exemplars of this tradition lack most of the long additions from synoptic passages, as well as exhibiting stronger affinities with the Egyptian textual tradition, which broke off and began its separate development much earlier than the Samaritan. The Samaritan text-type thus is a late and full exemplar of the common Palestinian tradition, in use both in Jerusalem and Samaria.

The Palestinian textual tradition of the Pentateuch sometimes comes in special dress. Often at Qumran it is inscribed in the Palaeo-Hebrew script. This script is now known from seals of the fourth century from Samaria (via Dâliyeh), an unpublished seal from Makmish,[47] and from late in the century from the so-called Hezekiah coin.[48] It is frequent in the official jar stamps of the third century B.C.E. from Judah, both in the stamps inscribed with *Yehūd*

---

[45] On the textual and palaeographical aspects of "Proto-Samaritan" texts from Qumran, see my early comments in *BASOR* 141 (1956), 12, n. 5a; *The Ancient Library of Qumrân,* pp. 172 f.; and "The Development of the Jewish Scripts," in *BANE,* p. 189, n. 4.

[46] See, provisionally, the writer's papers, "The History of the Biblical Text in the Light of the Discoveries in the Judaean Desert," *HTR* 57 (1964), 281–99, and "The Contribution of the Discoveries at Qumran to the Study of the Biblical Text," *IEJ* 16 (1966), 81–95.

[47] My knowledge of this seal is thanks to Professor Nahman Avigad, who will publish it. Its script shows a number of special traits in common with the Samaritan seals.

[48] Published by Ovid R. Sellers, *The Citadel of Beth-zur* (Philadelphia: Westminster, 1933), pp. 73 f.

plus symbol[49] and in the pentagram stamps bearing the legend *Jerusalem*.[50] In the second and first centuries B.C.E., this old national script is well known from published and unpublished manuscripts from Qumran as well as from Hasmonean coins. It is now possible to date roughly the periods in the typological sequence of the Palaeo-Hebrew scripts.[51]

In this sequence of scripts, it is evident that the ancestral Samaritan character branches off from the Palaeo-Hebrew script in the course of the first century B.C.E. There is no question of pushing the date higher. It may be noted that the Palaeo-Hebrew script is used only in copying Palestinian texts. Texts of other traditions never are copied in the script; on the other hand, Palestinian texts of the Pentateuch are also inscribed in the ordinary Jewish character.

A similar typology can be drawn in the development of spelling practices. The earliest Palestinian texts follow a highly defective mode of orthography. In the course of the early second century a special "Maccabean" spelling system emerged, which expands the use of vowel letters, sometimes in a startling fashion. This baroque style of spelling, in a relatively restrained mode well known in late manuscripts from Qumran, characterized the Samaritan Pentateuch.[52]

The language of the Samaritan Pentateuch also includes archaizing forms and pseudo-archaic forms which surely point to the post-Maccabean age for its date. From whatever side we examine the Samaritan Pentateuch, by whatever typological development we measure it, we are forced to the Hasmonean period at the earliest for the origins of the Samaritan recension of the Pentateuch.

This evidence suggests strongly that the definitive breach between the Jews and Samaritans must be sought in the special events of the Hasmonean era, before the Roman period, when Jew and Samaritan looked upon each other in loathing, or as corrupters of the faith.

[49] See most recently Lapp, *BASOR* 172 (1963), 22–35.

[50] J. S. Holladay, in a letter dated December 2, 1965, has called my attention to stamps on wine jars of the Greek islands, notably Thasos, which bear the pentagram and evidently influenced Jewish potters.

[51] See R. H. Hanson, "Palaeo-Hebrew Scripts in the Hasmonaean Age," *BASOR* 175 (1964), 26–42. With the publication of the full lot of Cave 4 manuscripts, more precision in dating these Qumran hands will become possible.

[52] On the orthography of Palestinian texts, see the second paper listed in n. 46, above, and D. N. Freedman, "The Massoretic Text and the Qumran Scrolls: A Study in Orthography, *Textus* 2 (1962), 87–103.

Once again we may look to the excavations at Shechem which yield evidence which, when correlated with texts from Josephus, provides a convincing setting. In 128 B.C.E. John Hyrcanus laid waste the temple of Mount Gerizim and imposed Judaean Judaism, so to speak, on the Samaritans; on the same campaign, he went so far as to circumcise by force the Idumeans living to the south of Judah. It is clear that his goal was to establish orthodoxy in the realm which once made up Israel. In 107 B.C.E. Hyrcanus again stormed north, destroying Samaria and probably Shechem as well.[53] Hyrcanus' attempt to extirpate the Samaritan cultus failed as signally as Spanish attempts to baptize Jews in another age. When Pompey in 64 B.C.E. freed Samaria from vassalage to the Hasmonean priest-kings, we may be sure the Samaritans severed all ties with Judaism, to traverse their own isolated and involuted path.

This reconstruction of the history of the Samaritans solves many problems which have perplexed us in the past. As we have suggested, it dissolves the mystery of the specifically Jewish character of Samaritanism. It explains the close ties of Samaritanism to Zadokite traditions, provides the background of Essene or apocalyptic Zadokite strains in late Samaritan law and doctrine. The historian is no longer required to contend with a parallel, but unrelated, evolution within two sects over a half millennium after their separation.

Similarly, the new reconstruction of the history of the Samaritans clears up confusion concerning the history of the text of the Pentateuch. In the distorted picture of this development still being defended in most circles, we were required to suppose that the Samaritan Pentateuch branched off as early as the fifth century, yet preserved a text exceedingly like the *textus receptus* of the Roman age, indeed a secondary or inferior form of the received text. The Greek version, branching off about the same time or slightly later, on the other hand, preserved a remarkably variant tradition, sometimes superior, sometimes inferior to the Rabbinic text of the first century of the common era. The Greek tradition conforms to all analogies in the transmission of ancient texts. The development of the Samaritan seemed at all points anomalous. These anomalies now disappear, with the happy result that the text critic's task is greatly facilitated.

[53] See E. F. Campbell in Toombs and Wright, "The Third Campaign at Balâṭah (Shechem), *BASOR* 161 (1961), 47, and G. E. Wright, "The Samaritans at Shechem, *HTR* 55 (1962), 358–59.

BIBLIOGRAPHY

Bickerman, E., *From Ezra to the Last of the Maccabees,* (New York: Schocken, 1962)

Cross, F. M., *The Ancient Library of Qumran,* rev. ed., (New York: Doubleday Anchor, 1961)

———, "The Development of the Jewish Scripts," in *The Bible and the Ancient Near East,* ed. G. Ernest Wright, (New York: Doubleday Anchor, 1961), pp. 133–202

———, "The Discovery of the Samaria Papyri", *BA* 26 (1963), 110–121

———, "Aspects of Samaritan and Jewish History in Late Persian and Hellenistic Times", *HTR* 59 (1966), 201–211

Wright, G. Ernest, "The Samaritans of Shechem", *HTR* 55 (1962), 366–77

The Early History of the Qumran Community

FRANK MOORE CROSS

I

After more than twenty years of discovery and publication, the study of the manuscripts from the desert of Judah has entered into a second, more mature phase.[1] The heat and noise of the early controversies have not wholly dissipated. One occasionally hears the agonized cry of a scholar pinned beneath a collapsed theory. And no doubt in the popular press, the so-called battle of the scrolls will continue to be fought with mercenaries for many a year. In fact, however, the period of initial confusion is properly past. From the burgeoning field of scroll research and the new disciplines it has created, certain coherent patterns of fact and meaning have emerged.

The scrolls and the people of the scrolls can be placed within a broad historical framework with relative certitude, thanks to external controls furnished by the archaeologist and the palaeographer. The historian must begin here, for the internal data from the scrolls pose special problems for the historian owing to their esoteric language, and the usual methods of historical criticism are difficult to apply without the intrusion of a considerable subjective element.

The archaeological context of the community of the Dead Sea, its caves, community center, and agricultural adjunct at 'En Feshkhah has been established by six major seasons of excavation. The ancient center has yielded a clear stratification, and in turn the strata are closely dated by their yield of artifacts, notably coins. In the era

[1] The most recent surveys may be found in *Scrolls from the Wilderness of the Dead Sea,* ed. F. M. Cross (Berkeley: American Schools of Oriental Research, 1965), pp. 5–12; and in Cross, *Die antike Bibliothek von Qumran* (Neukirchen: Neukirchener Verlag, 1967), pp. 20–60, and especially in the "Anhang zur deutschen Ausgabe, pp. 214–29, with bibliography.

of our interest, the site exhibits three phases. The first of these, so-called Period Ia, consists of the remains of the earliest communal structures. In Period Ib, the settlement was almost completely rebuilt and enlarged. The coin series suggests that the buildings of the second phase were constructed, as we shall see, in the time of Alexander Jannaeus (103–76 B.C.E.). The problem of the date of foundation of the settlement is an interesting and subtle one. So thoroughly were the structures of the first phase rebuilt that it is questionable whether any of the coins can be attributed to it. Moreover, it is notoriously difficult to date foundations since a certain time must elapse before debris, including lost coins, accumulates. This is complicated in the present instance by the short life of the first phase (Ia). At the same time coins have a considerable period of currency. When John Hyrcanus introduced the new Jewish coinage late in his reign, coins of the Seleucid kings continued to circulate, and John's own coinage did not cease to circulate on the day of his death. The earliest coins of Period I are five Seleucid coppers of imprecise date, coming down to the era of Antiochus VII Sidetes (138–129 B.C.E.), and some eleven silver coins of Seleucid stamp, five, at least, to be attributed to Antiochus Sidetes. The paucity of Seleucid coppers earlier than the reigns of John Hyrcanus and Antiochus Sidetes suggests that it would be most precarious to date the main buildings of Period Ib before their era, and one may argue that the main building phase belongs to the time of Alexander Jannaeus, beginning in 103 B.C.E. The series of Jewish coppers exhibits one certain coin of John Hyrcanus I[2], one coin of Judas Aristobulus (104–103 B.C.E.), 143 coins of Alexander Jannaeus, and ten coins of the remaining Hasmoneans (76–37 B.C.E.). These data suggest strongly that the second phase, that is, the main period of construction, is to be dated early in the reign of Alexander Jannaeus. The first phase, Ia, is evidently earlier. How much earlier is difficult to say; certainly it was short-lived. The rarity of coins dating before Antiochus Sidetes becomes more difficult to explain for every day we push back earlier than 138 B.C.E., the beginning of his reign. In short, we must place the foundation of the site in the wilderness of Qumran within the extreme limits 150–100 B.C.E., and probable limits of 140–120 B.C.E.

[2] This is a revised figure; in the preliminary report fifteen coins were attributed to Hyrcanus I. See now R. de Vaux, *L'Archéologie et les manuscrits de la Mer Morte* (London: Oxford University Press, 1961), pp. 14 ff.

In the second phase, Period Ib, the community center took its permanent form, though certain extensions or repairs of a minor sort were introduced before the destruction of its buildings in the earthquake of 31 B.C.E. reported by Flavius Josephus. After a period of abandonment, indeterminate in length, the site was reoccupied, rebuilt, and repaired precisely on the plan of the older communal complex, and flourished until C.E. 68 when it was stormed and occupied by the forces of Vespasian in the course of his raid on Jericho.

Theoretically, I suppose, the community occupying the ruins in each of these three phases need not have been related.[3] In fact the community of the second and third, and, no doubt, the little known first phase, was one continuing community. The peculiarity of the life at Qumran was such in these periods that the historian's normally vivacious imagination is overtaxed in trying to conceive of two such communities, as specified by the functions of the communal establishment in the wilderness, following one upon another without relationship. The very setting of the community requires a special explanation. Only powerful motivations would send a large group of persons into this wasteland. But more difficult to explain than the desolate environment chosen by the desert folk is the special character of the community center. The center was composed of communal facilities for study, writing, eating, domestic industries, common stores. The members of the community did not live in the buildings (for the most part at any rate) but in caves and shelters radiating out from the central buildings. That is to say, the architectural functions of the rooms and structures require a special mode of religious and communistic life. We can conclude only that the people of the scrolls founded the community in the second half of the second century B.C.E. and occupied it, with a brief interruption in the reign of Herod, until the dreadful days of the Jewish Revolt.

Corroboration of this reading of the archaeological evidence is immediately furnished by the paleographical analysis of some six hundred manuscripts recovered from Qumran. The main lines of the evolution of the late Aramaic and early Jewish bookhands were fixed on the basis of documents and inscriptions already in the interval between the two World Wars.[4] Now, thanks to the dis-

---

[3] As claimed by G. R. Driver, for example, in his erratic and arbitrary study, *The Judean Scrolls* (Oxford: Blackwell, 1965; New York: Schocken, 1966).

[4] W. F. Albright, "A Biblical Fragment from the Maccabean Age: The Nash Papyrus," *JBL* 56 (1937), 145–76.

coveries in the Judaean desert, the science of early Jewish palaeography has grown rich in materials for the typology of scripts.[5]
These discoveries include not only the manuscripts of Qumran in
Palaeo-Hebrew, Jewish, and Greek hands, but also the hardly less
important discoveries from the Wadi Murabba'ât and the Nahal
Hever written in both formal and cursive Jewish hands, as well as
in Greek, Latin, and Nabataean. While these discoveries have occupied the center of the stage, other discoveries from the Wadi
Dâliyeh north of Jericho,[6] from the excavations of Khirbet Qumran, from the tombs of Jerusalem, and from the excavations at
Masada,[7] to mention only the most important, have steadily pyra-
mided, extending our knowledge of the evolution and relative dating
of early Jewish scripts.

Not only do we now possess ample materials for precise typological analysis of the scripts of the Qumran manuscripts, we have accumulated also a series of externally dated scripts by which the
relative dates gained by typological study can be turned into absolute dates. Most striking no doubt are the documents bearing date
formulae of the late fourth century B.C.E. (Dâliyeh), and of the first
century and second century of the Christian era (Qumran, Murabba'ât, and Hever) which overlap in part and extend the Qumran
series backward and forward in time. To these may be added documents from excavations, notably from Qumran itself and Masada,
dated by archaeological context to the first century B.C.E and later.

The scripts of Qumran belong to three periods of paleographical
development. A very small group of biblical manuscripts belong to
an archaic style whose limits are ca. 250 to 150 B.C.E. Very frequent
are manuscripts in hands of the Hasmonean period, between 150
and 30 B.C.E. Manuscripts *composed* as well as copied by the sectarian community begin, most significantly, about the middle of the Hasmonean period, that is, about 100 B.C.E. Finally, there is a relatively
large corpus of Herodian manuscripts dating between 30 B.C.E. and
C.E. 70.

The spread of these manuscripts in date and in quantity furnishes

[5] See F. M. Cross, "The Development of the Jewish Scripts," in *BANE,* pp.
133–202.
[6] Cf. F. M. Cross, "The Discovery of the Samaria Papyri," *BA* 26 (1963),
110–21; and "Aspects of Samaritan and Jewish History in Late Persian
and Hellenistic Times," *HTR* 59 (1966), 201–11.
[7] Cf. Y. Yadin, *Masada: Herod's Fortress and the Zealots' Last Stand,*
tr. by Moshe Pearlman (New York: Random House, 1966) and *The Ben
Sira Scroll from Masada* (Jerusalem: Israel Exploration Society, 1965).

extremely important data for the historian. The life of the people
of the scrolls must be related to the dates of the books of their
library, especially to the books of sectarian content, many composed
and copied for the governance and teaching of the desert community.
The termination of the series with late Herodian hands correlates
precisely with archaeological data. The library was abandoned at
the time of the destruction of the community in c.e. 68. We must
in turn establish the origins of the community no later than the date
of the earliest extant sectarian compositions, that is, before ca. 100
B.C.E. Perhaps we can extract even more information from the series.
Non-sectarian scrolls, especially the biblical manuscripts, begin in
quantity about 150 B.C.E. Scrolls of the Archaic Period are exceedingly rare and are best reckoned master scrolls brought into the
community at the time of its founding. Extant copies of such characteristic sectarian scrolls as the Rule of the Community and the
Damascus Document go back to the beginning of the first century
B.C.E. Sectarian commentaries on Habakkuk, Nahum and other biblical works date mostly from the second half of the first century B.C.E.
and contain traditional lore of biblical interpretation developed in the
community in its earlier history, and precipitated into writing relatively late in the life of the sect.

We may say in summary therefore that the sect of Qumran came
into being between ca. 150 and 100 B.C.E. to judge purely on the
basis of palaeographical evidence.[8]

The relatively identical results of the independent disciplines of
the archaeologist and palaeographer establish the framework within
which we must reconstruct the history of the sectarian Jewish community. We are now prepared to plunge into the complex historical
data which may be culled from the manuscripts themselves and from
the classical texts dealing with the pre-Christian Jewish movements.

II

Extant classical texts which treat the history of the second century
B.C.E. mention four Jewish movements in Judaea, the Hasidim, a pious "congregation" which disappeared in the Maccabean era, and

[8] The chronological schema presented by the writer in "The Development of
the Jewish Scripts" (see n. 5) is proved to be minimal by the sequence of
fourth-century scripts from Dâliyeh, and may need to be raised slightly,
especially in the Archaic Period. Any attempt to date the events of the
origins of the sect in the late first century B.C.E., much less in the first
century C.E., can now be dismissed as unworthy of serious consideration.

three orders which emerge no later than the early Hasmonean era, and presumably have their roots in the Maccabean period. These are the Essenes, the Pharisees, and the Sadducees. Of these three only the Essene order can be described as separatist in the radical sense that they regarded themselves as the only true Israel and separated themselves fully from close contact with fellow Jews. Josephus informs us that the Essenes rejected even the sacrificial service of the Temple as unclean and "offered their sacrifices by themselves." Pliny (or rather his sources) tells us of their "city" in the wilderness between Jericho and 'En Gedi near the shore of the Dead Sea.

The last-mentioned datum is virtually decisive in view of the absence of strong counter arguments in fixing the identification of the sectarians of Qumran with the Essenes. We know of no other sect arising in the second century B.C.E. which can be associated with the wilderness community. Surface exploration of the Judaean desert between Jericho and 'En Gedi has turned up no rival settlement in the crucial era. Further the community of Qumran was organized precisely as a new Israel, a true sect which repudiated the priesthood and cultus of Jerusalem. Neither the Pharisees nor the Sadducees can qualify. The Essenes qualify perfectly. There is no reason to belabor the point here. A careful examination of the classical notices side by side with the texts from Qumran establishes the identification, in my opinion, beyond cavil. The strongest argument which has been raised against the identification of the Qumran sect with the Essene is as follows: since Palestine "swarmed" with obscure sects in the first century C.E., one must exercise caution in assigning the Dead Sea sect to a known group. The argument had plausibility only when a few manuscripts of uncertain date were known. The Qumran sect was not one of the small, ephemeral groups of the first century C.E. Its substantial community at Qumran was established in the second century B.C.E. and flourished some two centuries or more. Moreover it was not restricted to Qumran, but like the Essenes of the classical sources, counted its camps and settlements throughout the villages of Judah.

Its own sectarian literature was enormous, exercising a considerable influence upon later sectarian, including Christian, literature. The task, therefore, is to identify a major sect in Judaism. To suppose that a major group in Judaism in this period went unnoticed in our sources is simply incredible. The scholar who would "exercise caution" in identifying the sect of Qumran with the Essenes places himself in an astonishing position: he must suggest seriously that two major parties formed communistic religious communities in the same district of the desert of the Dead Sea and lived together in effect for two centuries, holding similar bizarre views, performing similar or rather identical lustrations, ritual meals, and ceremonies. He must suppose that one, carefully described by classical authors, disappeared without leaving building remains or even potsherds behind; the other, systematically ignored by the classical sources, left extensive ruins, and indeed a great library. I prefer to be reckless and flatly identify the men of Qumran with their perennial houseguests, the Essenes. At all events, in the remainder of our paper, we shall assume the identification and draw freely upon both classical and Qumran texts.

III

The Essenes of Qumran were a priestly party. Their leader was a priest. The archenemy of the sect was a priest, usually designated the Wicked Priest. In the protocols of their community, the priests took precedence, and in the Age-to-Come, a Messiah priest stood above the traditional Davidic or royal Messiah. There is some reason to believe that the sect conducted a sacrificial system in its community at Qumran. At any rate, the community was preoccupied with priestly lore, ceremonial law, the orders of the priests, the liturgical calendar, and many of their sectarian compositions reflect their almost obsessive interest in priestly orthopraxy.

The community referred to its priesthood as "sons of Zadok," that is, members of the ancient line of high priests established in Scripture. At the same time they heaped scorn and bitter condemnation upon the ungodly priests of Jerusalem who, they argued, were illegitimate. This animosity against the priests in power in Judah on the part of the priests of Qumran did not stem merely from doctrinal differences. Our texts rather reflect a historical struggle for power between high priestly families. In defeat the Essenes withdrew and formed their community in exile which was organized as a counter-Israel led by a counter priesthood, or viewed with Essene eyes, as the true Israel of God led by the legitimate priesthood. Even in exile the theocrat of Jerusalem, the so-called Wicked Priest, attacked the Essenes and made an attempt on the life of the Righteous Teacher, the priestly leader. For their part the Essene priests confidently expected divine intervention to establish their cause. They predicted that the Wicked Priest and his cronies would meet violent death at the hand of God and their enemies, and searched Scripture for prophecies of the end of days when they, the poor of the desert, would be reestablished in a new transfigured Jerusalem.

Mention of the Essene hopes of a New Age of glory leads us naturally to some comments on the special theological views of the Essenes which informed their understanding of history and gave to their community its peculiar institutions. The Essenes belong in the center of that movement which goes under the designation *apocalypticism*. The late visionaries of the Old Testament, notably the author of Daniel, as well as the later Baptist and Christian communities discovered themselves to be living in the last days of the Old Age, or rather in the days when the Old Age was passing away, the Kingdom of God dawning. The upsurge of evil powers in history reflected the last defiant outbreak of cosmic Satanic powers, and the gifts of the Holy Spirit, manifest in the community of the faithful, adumbrated the age of the Spirit to follow the final war in which the Spirit of Truth and his heavenly armies would put an end to the rule of the powers of darkness.

The constitution of the Essene community was a crystallized apocalyptic vision. Each institution and practice of the community was a preparation for, or, by anticipation, a realization of, life in the New Age of God's rule. On the one hand, their communal life was a ritual enactment of the events of the end-time, both the final days of the Old Age and the era of Armageddon. On the other hand, their community, being heirs of the kingdom, participated already in the gifts and glories which were first fruits of the Age-to-Come. The fashion in which all this was accomplished is extraordinary. It is not always easy to know the events, offices, and institutions which will come into being in the Age of the New Jerusalem. For the apocalyptist of Qumran the key to these future mysteries was at hand. One had only to read the Old Testament prophecies with the understanding given the inspired interpreter, that is, by pneumatic exegesis. For all the secrets of events to come in the last days were told by God through the mouth of his holy prophets. So the Essenes searched the Scriptures. They developed a body of traditional exegesis, no doubt inspired by principles laid down by their founder, which is reflected in most of their works, above all in biblical commentaries, *pesharim,* in which their common tradition was fixed in writing.

In apocalyptic exegesis, there are three important principles to be kept in mind. Prophecy openly or cryptically refers to the last days. Again, the so-called last days are in fact the present, the days of the sect's life. And finally, the history of ancient Israel's redemption, her offices and institutions, are prototypes of the events and figures of the new Israel.

On this basis, the Essene camp in the wilderness found its prototype in the Mosaic camp of Numbers. Here the Essenes retired to "prepare the way of the Lord" in the wilderness. As God established his ancient covenant in the desert, so the Essenes entered into the new covenant on their return to the desert. As Israel in the desert was mustered into army ranks in preparation for the Holy War of conquest, so the Essenes marshaled their community in battle array, and wrote liturgies of the Holy Warfare of Armageddon, living for the day of the Second Conquest when they would march with their Messianic leaders to Zion. Meanwhile they kept the laws of purity laid down in Scripture for soldiers in Holy Warfare, an ascetic regimen which at the same time anticipated life with the holy angels before the throne of God, a situation requiring a similar ritual purity.

The offices of the sect reveal this apocalyptic typology. The council of the community was numbered after the princes of Israel and Levi in the desert; at the same time they prefigured the judges who would rule the tribes of Israel in the New Age. As God had sent Moses, Aaron, and David, so they looked for three Messiahs, prophet, priest, and prince. The founder of their community bore a biblical sobriquet, the "Righteous Teacher" (from Hosea and Joel), apparently understood as the title of a priestly forerunner of the Messianic age. And even the enemies of the sect, the False Oracle, the Wrathful Lion, and so on, all bore designations culled ingeniously from prophecy.

The great external events of the history of their times were discovered in the Scriptures, predicted as signs of the last days: the Seleucid rule, the wars of the Hasmoneans, the rise of the Romans, and the conquest of Pompey. And the internal events of sectarian history were rehearsed even more dramatically in the sayings of the prophets. Here we come upon one of the major difficulties in writing their history. Major political events and, from our point of view, minor or private events in the life of the sect are mixed in their expositions of Scripture in dizzying fashion, and if this were not bad enough, the whole is presented veiled in the esoteric language of apocalyptic.

To sum up. The Essenes of Qumran were a community formed and guided by a party of the ancient Zadokite priests. In the latter half of the second century B.C.E., having lost hope of regaining their ancient authority in the theocracy of Jerusalem, and under active persecution by a new house of reigning priests, they fled to the desert, and, finding new hope in apocalyptic dreams, readied themselves for the imminent judgment when their enemies would be vanquished and they, God's elect, would be given final victory in accordance with the predictions of the prophets.

IV

There is surely no difficulty in discovering the general background of the rise of a dissident priestly party within the chronological limits which have been marked off. In the days of Antiochus Epiphanes (175–163 B.C.E.), the orderly succession of Zadokite high priests faltered and failed. The high priestly office became a prize dispensed by the Seleucid overlord, to be purchased by the highest bidder. The strife between rivals for the theocratic office shortly developed into civil war, and, in the resulting chaos, divine Antiochus found opportunity to carry out his fearful massacres terminating in the notorious desecration of the Temple and the Hellenization of Holy Jerusalem. The stage was now set for the rise of the Maccabees, whose destiny it was to lead the Jews in a heroic war of independence, and who, having won popularity by freeing Judah from foreign suzerains, usurped the high priestly office. In this fashion the ancient Zadokite house gave way to the lusty, if illegitimate, Hasmonean dynasty. Essene origins are to be discovered precisely in the struggle between these priestly houses and their adherents.

Perhaps the historian should say no more. However, the historical allusions in the expositions of biblical passages tempt one to attempt more precise reconstructions of the origins of the sect of Qumran. We should like to know the identity of the Wicked Priest of Jerusalem and to fix more exactly the occasion for flight and persecution of the sectarians; and we should like, if possible, to relate the

Essene sect to the other Jewish parties, especially to the Pharisees who came into being in the same historical milieu. Perhaps it is too much to ask the identity of the Essene Teacher or of other sectarian figures who from the viewpoint of general history played insignificant roles.

Before proceeding to the problem of sectarian beginnings, it should be noted that on occasion references to contemporary persons or events in the expositions of the sectarians are explicit or at least transparent. In a commentary on Nahum we read, "[This is to be interpreted as referring to Deme]trius, the Greek king who attempted to enter Jerusalem at the advice of 'Those Who Seek Flattery'. . . ." A little farther on the text continues, ". . . the Greek kings from Antiochus until the accession of the rulers of the Kittiyîm"; and a few lines later, ". . . This refers to the 'Wrathful Lion' . . . who hangs men alive. . . ."[9] We have sufficient information here to reconstruct the series of historical episodes to which the expositors applied the prophecies of Nahum. The text sets the broad framework: the Seleucid era between Antiochus and the accession of the Roman rulers, that is, from the time of one of the Antiochids of the second century B.C.E. until the Roman conquest in 64 B.C.E. The Demetrius in question is Demetrius III who was invited by the Jews to put down the villain Alexander Jannaeus in 88 B.C.E. The latter is well known for his mass crucifixions and hence qualified for the prophetic sobriquet, the "Wrathful Lion."

With the first discovery of this text a number of scholars including the writer seized on Alexander Jannaeus as a prime candidate for the archvillain of the sect, and attempted to place Essene beginnings in the civil strife which occupied six years of his reign. Upon further study, however, the reconstruction appeared less attractive. For one thing, it was becoming clear that the commentaries reflected the accumulated lore of Essene exegetes over a considerable period of time. Nowhere else is the title "Wrathful Lion" used of the so-called Wicked Priest, and the Righteous Teacher does not appear in the text at all. Furthermore, other names of Hasmonean rulers, as well as Aemelius Scaurus, Roman governor of Syria in 62 B.C.E., appeared in an unpublished text from Qumran so that the novelty

[9] The Nahum Commentary has been published by J. Allegro in "Further Light on the History of the Qumran Sect," *JBL* 75 (1956), 89–95, and in "More Unpublished Pieces of a Qumran Commentary on Nahum (4QpNah)," *JSS* 7 (1962), 304–8.

of the Nahum text wore off. Again, the strife in Jannaeus' time is clearly between the Pharisees and the Hasmonean house. There is good reason to believe from our texts that both the Pharisees and the Essenes derived from the older Hasidic congregation, and that their separation developed when the Pharisees supported or at least tolerated the rise of the Maccabean high priests while the Essenes fought until forced to separate from the Jewish community. The civil war against Jannaeus, the high priest, led by Pharisees does not appear a suitable occasion for the separation of the Essene and Pharisaic wings of Judaism. Therefore all that can be won from the Nahum commentary is a *terminus ad quem* for the foundation of the sect, and this might have been assumed all along from Josephus' reference to an episode in the time of Aristobulus I (103 B.C.E.) in which an Essene prophet took part. At the present stage of study, however, with the increasingly rigid controls furnished by paleography and archaeology, I believe the attempt to place sectarian beginnings in the time of Jannaeus falls out of consideration. We cannot descend beneath the reign of Jannaeus for the date of extant copies of Essene works including the Rule of the Community. This rule or so-called Manual of Discipline is not, moreoever, a programmatic work, but a codification of developed laws and institutions in use in the established community. And we have argued already that the archaeological evidence suggests limits between 140 and 120 B.C.E. for the construction of the desert community, and hence the foundation of the sect.

Another document, the so-called list of Testimonia[10] from Cave 4, Qumran, appears to contain transparent references. The document itself is of some interest. It consists of four quotations, three from the Bible, the fourth from a pseudepigraphical work, the Psalms of Joshua. The first quotation (a conflation of two quotations of Deuteronomy, 5:28–29 and 18:18, 19, found in one textual tradition at Exodus 20:21) records the prophecy of the coming prophet "like unto Moses," no doubt the eschatological Prophet expected by the Essenes. The second quotation is from the Oracles of Balaam (Num. 24:15–17) concerning the Star of Jacob and the Scepter of Israel. These figures are explained elsewhere in sectarian texts as respectively the priestly Messiah and the royal Messiah. The third testimonium is taken from the Blessing of Moses on Levi (in Deut. 33:8–11) ". . . for he guarded thy word and guarded thy

[10] Published by J. Allegro in "Further Messianic References in Qumran Literature," *JBL* 75 (1956), 174–87.

covenant; and he taught [or illuminated][11] thy judgments to Jacob, thy teaching (Torah) to Israel." The words are clearly applicable to a priestly teacher and presumably are taken to apply to the Righteous Teacher of the last days. The fourth testimonium is the most extraordinary. It refers to the "Cursed One" predicted in Joshua 6:26 as elaborated in the Psalms of Joshua, one of the sectarian pseudepigrapha. Presumably, in view of the other figures to whom testimonia apply, the Messianic prophet, priest, and prince, and the priestly forerunner of the New Age who founded the sect, the "Cursed One" must be a central figure in the sect's history, perhaps their archenemy, certainly a figure worthy of juxtaposition with the Righteous Teacher.

The quotation from the Psalms of Joshua first quotes Joshua's curse of Jericho, or rather of one who builds the destroyed city: "Cursed before the Lord be the man who shall build this city; at the cost of his first-born shall he lay its foundation, and at the cost of his youngest son shall he set up its gates." As is well known, the prophecy was fulfilled, or rather the curse was effective when in the ninth century B.C.E. Jericho was rebuilt by a certain Hiel with the loss of his sons. It is all the more remarkable that the Essenes chose this particular text, once fulfilled, and reapplied it to their own time. Yet as their language shows, they were aware that the building of the city in their day was a second rebuilding. Presumably they supposed that the curse held permanently. At all events, the exposition, partly broken, runs as follows: "and behold an accursed man, a son of Belial, shall come to power to be a trapper's snare and ruin to all his neighbors, and he shall come to power and [his sons] . . . [with him] (partially reconstructed),[12] the two of them becoming violent instruments. And they shall build again the [city . . .] and set up a wall and towers for it to make a stronghold of wickedness [ ]." The latter part of the text is too badly broken to be reconstructed completely. It refers to the effects of horrors done in Israel, and Judah, "sacrilege in the land," and finally bloodshed in Jerusalem. Apparently these dreadful things are the upshot of the behavior of the cursed man and his sons.

[11] There is a familiar Hebrew pun here playing on the word light, or illuminate, and Torah or teaching.

[12] For a detailed discussion of the passage, see F. M. Cross, *The Ancient Library of Qumran,* rev. ed. (New York: Doubleday Anchor, 1961), p. 149, n. 83a.

If we follow the pattern of close apocalyptic exegesis which normally obtains in sectarian exposition of Scripture, we must look for an event connected with the fortification of Jericho by a major enemy of the sect when the dreadful curse of Joshua repeats itself. And properly, we must look for a high priest of Jerusalem who associated his sons with him in his rule. These requirements are sufficiently explicit, thanks to the unusual and specific character of the ancient curse, that we should be able to identify the persons and events.

Within our historical limits, one series of events immediately comes to mind which fulfills the requirements of the passage as I have outlined them: the death of Simon the Maccabee and his two sons in Jericho in 134 B.C.E. The circumstances are worth our attention. In 138 B.C.E., Antiochus VII Sidetes was successful in ousting Tryphon, pretender to the Seleucid diadem, and he consolidated the Seleucid state. He immediately took steps to reassert Syrian control of Judaea, sending an army against Simon Maccabeus. Simon, the last and perhaps the greatest of the five Maccabean brothers, was quite aged. He had set his sons over the Jewish armies and associated them with himself in the administration of the country. Antiochus' army under Kendebaios was defeated, and both Antiochus and Simon immediately began preparations for a second round. In February of 134 Simon together with Judas (probably his eldest) and Mattathias his youngest toured the cities of Judah, evidently reviewing fortifications which he had built or which were in process of construction. Antiochus Sidetes was to strike and conquer Judea and Jerusalem later in this same year. On their tour Simon and his sons descended to Jericho. Jericho was administered under Simon by one Ptolemy son of Abubos. The district of Jericho was heavily Idumean in population in this period and formed a political unit separate from Judea proper. Ptolemy appears to have been an Idumean and in certain ways reminds us of his fellow Idumean, Herod the Great, who was finally to succeed in reestablishing the Idumean power. Ptolemy like Herod was more or less Judaized, to judge from his marriage to Simon's daughter, though it is clear that the marriage was a political one. Ptolemy had ambitions to rule Judah, and he organized a plot of considerable proportions, no doubt with the complicity of Antiochus Sidetes.

Ptolemy's opportunity came upon the occasion of Simon's visit to Jericho. Ptolemy held a banquet for his victims in a newly completed fortress guarding Jericho. When Simon and his sons were drunk, Ptolemy's men murdered Simon, and later his two sons. Ultimately, Ptolemy's plot failed. John Hyrcanus, Simon's remaining son, was resident governor in Gezer. A runner informed him of the plot, and John was able to elude assassins sent to slay him, and to escape to Jerusalem in time to rally loyal Jews against the forces sent by Ptolemy to take the city. Meanwhile, Ptolemy had sent word to Antiochus of the coup, asking immediate aid and official appointment over Judea. Antiochus arrived too late to succor Ptolemy, but was successful in reducing the country and in forcing Jerusalem to surrender.

The events seem to explain adequately the resurrection of the old curse on Jericho by the Essenes. Most of the elements of the prophecy fit strikingly: the association of a cursed man with two sons in the fortification of Jericho, their death at the hands of the Idumeans as evidence of the effectiveness of the curse, the subsequent devastation and bloodshed in Judah and Jerusalem. I find it very difficult not to conclude that Simon is hereby established as the Cursed Man of the Testimonia, and to the distinction of being an archvillain of the sect. Is this "Cursed Man" identical with the Wicked Priest? His juxtaposition with the other central figures of the sect strongly suggests the identification, but perhaps we should proceed with caution, since at least one other high priest, Jonathan, may qualify as an alternate to Simon.

Jonathan (162–142 B.C.E.) was the second of the Maccabean brothers, the first to usurp the high priestly office. In 152 B.C.E. by appointment of Demetrius, one of two rivals for the Syrian throne, he assumed the robes of the theocratic office. While there is no direct evidence, it is quite impossible to suppose that Jonathan's flagrant violation of Zadokite rights to the high priesthood did not bring immediate and violent opposition from the Zadokite house and the Hasidic elements of Jewry who had never supported the Maccabees more than half-heartedly. It would appear probable that the ministry of the Righteous Teacher goes back to this ominous turn of events.

Furthermore, Jonathan's death fits precisely with Essene comments on the violent end of the Wicked Priest. In the commentary on Habakkuk we read, "This is to be interpreted as referring to the Wicked Priest whom, because of transgression against the Righteous Teacher and the men of his party, God gave into the hand of his enemies to bring him low with a mortal blow. . . ."[13] Tryphon captured Jonathan by treachery and after holding him a prisoner for a time, murdered him in 142 B.C.E. In another commentary, the Wicked Priest is said to be given "into the hands of violent foreigners,"[14] a cliché from Ezekiel's prophecies (Ezek. 28:7; 30:11, etc.). It has been argued plausibly that these texts fit perfectly only when applied to Jonathan. It is true that Ptolemy himself was probably Judaized despite his Idumean affiliations, and that the Syrian role in the affair was indirect. Hence, while Simon's demise can be fitted with these biblical phrases applied by the Essenes to the Wicked Priest's death, Jonathan's end fits equally well or better.

For a number of reasons Simon makes the better Wicked Priest. Jonathan became *de facto* high priest at the appointment of one of the Seleucid contenders for kingship. His position was tenuous, however, throughout his tenure in the office. Jewish independence was not to be fully won until the reign of Simon. To the end of his days Jonathan struggled to maintain himself against foreign foes. It seems unlikely that he was sufficiently secure to turn upon his fellow Jews and persecute the Zadokites; moreover, in view of the *de facto* nature of his theocratic rule and the uncertainty of the times, the Zadokite priests would not have abandoned hope and fled Jerusalem upon the occasion of Jonathan's donning the high priestly robes. On the contrary, we should expect the move to initiate hostilities between the orthodox and the Maccabean nationalists.

The lot fell upon Simon, Jonathan's successor, to bring his brothers' national dreams to fulfillment. In the second year of his rule he succeeded in driving out the Syrian garrison from the citadel in Jerusalem. Judea was at last free of the Seleucid yoke. Simon now ruled in peace and was at liberty to consolidate his realm. In 140 B.C.E., the third year of his reign, a great assembly was held "of the priests and peoples and heads of the nation and the elders of the country." The decree of the assembly was engraved in bronze and set up on stelae in Mount Zion. The work of the assembly and the significance of the decree for the history of the high priesthood cannot be overestimated. Simon was made high priest, *de jure,* by the assembly's decree, and high priesthood was given to Simon's house forever, "until a faithful prophet should arise."[15] The claim is made here to a legal transference of the high priesthood from

---

[13] 1QpHab. 9:9–12.
[14] 4QpPs. 37 (to 37:32–33).
[15] I Macc. 14:30–39.

the Zadokite dynasty to the Hasmonean dynasty. The illegitimacy of Simon's house is admitted tacitly in the phrase "until a faithful prophet arise," that is, until a final arbiter between the rival houses appears in the Age-to-Come. Further, the decree warned against any opposition to Simon by layman or priest, prohibited private assembly, and threatened punishment to anyone who acted contrary to the stipulations of the decree.

In this decree we can discern clearly the new high priest's determination to stamp out, indeed to persecute, those who refused to recognize the full legitimacy of his office. This program, falling in the early years of Simon, seems to give the appropriate occasion for the crystallization of the Essene sect, its persecution and the persecution of the Righteous Teacher, and the exile in the wilderness of Judah. Simon had the leisure, power, popularity, and inclination to root out Jewish opposition to the ascendancy of his party and his house. Certain texts, especially the Testimonia, give evidence in support of our identification of the Wicked Priest with Simon. Finally, it should not be overlooked that the archaeological evidence for the dating of the foundation of the community fits more easily with a date in Simon's reign than with a date in Jonathan's reign.

We have not dealt, of course, with a large number of texts relating to the Wicked Priest and his relations with the Righteous Teacher and the exiled community. Most fit equally well with Jonathan or Simon, or indeed with a number of other priests. In this era one cannot complain of a shortage of wicked priests. One final text, however, deserves mention. In a passage of the commentary on Habakkuk, the expositor comments, "This means the priest whose dishonor was greater than his honor. For he . . . walked in ways of drunkenness in order to quench his thirst. But the cup of God's wrath will swallow him up . . . !"[16] The high priest caroused once too often. In the hands of Ptolemy the cup of pleasure turned into the cup of wrath and swallowed Simon. Or so I should interpret the text.

Our space is exhausted and the task of writing a history of the Essenes is only begun. We have been able to fix the general framework of the community's life in the desert. Perhaps we have succeeded in identifying the villain of the esoteric commentaries. I dare say we have succeeded far better in introducing the complexities and frustrations which face the student of the Essene library from Qumran.

[16] 1QpHab. 11:12–15.

Twenty Years of Discovery

ROBERT G. BOLING

The exciting story of the recovery of ancient scrolls, beginning with the first spectacular discoveries in 1947, made by the most spectacular of all explorers, the Ta'amireh tribesmen, is bound front and back by intrigue and tragedy. Most recent has been the report from Israel, in the wake of the 1967 Six-Day War, concerning the acquisition of a magnificently preserved copy of another work previously unknown to the modern world and belonging to a genre all its own. It is temporarily nicknamed the "Temple Scroll" because of its interest in religious rules on various subjects and its "enumeration of sacrifices and offerings according to the festivals," as well as its own detailed reporting of *divine instructions for building the temple.*[1]

Qumran: A Way in the Wilderness

The story of the accidental beginning of the finds, with the chance discovery by a half-curious, half-frightened bedouin boy venturing into a cave, is now well known. Among the seven scrolls of the original lot (Qumran Cave 1), purchased from tribesmen by various individuals and institutions during the fighting in Jerusalem in 1947–48, were a couple of magnificently preserved copies of Isaiah[2] from the last pre-Christian centuries, together with a variety of non-biblical works. The latter are now famous: a Commentary on

---

[1] For the quotations and all information here about the Temple Scroll, we are indebted to Professor Y. Yadin for the preliminary report, first published in *BA* 30 (1967), 135–39, that appears on pp. 139–48.

[2] For sheer impressiveness, nothing equals the sight of the great Isaiah scroll (IQ Is^a), *The Dead Sea Scrolls of St. Mark's Monastery*, I, ed. by M. Burrows, *et al.* (New Haven: American Schools of Oriental Research, 1950). For the other Isaiah manuscript in the original group, see E. L. Sukenik, *Ozar hamegillot hagenuzoth* (Jerusalem: Bialik Foundation, 1955).

Habakkuk,[3] a Genesis Apocryphon,[4] a collection of extracanonical Thanksgiving Psalms,[5] an apocalyptic plan for the eschatological War of the Sons of Light against the Sons of Darkness,[6] and a Manual of Discipline.[7] The Manual was designed to regulate the life of a partic- ular religious community which understood itself as living in the last days, the community of Jeremiah's "New Covenant" promise, heirs to all that had gone on from Genesis to Daniel, ready for the con- summation of God's rule over all peoples.[8]

The character of this sectarianism has been clarified as Essene, belonging to a segment of Jewish society described by Josephus and other early historians but curiously not mentioned in the New Testament. The Essene influence, however, is becoming startlingly clear, and among the participants in the reconciliation discussed by Paul, the former Pharisee, was many a reconstructed Essene.

The location of Qumran Cave 1 directed scholarly attention to the nearby ruin (Khirbet Qumran) sitting high atop the marl terrace which the Wadi Qumran has cut through to the level of the Dead Sea. The marl terrace in turn runs right up against the abrupt lime- stone cliffs which form the eastern limit of the Palestinian hill country and the western limit to the valley of the Jordan River- Dead Sea rift. (These geographical notes are necessary to high- light the subsequent interplay of scholarly wisdom and bedouin wit.)

Systematic excavations of the Qumran Ruin were undertaken from 1951 to 1956 with results that have shed a flood of light on the

---

[3] Burrows, *op. cit.* English translations in T. H. Gaster, *The Dead Sea Scriptures,* rev. ed. (New York: Doubleday Anchor, 1964), pp. 244–252, and M. Burrows, *The Dead Sea Scrolls* (New York: Viking, 1955), 365–70.
[4] N. Avigad and Y. Yadin, *A Genesis Apocryphon* (Jerusalem: Magnes Press, 1956), with translations from the Aramaic into English and Modern Hebrew.
[5] English translations in Gaster, *op. cit.,* pp. 123–225, and Burrows, *The Dead Sea Scrolls,* pp. 400–415. Plates in Sukenik, *op. cit.*
[6] Y. Yadin, *The Scroll of the War of the Sons of Light against the Sons of Darkness,* tr. by B. and C. Rabin from the Hebrew (Oxford University Press, 1962).
[7] M. Burrows, *et al. The Dead Sea Scrolls of St. Mark's Monastery,* II, (New Haven: American Schools of Oriental Research, 1951). Translations in Gaster, *op. cit.,* Burrows, *The Dead Sea Scrolls,* and William H. Brownlee, *The Dead Sea Manual of Discipline* (New Haven: American Schools of Oriental Research, 1951).
[8] Subsequent excavation of Cave 1 yielded fragments belonging to some seventy documents. See F. M. Cross, *The Ancient Library of Qumran,* rev. ed. (New York: Doubleday Anchor, 1961). This work should be consulted both for its vivid and careful detail in narrating the course of discoveries and for the whole range of introduction to Qumran studies.

identity, outlook, and life-style of the people who owned the scrolls. In the meantime the Bedouin were busy elsewhere, and as early as 1951 a new lot of scrolls was for sale in Jerusalem. The source was traced to caves in another wadi some twelve miles south and west of Qumran.

Wadi Murabba'at

In January of 1952 the tribesmen led scholars under police escort to the newest source of finds. Among the Murabba'at scrolls, some purchased from the nomads and some recovered in excavation, is the earliest (seventh century B.C.E.) papyrus text in Hebrew yet found in Palestine. More sensational was a series of texts of the late first and early second centuries C.E., written in Greek, Hebrew, and Aramaic, belonging to remnants of the forces of Simon bar Kokhba, leader of the Second Jewish Revolt against Rome (132– 135 C.E.).[9]

Meanwhile, back at Qumran

With scholars concentrating their efforts on the ruins at Qumran and the caves at Murabba'at, the Bedouin were free to explore for additional riches and in February of 1952 found Qumran Cave 2. The original discovery had so far exceeded the expectations of specialists that in some quarters there had been suspicions and charges of forgery. It is therefore not surprising that scholars did not hasten at first to launch a thorough exploration of the Judaean badlands. But with the rapid pace of developments in the winter of 1951–52 the various archaeological schools in Jordan were spurred on to a systematic search of all nooks and crannies to the north and south of Qumran on a line stretching for five miles. Soundings were made in some two hundred caves, twenty-five of which produced pottery that could be directly related to that of the Qumran Ruin.

In March of 1952 Qumran Cave 3 was explored and produced the now famous Copper Scroll with its folkloristic account of the location of royal temple treasure.

The scholarly search was finally brought to a conclusion by the combined effects of heat, disease, and plain physical exhaustion,

[9] Cross, *The Ancient Library of Qumran,* 12–30. The Murabba'at finds have been edited by P. Benoit, J. T. Milik, and R. de Vaux, *DJD,* II (Oxford University Press, 1961).

plus the shortage of funds and the observation that all the finds had been made in the natural caves of the limestone cliffs above the plateau on which the Qumran Ruin is situated.

The Bedouin, however, with sturdier constitutions for their clime and less devotion to science and logic, continued their unsponsored searching in a series of man-made caves in the marl terrace beneath the Qumran Ruin. They hit pay dirt once again—caves 4, 5, and 6. Then in 1955, during the fourth season of excavation at Qumran, caves 7–10 were discovered by the archaeologists, all in the marl terrace to which the enterprising Bedouin had pointed them. After the initial discovery, pride of place goes to Cave 4, with tens of thousands of fragments belonging to some four hundred manuscripts.

Finally the tribesmen found Cave 11 and came away with two magnificently preserved scrolls, one of them a compilation of psalms that is utterly distinctive for its variations in order and content from any known recension of the canonical book.[10] The character of the second scroll has not yet been announced. The tribesmen and archaeologists between them found significant fragments of at least five other scrolls.

The Qumran finds have now been so long with us that it is easy to overlook the full range of their contents. Every Old Testament book is represented, with the single exception of Esther. The Qumran folk also studied the deutero-canonical literature as well as a variety of previously unknown works and some, indeed, of heretofore unknown genre. In addition to the literature, there are extensive remains of records, receipts, contracts, letters—a vast deposit of private and public memoranda that beggars description.

Khirbet Mird: Christian Monastics

The Qumran Ruin, which after excavation was clearly to be identified as the community center for the owners of the scrolls stored in the Qumran caves, was destroyed by Vespasian's troops during the First Jewish Revolt, c.e. 68–70, and it seems never again to have known a major occupation or sustained settlement.

During the subsequent centuries there were many Christian monastics who inherited life in the wilderness, and the trail of recent

[10] Recently published as *DJD*, IV (Oxford University Press, 1965), by J. A. Sanders, who has also produced a popular American and less technical edition, *The Dead Sea Psalms Scroll* (Cornell University Press, 1967). See also Sanders' article on pp. 101–16.

manuscript discoveries leads next to the site called Khirbet Mird. The Mird Ruin is situated high inland from Qumran on one of the peaks in the western flank of the Judaean hills. This was the site of the fortress Hyrcania on the ruins of which was built, late in the fifth century, the monastery of Kastellion. Texts recovered in 1952–53 in an underground cavern at Mird are written in Arabic, Greek, and Palestinian Aramaic and belong to the eighth–tenth centuries, the "Golden Age" of the monastery there. Among these documents are the first Christian Aramaic texts found in Palestine and the first papyrus and non-literary documents in this dialect to be edited, indicating that here Aramaic was in use in both liturgy and daily life.[11]

Wadi ed-Dâliyeh: Samaritan Refugees

Long before the age of the monks at Khirbet Mird and the much earlier Essene experiment at Qumran, the desolate edge of the wilderness had provided refuge for other folk fleeing the hand of the overlord—this time represented by the troops of Alexander the Great. In the spring of 1962, negotiations with the Bedouin opened a trail into the rugged country some ten miles north of old Jericho. Papyrus documents from the Wadi ed-Dâliyeh include commercial and legal instruments—records of real estate transactions, loan agreements, and judicial settlements of broken contracts.[12]

In Professor Cross's view, these Samaria papyri are to be understood as records taken into the Dâliyeh cave by patrician families fleeing from Alexander's punitive expedition against Samaria and taking refuge in the cave where they were trapped and died en masse. Their records shed a bit of brilliant light on the fourth century B.C.E.—one of the most obscure segments of the biblical period— bringing new clarity to the history of the Jerusalem priesthood and enabling students for the first time to make some sense out of a number of differences between the Bible and early historians, especially Josephus.[13] Among other results the decisive Samaritan

[11] G. R. H. Wright and J. T. Milik, "The Archeological Remains at El Mird in the Wilderness of Judaea," *Biblica*, 42 (1961), 1–27.

[12] F. M. Cross, "The Discovery of the Samaria Papyri," *BA* 26 (1963), 110–121. See also Cross's essay, above.

[13] F. M. Cross, "Aspects of Samaritan and Jewish History in Late Persian and Hellenistic Times," *HTR* 59 (1966), 201–11, a new synthesis of the philological and archaeological data. For the latter, see G. Ernest Wright, *Shechem: The Biography of a Biblical City* (New York: McGraw-Hill, 1965), 179–81.

"schism" must be brought well below the era of Alexander where it belonged to the same productive matrix that nourished Pharisees, Sadducees, Zealots, Essenes, and eventually the emerging Christian community.

Nahal Hever, Nahal Seelim, and Nahal Mishmar

With the shift from Arabic *wadi* to Hebrew *nahal* we have now to review the course of discoveries on the Israeli side of the border, which emerged from the fighting that complicated the earliest negotiations for scrolls and the attempt to trace their discovery.

The Bedouin is famous for his way of relating to borders. In 1960 the state of Israel launched an exploration of the system of deep ravines running down from the Judaean hills to the Dead Sea, south of the line which then separated Israel from its Palestinian neighbors. The territory from En-gedi to Masada was systematically searched, spurred on by mounting intelligence reports about materials accumulating in the hands of Bedouin.[14] In order to offset their native disadvantage, the scholars used everything from hard footwork to helicopters and moved tons of cave dirt (with the usual high admixture of bat dung).

Two teams reported in with spectacular finds, and a third quickly earned the rating "sensational" in antiquity-conscious Israel. The caves in the dry gulches Hever, Seelim, and Mishmar were strewn with skeletal remains and various equipment as well as official documents of men who had suffered an end similar to those of an earlier period taking refuge in the Dâliyeh cave.[15] Here, however, the historical context was the Second Jewish Revolt (cf. section on Murabba'at, above), under the leadership of Simon bar Kokhba. The sensational finds were the "Bar Kokhba Letters,"[16] pieces of that great revolutionary's communications with his officers and men.

Another most priceless item from Hever is a magnificent scroll of the Minor Prophets, a copy produced in the second century C.E., and one which is already providing a breakthrough in the study of textual criticism and the recensional history of the Old Testament

[14] *IEJ* 11 (1961), 3–72 and Plates 1–24.
[15] And thus appropriately labeled by the explorers "The Cave of Horrors." See reports in *IEJ* 12 (1962), 186–214.
[16] Y. Yadin and H. J. Polotsky, *IEJ* 12 (1962), 227–62 and Plates 15–48. Yadin discusses the letters in *BA* 24, 2–3 (May and September 1961).

in early Rabbinic and Christian circles.[17] The Minor Prophets scroll
came to modern attention in 1955, when it was purchased from
tribesmen who had recovered it from the Cave of Horrors, as proved
by a handful of additional fragments found later by the Israeli
team.

This whole segment of Palestinian history is brought into still
sharper focus by the next and last site of manuscript discovery that
I shall discuss.

Masada: Zealots' Last Stand

Perhaps no place name has ever regained its ancient significance
as rapidly and as widely as has Masada, thanks to the expedition's
organizing genius and the rapid publication and popularization of
the results. For the results are breath-taking, regarding both the
luxuriance of Herod's earlier building program there and the evidence of the timbre of Palestinian resistance to the bitter end,
against Rome.[18]

The biblical manuscripts from Masada are: part of a Psalms scroll
(81:3–85:10), a Leviticus fragment (4:3–9), and pieces of a
Genesis scroll (46:7–11).[19]

Also from Masada are a series of apocryphal and sectarian writings, some as yet unidentified, one tentatively suspected to be a
Samuel Apocryphon. Extremely significant is a scroll of "Songs of
the Sabbath Sacrifice," a collection of psalms correlated with the
special sacrifice appropriate to each Sabbath. Fragments of another
four copies of this work have been identified among the mountains
of scraps from Qumran Cave 4 and indicate that among the participants in the Great Revolt were some whose heritage can now
be traced as far as the earlier sectarianism of the Qumran type.[20]

By far the most impressive of the Masada manuscript finds is
the recovery of sizable Hebrew portions of Ben-Sira ("Ecclesiasticus"), "copied only one or two generations after the grandson

[17] F. M. Cross, "The History of the Biblical Text in the Light of Discoveries in the Judaean Desert," *HTR* 57 (1964), 281–99. See the article
by P. W. Skehan on pp. 89–100.
[18] Y. Yadin, *Masada: Herod's Fortress and the Zealots' Last Stand,* tr. by
Moshe Pearlman (New York: Random House, 1966).
[19] Y. Yadin, "The Excavation of Masada—1963/64," *IEJ* 15 (1965), 103–5,
Plate 19.
[20] *Ibid.,* 105–8.

of Ben-Sira had translated the book into Greek,"[21] leaving traces now clearer than ever that at points he did not understand the Hebrew original.[22]

In addition to these parchment scrolls from Masada, we have papyri in Hebrew, Greek, and Latin (letters, lists, receipts), and ostraca which expand the linguistic equipment of Masada's defenders to include Aramaic.

And more to come?

It is clear that not all precincts have reported in. And while we wait and work and search for funds, hoping that such priceless treasures will not suffer irreparable damage in the processes which must be followed in their acquisition, little things mean a lot— thousands of them! Palestine in the last centuries before the Common Era saw an unexceeded flurry of hard religious thinking and reverent speculation, with a variety of experiments at honoring historical memory and facing the future—a truly exciting variety in the midst of which moved Jesus of Nazareth, a variety which we can ignore only to our own theological impoverishment.

[21] *Ibid.,* 109.
[22] The text has been promptly published by Y. Yadin, *The Ben Sira Scroll from Masada* (Jerusalem: Israel Exploration Society, 1965).

The Scrolls and the Old Testament Text

PATRICK W. SKEHAN

"Will the Dead Sea scrolls mean changes in the Bible?" The question is as frequent as it is naïve; and since in this form it is likely to be asked only by believers, as a polite conversation piece, it is clear that the expected answer is "No!" Yet if one says, "Well, they will help us in the understanding of many details of the Old Testament text," the questioner decides he is being put off: changes, and he's not being told; or no changes, and it's not being admitted.

An insight, however glimmering, into four centuries of transmission of the Hebrew text (from ca. 300 B.C.E. to ca. C.E. 100) that was previously unattainable is, however, not a bad thing.[1] There is further significance to this when the periods best represented in the new evidence (100 B.C.E. to C.E. 68) are those which form the backdrop for the New Testament use of the Hebrew Scriptures. And when, at the same time, light is increasingly shed on the development during those centuries of the ancient Greek translation of the Old Testament books, which was the direct source for many New Testament citations and has also been the main term of comparison in looking for possible accidents of transmission that may have affected the received Hebrew, the gain indeed becomes rather considerable.

The matters of detail can be very small. In Genesis 1:9, current translations read, "Let the water below the sky be gathered into one area" (*The Torah,* Jewish Publication Society, 1963), or, "a single area" (Anchor Bible, *Genesis,* 1964), or, "one place" (RSV).

[1] ". . . the period of manuscript documentation. According to the state of our knowledge at present, this period begins at 300 B.C.E. . . ." M. H. Goshen-Gottstein, *The Book of Isaiah, Sample Edition* . . . (Jerusalem: Hebrew University, The Magnes Press, 1965), p. 13.

There is, however, an alternative reading to "area, place" which both equal Hebrew *mqwm;* it is "gathering, reservoir," Hebrew *mqwh.* The former is the reading of all Hebrew manuscripts known before 1947; the latter is suggested by the ancient Greek (Septuagint, LXX) translation. The sense is hardly affected at all; there are considerations of literary style and consistency in the narrative favoring *mqwh,* but the tendency of translators, as shown above, would indicate that these cannot be urged too far. And on the other hand, one could, if put to it, so explain the second *m* in the received reading as to get *miqwe-mi,*[2] the term for "gathering" with a correlative or reinforcing particle tacked on, without changing the consonants of the standard Massoretic Text (MT). The fact that a manuscript from Cave 4 at Khirbet Qumran has the *miqweh* reading[3] in this place tells us only that one copyist in Palestine about the beginning of the Christian era offered the same reading seen by the LXX translator, presumably in Egypt, a couple of centuries before. It adds a touch of concrete objectivity to the evidence for the variant reading, but it hardly alters the terms of the choice.

Small or large, letters or words or phrases or verses, the variant readings from Qumran usually prove to be not unexpected: that is to say, somewhere in the bulk of copied and quoted and translated materials which we already possessed, from ancient and early medieval times, a parallel exists to nearly all the readings the new texts give us, barring copyists' errors or historical oddities of spelling. The textual critic has somewhat the feeling that a door has been opened for him to penetrate back into a remoter antiquity, and that, as he does so, nearly all his alternatives and all his problems move back with him and regroup themselves into small clusters of old friends, all of them familiar, but some of them not seen in each other's company before. Even after all the evidence is published, it will be some time before the new lines of evaluation they make possible will become clear and gain a consensus of scholarly recognition. At present, one can suggest directions.

Besides the LXX translation, the one textual source with some credentials as pre-Christian evidence has been the Samaritan text of the first five biblical books. Often ascribed to the fifth century B.C.E. for its origins, this reworking, for such it is, of the Pentateuchal materials has been supposed to be an independent witness of ap-

---

[2] For a slightly different analysis and interpretation of the word, see D. N. Freedman in *ZAW* 64 (1953), 190–91.

[3] Professor F. M. Cross has kindly allowed me to use this information.

proximately that antiquity. A copy of Exodus (4Q paleoEx[m]) from Qumran does indeed attest that the text of this recension has been handed down with remarkable faithfulness from about the mid-second century B.C.E. But the Qumran text is not Samaritan in origin; the Samaritan Pentateuch contains a sectarian item about the unhewn altar on Mount Gerizim following the Ten Commandments, at Exodus 20:17, which was never present in this manuscript.[4] Besides, its expanded treatment of the received Pentateuch can be paralleled from other Hebrew manuscripts from Qumran, notably 4Q Num[b], which are otherwise quite different from the Samaritan text. Following W. F. Albright, F. M. Cross has several times pointed out[5] that the script, the orthography, and the state of the text of the Samaritan Pentateuch, along with the history of the sect as we know it from Josephus and elsewhere, make it sure that the sectarian tradition branched off from an extant Palestinian form of the text (such as is witnessed by 4Q paleoEx[m]) only subsequently to the destruction of Samaria under John Hyrcanus in 107 B.C.E. The expansions, which are of a harmonizing nature, using data from one biblical passage to build up a related passage elsewhere, in this recension are an extreme example of the processes of text transmission in Palestine which went on for several centuries up to the first century C.E. when one manuscript tradition, the MT which is the form of our printed text, became normative and, finally, exclusive. An instance of this tendency to expand and harmonize, within the Pentateuch but apart from the Samaritan tradition, can be found in the seventy-five, rather than seventy, persons who went down into Egypt, according to the Hebrew manuscript 4Q Ex[a] at Exodus 1:5, paralleling LXX readings on the same point at Genesis 46:19–20, 27, and in Deuteronomy 10:22 as well as in Exodus. Another is in the late first century B.C.E. manuscript 4Q Deut[n], where Deuteronomy 5:15 is followed by an excerpt from Exodus 20:11, giving an additional reason for the commandment about the Sabbath. The Samaritan text does not do this, and in the Greek tradition the same borrowing from Exodus turns up as an insert in Deuteronomy 5:14, in Codex Vaticanus alone, and in

[4] The manuscript is fragmentary; the way this particular expansion can be shown to have been absent from it has been described in *JBL* 78 (1959), 22–23.
[5] See for example "The History of the Biblical Text in the Light of Discoveries in the Judaean Desert," *HTR* 57, (with J. G. Janzen), (1964), 285; and *The Ancient Library of Qumran*, rev. ed. (New York: Doubleday Anchor, 1961), 172–173, 192–193.

no other manuscript. Similar instances from 4Q Num[b] are cited by Cross; and even in 4Q Ex[f], the oldest biblical manuscript known to us, the insertion of "from their leaving Egypt" into Exodus 40:17, though shared with both the Samaritan and the LXX texts, must be judged a harmonizing expansion from Exodus 16:1; 19:1.[6] Thus it comes about that in evaluating expanded readings in the first five books, the textual critic will readily acknowledge a whole period of copying the texts, during which explaining the Bible by the Bible, within the text itself, was regarded as truly reverential treatment; but he will not accept readings arrived at in this way despite their antiquity, as the equal of the tightly organized, close-knit text of these books preserved in our printed Bibles. And when confronted by the variant text of the Pentateuch presupposed by Acts 7, he will not jump to the conclusion that Luke (or Stephen) was under Samaritan influence. Instead one should infer only that the New Testament tradition knew a developed Palestinian text (so Professor Cross, orally), whether that text was in Hebrew still or now in Greek (see below).

In our Bibles, the one section of Pentateuch text which consistently illustrates the "expansionist" procedure, and carries it back from the work of copyists to form a link with the editing process in the formative period of the collection, would be Exodus 36–39, where all the directives given by God to Moses for the building and equipping of the desert Tabernacle (Exod. 25–31) are presented as being carried out in equally minute and exact detail. Though it has been thought that the somewhat shorter and differently or-dered LXX treatment of these chapters may represent an earlier stage, this is perhaps unlikely.[7]

That all critics are not about to achieve a consensus readily, even when the Qumran evidence is explicit, may be inferred from the reception accorded to a fragment of the Song of Moses in Deuteronomy 32 (4Q Deut[o]) published by the present writer in 1954.[8] Its text, though conflate, with certain poetic lines repeated and with an apparent borrowing from Psalms 97:7, agrees in some details with the LXX tradition, which has double renderings of its

---

[6] See Cross, *The Ancient Library of Qumran*, pp. 184–86, with n. 36; and the exhibit catalogue, *Scrolls from the Wilderness of the Dead Sea* (Berkeley: American Schools of Oriental Research, 1965), pp. 23, 31–32.

[7] D. W. Gooding, *The Account of the Tabernacle* (Cambridge University Press, 1959); P. Katz, *TLZ* 85 (1960), 330–35.

[8] *BASOR* 136 (1954), 12–16; subsequent information in *JBL* 78 (1959), 21–22.

own. In the writer's judgment, with which he is happy to have the agreement of F. M. Cross,[9] it is both possible and necessary to reconstruct at the end of the poem (vs. 43) four half-lines of Hebrew verse:

> Rejoice, O heavens, with him,
> And ascribe might to him, [all] you sons of God;
> For he avenges the blood of his sons
> and purges his people's land.

For this, the Qumran text has six half-lines, the LXX eight, and the standard Massoretic four; only LXX includes all four of the above. On the other hand, W. F. Albright, who sees the primary danger to a text of this antiquity as the loss of elements in transmission, has opted for a full text that would contain all of the known units[10]; whereas E. S. Artom in *Rivista degli studi orientali*[11] has a systematic defense of the MT on all points. To press for no more, the poem begins (vs. 1) with an address to the heavens, and Qumran and LXX evidence support a reading, "sons of God" at the end of its verse 8; hence the MT, which has "Rejoice, O nations, with his people," and omits the "sons of God" in the poem's ending, is engaged in the not exclusively modern practice of demythologizing. This example might also serve to suggest a maximum in the degree to which any biblical text may appear transformed as a result of the new data; the more usual case would be of far less substantial "changes," scattered over much larger portions of the text.

If in the Pentateuch our standard text is on the whole close-knit and excellent, it would seem on the contrary that the Major Prophets Isaiah, Jeremiah, and Ezekiel have come down to us in texts arrived at by systematic expansion, harmonizing, and reworking. This has long been thought to be the case for Ezekiel on internal grounds, and so far the Qumran texts have not advanced the evidence for it very much, except by widening the perspectives through actual illustrations of the process in the other two books. For Jeremiah, the case centers around the shorter edition of the book, known previously from LXX; the fact that this shorter form is now found in one of four Hebrew manuscripts of Jeremiah from Qumran (4Q

[9] *The Ancient Library of Qumran*, pp. 182–84.
[10] Most recently, seven units extant, with an eighth lost: *VT* 9 (1959), 339–41.
[11] *RSO* 32 (1957), 285–91.

Jer[b]) has led to renewed study. As a result of this, Professor Cross and J. G. Janzen affirm that "a large portion of the plusses of MT in Jeremiah stem from expansionist tendencies of the type familiar for example in the Samaritan Pentateuch. On the contrary, the short text represented at Qumran and in the Septuagint is exceedingly well preserved."[12] The large Isaiah scroll from Qumran has proved textually disappointing to many, who were hoping that a text of such antiquity (ca. 100–75 B.C.E.) might stem from an earlier line of transmission of the book than that represented in our Bibles, and thereby solve some of the known difficulties. But once the hurdles of its unfamiliar orthography are surmounted, the text itself in this scroll either preserves the difficulties intact, or resolves them with a secondary reworking that gives no evidence of a better insight into the form and meaning of a passage than later centuries have been able to obtain by other means. There are, for example, some twenty-seven passages, chiefly in the second half of Isaiah,[13] that present in the text of the big scroll unique readings, each of them dependent on some other passage within Isaiah, or on an identifiable phrase from some other prophetical book. A good instance is in Isaiah 34:4, where RSV gives us the line, "All the host of heaven shall rot away." For "shall rot away" IQ Is[a] substitutes "and the valleys will be cleft" from Micah 1:4; it then supplies "the host of heaven" with a new verb, "shall fall (like leaves)," drawn from the same verse of Isaiah, in a later clause.

The treatment just illustrated is expansionist, and also harmonizing; it represents a policy of introducing exegesis within the text itself. A similar technique can be seen in the LXX translation of Isaiah, where both the Greek translator and the copyists from whom he received the Hebrew prototype for his work must be credited with this kind of activity.[14] One may go farther afield and suggest that not only is there a period of transmission for a number of Old Testament books during which this tendency may be identified, but that the harmonizings and expansions in early texts of the four Gospels are attributable, beyond the influence of Tatian and his Diatessaron, to a carryover from this fairly widespread previous Jewish practice in the transmission of sacred texts. As to Isaiah itself,

[12] HTR 57 (1964), 287, n. 28.
[13] VTS, IV (Leiden: Brill, 1957), 152.
[14] See J. Ziegler, *Untersuchungen zur Septuaginta des Buches Isaias* (Münster in Westfalen, 1934), 103–75.

however, one may note that, though there are many (some eighteen) fragmentary manuscripts of it from Qumran, only the large scroll from the first cave shows the characteristics here described. Though our standard form of the Hebrew text of this prophet does show some evidence of harmonizing between supposedly related passages, this feature assumes nothing like the proportions that are suggested for expansionist treatment in Jeremiah and Ezekiel.

The Psalms at Qumran have been excellently studied and placed in perspective by Professor J. A. Sanders.[15] Active liturgical adaptation on the part of the Qumran community, with responsory treatment, litany-like arrangements, and the introduction of non-canonical hymns or psalms to supplement the standard collection are indicated. Since the end of the Psalter in its canonical arrangement is not yet attested from Qumran (though it is stated to be so from Masada), the question has been raised whether the full canonical collection in the usual arrangement was known there. The present writer thinks there are adequate indications that it was,[16] and that the standard arrangement is presupposed by the liturgical adaptations and by a subsequent "library" edition honoring David as the sponsor and author of Psalm materials. This last is how he understands the scroll (11Q Ps^a) published by Sanders. Both the number of Psalms credited in it to David, 3,600, and the total number of his alleged compositions, 4,050, are multiples of 150, the canonical number.

Far from enlarging the textual critic's confidence in his ability to retrieve an original reading when the received text has suffered damage, the Qumran manuscripts suggest to him a greater degree of caution. When, for example, there is an absolute gap in the transmitted text, the recollection that some generations of pre-Christian scribes evinced a tendency to smooth, harmonize, and supply may make the most obvious-seeming supplementary reading in LXX or at Qumran, or both, no better than today's shrewd guess, and with no better guarantees of authenticity. In Genesis 4:8, for example, the MT has, "Cain said to his brother Abel. . . . And when they were in the field. . . ." The RSV supplies Cain's utterance, on the basis of the ancient versions, as "Let us go out to the field." This is what he had to say, we tell ourselves; but suppose the LXX

---

[15] Notably in the "popular" edition of 11Q Ps^a, *The Dead Sea Psalms Scroll* (Cornell University Press, 1967), and in *HTR* 59 (1966), 83–94.
[16] See *BA* 28 (1965), 100.

translator thought so too? Who then can assure us that this is how the Hebrew editor of Genesis had him say it? In Psalms 72:17, not thus far known from Qumran, RSV has the parallelism,

> May men bless themselves by him,
> all nations call him blessed!

But the "men" are supplied, and the Hebrew half-line limps for lack of a subject. Many have seen with satisfaction that LXX offers, "May all the clans of the earth bless themselves by him" for the first unit. A bit heavy, but it fills the gap; until, that is, we realize that this is the language of Genesis 12:3 and was probably borrowed from there. Then another look at the Psalm itself will show us that the LXX critic need not have gone so far; verse 11 would have given him "May all kings bless themselves by him" as the parallel to "all nations" in the second unit, with more point in the context, better balance, and a clue as to how the loss took place (*kl mlkym* dropped out before *kl*).[17] In 11Q Ps^a, Psalm 145, an alphabet acrostic, has its full complement of lines, each with a refrain. In the current Hebrew text of Psalms, the line beginning with *n* is missing. This lack is remedied in most translations with a verse that reads,

> Faithful (*n'mn*) is the Lord in all his words,
> and holy in all his works.

The warrant for this has been the LXX; one medieval Hebrew manuscript is cited for it also. It is found in 11Q Ps^a. But when one looks at verse 17 of the same Psalm, there with the adjective "just" to begin it is an otherwise nearly identical Hebrew line ("ways" and "words" are very similar in Hebrew). Anyone could guess at the word beginning with *n-* to substitute for "just"; but did the Psalmist really make the rest of these lines do double duty in his composition?

When we turn to the Books of Samuel, we are on firmer ground. Here the keenest critics (J. Wellhausen, S. R. Driver, P. Dhorme) have never been in any doubt that the LXX, and its Lucianic form in particular, is needed to eke out a weak and truncated text in our Hebrew Bibles. The Qumran texts of Samuel confirm this in generous measure, and the most fruitful results to be obtained

[17] *Biblica* 40 (1959), 302–8.

25. Figurine, probably
female.

26. Male figurine.

27. Male figurine.

28. Figurine of a lyre
player.

29. An eighth-century sherd
—inscribed in Hebrew
characters.

31. Fragment of stele of Sargon II.

30. Area D—mass burial under floor of an Iron II building.

32. Iron II kiln with holemouth
jars.

33. Kiln reused as grave in late seventh–early sixth century.

34–35. The Seal of the Governor of Samaria. Its legend reads:
[yšʿ?]yhw bn [snʾ]
blṭ pḥt šmr ⌈n⌉
[Yašaʿ]yahū son of [San-]
ballaṭ governor of Samaria

It was affixed to Papyrus 5, a contract relating to the sale of a vineyard, dating probably from the early reign of Artaxerxes III (358-338 B.C.E.).

in any biblical book from the scroll finds, for the straight wording of the text, will be those obtained from a comparison of the Qumran Samuel manuscripts with the very variable LXX evidence (again, see below). Not that the results are always positive. We learn, for example, that the reason the name of Saul's son Ishbaal is missing from the MT of II Samuel 4:2 (where the syntax of the sentence has been mangled by a deletion, compare also vs. 1) is because the *wrong* name Mephibosheth stood in that place in a parent text of the MT, as it still stands in some of the LXX evidence and in 4Q Sam[a]: witness verse 4 of the same chapter in the MT, which would be wholly out of place if Ishbaal were named in verses 1, 2.[18] Besides, this most extensive Qumran manuscript of Samuel represents a developed Palestinian form of text, quite at home in the first century B.C.E., but needing to be measured against the older strata of LXX evidence as well as against the MT before it can carry us back to the earliest attainable text of the books.

The most complex and far-reaching development in textual studies set in motion by the new manuscript finds has to do with the history and evaluation of the LXX. From what has since been identified as a cave in the Wadi Khabra, west of Engedi, the Ta'amire Bedouin brought to Jerusalem in 1952–53, among other things, a fragmentary Greek scroll of the Minor Prophets. Studied by D. Barthélemy,[19] this proved to be of first century C.E. date, and to contain a rendering of the Minor Prophets based indeed on the LXX translation, but systematically revised toward a narrower and more consistent equivalence with the Hebrew. Seeking comparable materials elsewhere, Barthélemy found them in the text of the Freer codex in Greek, the citations of the *quinta editio* (V[a]) of Origen's Hexapla, the Sahidic Coptic version based on the Greek, and the quotations in Justin Martyr's mid-second-century writings. Certain characteristic turns of expression in this recensional work made it possible for him to identify it again outside the Minor Prophets in parts of the Samuel-Kings text in most manuscripts and in our printed Greek Bibles, between II Samuel 10 and I Kings 2:11, and again from I Kings 22 through all of II Kings. Further ramifications include the supplements to the short LXX texts of Job and Jeremiah, the "Theodotionic" text of Daniel, and the LXX render-

---

[18] Cross, *The Ancient Library of Qumran*, p. 191.
[19] *Les devanciers d'Aquila, VTS*, X (Leiden: Brill, 1963).

ings of Lamentations and (probably) Ruth. Barthélemy goes on to identify the editor of this recension with the name Theodotion, and to identify Theodotion with the Jonathan ben Uzziel of rabbinic tradition. The recension would have been produced between about C.E. 30 and 50.

We may refrain from passing judgment on the Jonathan identification, and still acknowledge that what the new evidence has done (with the aid of a remarkable earlier critique of the LXX Samuel-Kings, on internal grounds, by H. St. J. Thackeray[20]) is to reveal to us that a large bulk of the revision work on the LXX associated with Origen's Hexapla in the mid-third century C.E. is actually a compilation of Jewish revision attempts, presumably in Palestine, dating from before the turn of the era until the days of Aquila, ca. C.E. 130–135. Symmachus toward the end of the second century C.E. and Origen in the third are latecomers; some of the revision work was under way even before the date proposed by Barthélemy (the "Lucianic" strain of texts, followed in Samuel-Kings by Josephus, occupies an intermediate position in some cases between the earliest LXX and the "Theodotionic" revision of Thackeray-Barthélemy). This development culminated in the work of Aquila, who *follows* and builds on most of what we have been calling Theodotion. The tangled web of "Septuagint" materials still dates from about 300 B.C.E. to about C.E. 130; but we now have quite valuable criteria by which to sort it out and establish a relative time scale for its individual strands. This is very important for its effective use in relation to the original Hebrew of the Old Testament. As a first and superficial result, it eliminates finally the false problem of how a "Theodotion" text of Daniel, supposedly produced toward the end of the second century C.E., could be cited in the New Testament and by Clement of Rome. It places the critical study of Samuel and Kings on a firmer basis than ever,[21] just when the distinctive pre-Christian Hebrew texts from Qumran are added to our re-

[20] *The Septuagint and Jewish Worship* (Oxford University Press, 1923), pp. 16–28 and 114–15.

[21] J. D. Shenkel's *Chronology and Recessional Development in the Greek Text of Kings,* (Harvard University Press: 1968), is a valuable study on the separate systems of cross-dating between the reigns of Judaean and those of northern Israelite kings followed by the Lucianic LXX and by MT respectively. This is particularly significant for the end of I Kings and the beginning of II Kings (dates for Jehoshaphat).

sources.[22] Beyond that, there are surely not enough skilled LXX students today to work out all the needed refinements and reassessments of our knowledge within one generation.

The text of Isaiah 42:1–4 used in Matthew 12:18–21 is not, as is well known, the LXX text of Isaiah. There is a risk of too hasty conclusion on too narrow a basis; but it does seem that the phrase *eis nikos* which the Matthew text contains is a clue to recensional treatment by a reviser of the proto-Theodotion type. St. Paul quotes the same phrase from Isaiah 25:8 to good effect in I Corinthians 15:54, where it is juxtaposed with a Minor Prophets quotation (Hosea 13:14) containing also the word *nikos*. The point is that while not only the word, but the *eis nikos* phrase, would be quite at home in the basic LXX translation of the Minor Prophets, it does not occur in LXX Isaiah, but appears from hexaplaric evidence to have been introduced into that book by a reviser prior to Aquila, who may or may not have been the first century "Theodotion." Thus the knowledge of this sort of recensional activity will seemingly have something to contribute to the vexed question of Old Testament citations in the New Testament, and how they were arrived at.

The bearing of the Qumran texts on the history of the canon of the Old Testament books is bound up in large measure with the actual contents of the Qumran library (which did not have Esther).[23] It is bound up also in the decision as to what force one attributes to the use of non-scriptural material (from our point of view) in liturgical practice in combination with the Psalms. Early Jewish and Christian usage in this regard seems to run counter to any far-reaching conclusions from the Qumran practice as suggested by 11Q Ps[a].

Two points regarding the Old Testament Apocrypha are of some moment for questions of textual transmission. The first is the witness of the Qumran Tobit texts (three in Aramaic, one in Hebrew) to the

---

[22] See Cross (with J. G. Janzen) *HTR 57* (1964), 281–98. See also F. M. Cross, "The Contribution of the Qumran Discoveries to the Study of the Biblical Text," *IEJ* 16, (1966), 81–95. The set of Hebrew textual notes for I–II Samuel appended to the typical edition of the CCD translation of these books (*The Holy Bible: Samuel to Maccabees,* Paterson, New Jersey: 1969), prepared in consultation with Professor Cross, affords a good preliminary sampling of the insights provided by the Qumran manuscripts into the state of the text.

[23] This has been discussed recently enough to be still current information in *BA* 28 (1965), 87–90.

long Sinaiticus-Old Latin form of the book. In later times, shorter recensions of this book were those commonly circulated. This would not be a case in point for W. F. Albright's working hypothesis regarding the shortening of ancient texts through the accidents of transmission. It illustrates rather the difference in viewpoint between a Semitic storyteller and Wisdom-compiler on the one hand, and the literary redactor of the Hellenistic age on the other. The modern textual critic will find much more immediacy in the longer narrative, whatever the *Reader's Digest* might think of it.

The other point has to do with Ben Sira (Sirach, Ecclesiasticus), for which the principal new evidence comes from Masada rather than Qumran.[24] This is a notoriously complex book for textual study. If we may single out one fact emerging from the new texts[25] as primary, it would be that the rather considerable range of variants in the later texts and translations finds its basic explanation in the adventures the book had already undergone within a hundred years of its composition. Thus the jumbled evidence of the Cairo Genizah witnesses, the secondary recension in Greek and Latin, and the divergences between the grandson's Greek translation and the Syriac version of the text, after all due allowances for faulty copying have been made, still have their fundamental source in reworked or divergent texts that were already circulating in Hebrew early in the first century B.C.E., and in Greek early in the following century. A survey of the various estimates of the book and its textual problems[26] from 1900 to today could be humbling to specialists in textual study, and should be instructive.

[24] Y. Yadin, *The Ben Sira Scroll from Masada* (Jerusalem, 1965).
[25] Another new text not sufficiently known in time to be included here is the Leviticus Scroll from Cave 11 of Qumran. It may be described as follows:
1. The extant parts of the Scroll consist of a long strip containing parts of the last six chapters of the Book of Leviticus, and several smaller pieces containing parts of earlier chapters.
2. The script is the so-called paleo-Hebrew or proto-Samarian; the document may tentatively be assigned to the first century B.C.
3. As might be expected, the text follows MT closely; where it diverges it tends to agree with LXX and/or the Samaritan. There seem to be a few unique readings.

To summarize, 11Q Lev seems to be a suitable exemplar of the so-called Palestinian recension identified by F. M. Cross and others; it is also a major witness to the paleo-Hebrew script. (David Noel Freedman)
[26] Available in A. A. Di Lella, *The Hebrew Text of Sirach* (The Hague: Mouton, 1966; New York: Humanities Press, 1967).

Cave 11 Surprises and
the Question of Canon

JAMES A. SANDERS

I

The last Qumran cave, the one designated Cave 11, has yielded a bonanza of surprises. Material from it first came into Jerusalem through the Bedouin of the area in February, 1956. As the various pieces were identified and studied, it became clear that new possibilities in Bible study, and in the study of the Qumran sect, were being opened. For a variety of reasons, financial and otherwise, detailed scientific work on the Cave 11 materials did not begin until the fall of 1961. The preliminary reports published the following year, on the Psalms and on Job, provoked considerable interest and many questions.[1]

Since 1962 a scroll of Ezekiel, three scroll texts of Psalms and a florilegium on the figure of Melchizedek have been published.[2] Only the Job and Ezekiel pieces have so far failed to generate some excitement: the Ezekiel because what little is legible from the ossified knot of leather on which it was written seems identical to

[1] J. van der Ploeg, *Le Targum de Job de la grotte 11 de Qumran* (Amsterdam, 1962); A. S. van der Woude, "Das Hiobtargum aus Qumran 'Höhle XI'", *VTS* IX (Leiden: Brill, 1963), 322–32. J. A. Sanders, "The Scroll of Psalms (11QPss) from Cave 11: A Preliminary Report," *BASOR* 165 (1962), 11–15.

[2] W. H. Brownlee, "The Scroll of Ezekiel from the Eleventh Qumran Cave," *RQ* 13 (1963), 11–28. J. A. Sanders, *The Psalms Scroll of Qumran Cave 11*, *DJD* IV (Oxford University Press, 1965), and *The Dead Sea Psalms Scroll* (Cornell University Press, 1967). J. van der Ploeg, "Le Psaume XCI dans une recension de Qumran," *RB* 72 (1965), 210–17, and "Fragments d'un manuscrit de psaumes de Qumran (11QPsᵇ)," *RB* 74 (1967), 408–12. A. S. van der Woude, "Melchisedek als himmlische Erlösergestalt in den neugefundenen eschatologischen Midraschim aus Qumran Höhle XI," *OTS* 14 (1965), 354–73.

the received text, and the targum[3] of Job because it turns out to be a simple Aramaic translation rather than a full targum.[4]

The importance of the text dealing with Melchizedek, on the other hand, can hardly be exaggerated, for it reaches beyond the linguistics of New Testament study into its Christological thought forms. The preserved fragment is a midrash on a cluster of ten Old Testament passages centering in Isaiah 61 and the jubilee-year text in Leviticus 25; but it also quotes, or alludes to, and interprets verses from Psalms 8 and 72 as well as Isaiah 52 and Deuteronomy 15. It is a rich storehouse of material, along with similar texts from Cave 4, showing how some Palestinian Jews contemporized Old Testament texts. But its importance for Christianity, especially for understanding the Epistle to the Hebrews, is as yet beyond reckoning. Melchizedek is presented as a heavenly Redemption figure who will execute divine judgment and salvation in the drama to take place in the anticipated eschatological Jubilee year. He is presented as a member of the heavenly council of the holy ones of God and even exalted above them, fulfilling, in the judgment and salvation drama, the role later associated with the archangel Michael. In the same text the bearer of good tidings (Isa. 52) appears to be identified with one anointed (a Messiah) by the Spirit (Isa. 42 and 61). This same cluster of scriptural figures is, of course, related in the New Testament to Christ, but we have now in this very important Cave 11 fragment the evidence of their first being interwoven in this manner. The heavenly Son of God of Hebrews 7, who rules above all heavenly and earthly powers, and lives forever to make intercession for those who put their trust in him, has his counterpart now in the heavenly Melchizedek at Qumran.[5]

There are still two manuscripts brought in from Cave 11 in 1956 which have not yet been worked on: a fragmentary copy of the Apocalypse of the New Jerusalem also known from Caves 1, 2, and 4; and fragments of the Book of Leviticus written in the

---

[3] See Glossary (Ed.).

[4] If the Job piece is the same as that interdicted by Rabban Gamaliel in the first century, as the Dutch scholars both think, it is something of a disappointment rather than an excitement. Its importance, however, along with the Genesis Apocryphon of Cave 1, as a primary source for study of the Palestinian Aramaic Jesus might have spoken, cannot be gainsaid; see now the excellent edition of the latter by J. A. Fitzmyer, *The Genesis Apocryphon of Qumran Cave 1* (1966), and especially pp. 17–25 and 171–206 on first-century Palestinian Aramaic.

[5] M. de Jonge and A. S. van der Woude, "11Q Melchizedek and the New Testament," *NTS* 12 (1966), 301–26, especially pp. 322–23.

archaic Hebrew script. Professor David Noel Freedman, dean at the San Francisco Theological Seminary and an editor of this volume, is scheduled to begin work on the Leviticus materials soon.

The Six-Day War brought further Cave 11 surprises. Professor Yigael Yadin, of the Hebrew University in Jerusalem, Israel, had somehow learned in the early nineteen-sixties about a cache of scrolls which were still in the hands of an antiquities dealer in Jordanian Palestine. While we are not absolutely certain, it is highly probable that they were also part of the Cave 11 library. One of the scrolls turns out to be the largest yet found at Qumran, which Professor Yadin has entitled "The Temple Scroll" and which he describes in the report on p. 139.

II

But the greatest surprise provided by the amazing Cave 11 is in its Psalter materials.[6] Three manuscripts of Cave 11 Psalms have been published to date, and they all three exhibit very interesting variations in the order and content of the psalms they include. Two of the manuscripts are copies of the same recension or edition of psalms; of the third so little has to date been published that it is difficult to judge whether it reflects the same revision, or collection, or not. The large Psalms Scroll from Cave 11 (11QPs^a) has been published in two editions, in 1965 and early in 1967; the other copy of the same recension (11QPs^b) has only just recently appeared in print. The fact that 11QPs^b where it is extant, duplicates 11QPs^a in both order and content of psalms is highly significant; it proves at the very least that the recension of psalms to which they witness was not a private or maverick collection. 11QPs^b includes psalms found in columns 16, 18, 19 and 23, of 11QPs^a. Column 23 of the larger scroll contains Psalms 141, 133 and 144 in that order, and that is precisely the order of the same psalms on a single column in 11QPs^b. Just as interesting is the fact that in the very words of the psalms where 11QPs^a differs from the received Massoretic Text (MT), 11QPs^b agrees with its Cave 11 companion. In fact, there is good reason to think that the 11Q

[6] See n. 2 above for bibliographic details: 11QPs^a (the large Psalms Scroll) Sanders; 11QPs^b (its identical mate but only parts of three columns preserved) van der Ploeg, in *RB* 74; and 11QPsAp^a (or possibly 11QPs^e) van der Ploeg in *RB* 72.

texts were identical even where 11QPs[b] has lacunae, except in the minor and obvious scribal errors.[7] Column 19 of the larger scroll contains a non-Massoretic and heretofore unknown psalm to which we have given the title "Plea for Deliverance." 11QPs[b] includes the same psalm in a more fragmentary form, except that it provides us now with a line at the top, which in the larger scroll was in the lost lower third of the previous column 18.[8] The two copies of the psalm are identical (even to the point of almost having the same line divisions on the leather) with the exception of two very minor and very similar orthographic variants.

Finally, column 16 of the larger scroll contains what is possibly a new non-Massoretic psalm composed of floating bits of liturgical material familiar from Psalms 118, 136 and elsewhere. In this regard it rather approximates the psalm in I Chronicles 16:8–36 which is itself a pastiche of Psalms 105:1–15; 96:1–13; 106:1 and 47–48. Its close relation in the scroll to Psalm 136 reminds one of the very short Psalm 117 which many scholars have suggested should be seen either as a coda to Psalm 116 or an incipit to Psalm 118; and it should be remembered that Psalm 117 is itself reminiscent of Psalms 67:4 and 103:11. Professor Peter Ackroyd has made a very worthy translation of the little poem:

> Praise Yahweh for he is good,
>   his mercy is for ever.
>
> The sound of a shout of salvation
>   is in the tents of the righteous.
>
> The right hand of Yahweh acts valiantly
>   the right hand of Yahweh is exalted
>   the right hand of Yahweh acts in power.
>
> It is better to trust in Yahweh
>   than to trust in men.

---

[7] Careful measurements across fragments *d* and *e* of 11QPs[b] (Plate XVIII) indicate, *pace* van der Ploeg, that *ḥayyim* was lacking in Ps 133:3b there as well as in 11QPs[a]. (Note that it has long been questioned by scholarship because of scansion.) By contrast, 11QPs[b] does not duplicate the obvious scribal goof of 11QPs[a] in the following line (*ha-melammed* of 144:1). Finally, again *pace* van der Ploeg, I am not at all sure that MT *ledawyd* can be presumed in the immediately preceding lacuna where 11QPs[a] lacks it.
[8] *'ebyon/'any wedal 'anoky ky* . . . "Humble and poor am I, for . . ."

It is better to confide in Yahweh
  than to trust in noble men.

It is better to trust in Yahweh
  than to trust in a whole army.

Praise Yahweh for he is good,
  his mercy is for ever.
    Hallelujah.[9]

This same new psalm also appears in 11QPs[b]. What is preserved of it in the smaller scroll is verbatim what appears in 11QPs[a]. The sum of it is that our surprising Cave 11 contained two copies of the one really imposing witness to the Hebrew Psalter in pre-Massoretic times.[10]

The titular designation "Psalm of David" familiar from the seventy-three psalms where it appears in the Massoretic Psalter provides interesting observations in the Qumran Psalter. It appears at the head of a non-Massoretic psalm in 11QPsAp[a], and a variant of it also appears in the first line of Psalm 151 in the large Psalms Scroll. Also in the larger scroll Psalms 104 and 123 begin "Psalm of David," whereas the Massoretic Psalter does not have the title for either. Conversely, the designation is lacking in the Psalms Scroll (11QPs[a]) for Psalm 144; there is a lacuna at that point in 11QPs[b] and no secure way of knowing if it originally had the Davidic ascription, but the two scrolls are so identical in most other respects that it is best not to assume it simply because the

---

[9] P. R. Ackroyd, "Notes and Studies," *JTS* 17 (1966), 396–99.

[10] It should be very carefully noted, *pace* Yadin, "The Temple Scroll," p. 139, and S. Talmon, *Tarbiz* 37 (1967), 100, that the Tetragrammaton whether in archaic or block script is indeterminate for judging if a scroll was considered "canonical" at Qumran. Where 11QPs[a] always has it archaic, 11QPs[b] (identical otherwise) has it block (frag. *d*) 11QPsAp[a] (?11QPs[e]) apparently has it block, according to van der Ploeg, top p. 211; and 4QPs[f] has it block (columns vii 5, ix 5, ix 14, x 13) precisely in the non-Massoretic psalms. In point of fact, I am not actually disagreeing with Yadin's conclusion; I would, however, disagree with Talmon's conclusion that the divine name in archaic script always indicated that the manuscript was considered somehow non-canonical at Qumran.

The simple fact of the matter is that we can no longer read our post-C.E. 70 concepts back into the earlier period at all points. *Contra* the conclusions of M. H. Goshen-Gottstein in *Textus* 5 (1966), 22–23, and Talmon in *Tarbiz* 37 (1967), 99–104, in this regard, see the more cautious remarks by Ackroyd, in *JTS* 17 (1966), 396–99, B. J. Roberts in *JTS* 18 (1967), 183–85, van der Ploeg in *RB* 72 (1965), 216–17, and Sanders, *The Dead Sea Psalms Scroll*, pp. 156–58.

received Massoretic Psalter has it. Similarly, the interjection "Hallelujah" is omitted from the superscriptions in Psalms 135, 148, and 150 where MT has it, but appears in Psalm 93:1 where it does not. It appears, therefore, either that there was fluidity in the first century even in the Davidic ascriptions or that the Qumran Psalter represents, in complex ways, another text tradition or stage of Psalter canonization earlier than any we had heretofore. For, on the face of it, if there had already been a closed canon of Psalms since the fourth century, or since late Persian times, in which such matters were already invariable, even a "liturgical collection" of canonical and non-canonical psalms would surely reflect the accepted canon where it existed.[11] Composers of the pesharim and midrashim of the age did, apparently, "contemporize" biblical texts, and thus mold them to their convictions; but these Qumran Psalters are simply not sectarian in that sense, nor are they "sectarian" in any sense in which we have yet used that word in Qumran studies. To suggest that they are sectarian liturgical collections, forerunners of Jewish and Christian prayer books, far from being a simple, conservative, self-authenticating solution to the problem of Qumran psalmody, is a bold, venturous hypothesis fraught with as many difficulties as any other yet suggested.

The highly liturgical type materials in the Psalms Scroll which appear as addenda to known Massoretic psalms seem at first blush to lend themselves to the proto-prayer book suggestion. The new psalm at the top of column 16, made up of many liturgical phrases from a number of sources, especially those familiar from Psalm 118, has already been cited. Psalm 135 has two apparent insertions, in verses 2 and 6, which commend themselves as cultic anacolutha. In italics in the following are the words peculiar to 11Q:

> What the Lord pleases he does in heaven,
>> and on earth *to do, he does;*
>> *there is none like the Lord,*
>> *there is none like the Lord,*
>> *and there is none who does as the King of gods,*
> in the seas and *in* all deeps (11Q Ps 135:6).

[11] The suggestions that 11QPs^a is to a "proper" Psalter what 1QapGen is to Genesis, and a pesher text to canonical texts, are comforting but misleading analogies. The matter is much more complex as we shall attempt to indicate. The suggestion that it is evidence of another "first," that is, a forerunner of later Jewish and Christian prayer books is so attractive in certain ways as to deserve careful criticism (Goshen-Gottstein, *Textus* 5 (1966).

That is, of course, liturgical material very similar to what one finds in later Jewish prayers and songs. But it is also like what one finds in I Samuel 2:2, which is not better syntactically related to the rest of the Song of Hannah than the above italicized material to MT Psalm 135:6.

> There is none holy like the Lord,
>> indeed there is none beside thee,
>> and there is no rock like our God (I Sam. 2:2).

There is a similar spate of material in 11Q Psalm 146 between verses 9 and 10 which is so poorly preserved that it is untranslatable but which reflects the same biblical-liturgical type literature. Other such bits and pieces should undoubtedly also be viewed in the same manner.[12]

The most interesting, perhaps, and the most obviously liturgical aspect of the scroll is in the refrain and the subscription to Psalm 145. The subscription is very frustrating because in it we have, for the first time, a suggestion as to ancient categories of psalm types: in it Psalm 145 is called a *zikkaron,* a "memorial psalm," but that is as far as the text goes at the bottom of the column of decomposed leather. We can imagine all sorts of possibilities, especially since the word *zikkaron* is so central to our current understanding of the theology of ancient Israel and her cultic life at all stages. But the refrain presents no difficulties in reading: after each verse of the psalm, as after each verse of Psalm 136, a constant refrain recurs through all the verses: "Blessed be the Lord and blessed be his name forever and ever." If one assumes an invariable canon of Psalms from the Persian period, then he is inclined to view this refrain as an addition to the Massoretic psalm, whereas the refrain to Psalm 136 he is inclined to view as more ancient.[13] However, the problem is considerably more complicated, for verse 21 of the Massoretic recension of Psalm 145 contains a clear historic memory of the last two words of the Qumran refrain, whereas verse 21 in Qumran Psalm 145 lacks the two words precisely because it has the whole refrain. One wonders if the refrain now available for Psalm 145 is not just as ancient as that available all the while for Psalm 136, relative only perhaps to the date of composition of the two psalms. Why, then, if the Massoretic Psalter has a refrain to Psalm 136,

---

[12] Sanders, *The Dead Sea Psalms Scroll,* pp. 15–21, 158–59.
[13] J. van der Ploeg reports that 11QPsAp[a] (or, in my designation, 11QPs[e]) has Ps 118 also with a constant refrain.

does it not have the refrain to Psalm 145? At first glance, one feels comforted to say that someone at Qumran simply added the Psalm 145 refrain to an already set Psalter. And yet the cautious student knows that he must leave very much open the possibility that it was the Massoretic, or proto-Massoretic, tradition which omitted the Psalm 145 refrain because the refrain would have been retained in liturgical memory and signaled otherwise in the psalm.[14] So far, only Psalm 136, of all Hebrew psalmody, has even the suggestion of a refrain after each hemistich or colon rather than after a full bicolon. To transmit Psalm 136 without its refrain could have created a gross misreading: the refrain in Psalm 136 is integral to the scansion of the psalm in a way not the case with Psalm 145, or with any other psalm for which we might posit an ancient refrain.

The greatest "addendum" of all in 11QPs[a] is in column 27, the prose composition which says that David composed "through prophecy" 4,050 psalms and songs. The paragraph indicates the liturgical usage of the songs (*shir*) which David composed, and follows the calendar in use at Qumran and elsewhere in the late Second Temple period. It might be comforting to suppose that all the non-Massoretic materials in the Qumran Psalter could be relegated to the category of "song" and thus dismiss the problem which it presents. No supposition could be more unscientific: there are songs so designated in the Massoretic Psalter (cf. Pss. 18, 92, 120–134, etc.). And 11QPs[a] includes forty Massoretic psalms all from Books IV and V, or the last third of the Psalter.[15] To point out that later prayer

---

[14] Precisely in the overloaded MT Ps 145:21. Note the presence of the enigmatic *Selah,* after Ps 91:4 in 11QPsAp[a], lacking in MT 91:4.

[15] As is carefully noted by Goshen-Gottstein, *Textus* 5 (1966), 32, n. 42. Apropos Professor Goshen-Gottstein's further (less careful) remark on the same page, n. 43, that the term Psalms Scroll itself uncritically influenced early judgments, it should be noted that our first designation was "Scroll of Psalms" and the first siglum assigned was 11QPss, as attested in *BASOR* 165 (1962), 11. Interesting in this regard is a conversation I had in May 1963 with Professor Brownlee in Claremont. He asked, after a lecture I gave on the non-Massoretic psalms, why I used the confusing siglum 11QPss, why not 11QPs[a]. I told him that the decision had since been made, in conjunction with the Dutch, to use 11QPs[a]. I had decided that the presence of thirty-six (now forty) Massoretic psalms in the scroll could not be ignored, and that since the style of the non-Massoretic psalms was "biblical" and not sectarian (compare Hodayot), I had a complex problem on hand not easily solved. The manuscript for *DJD,* IV had already been mailed, and I was content to have time to give the problem thought and to hear reactions. My thinking at that time appeared later in tentative form in *HTR* 59 (1966),

books include forty psalms to be recited at a single service is less than illuminating, for no prayer book service would exclude all psalms from the first two-thirds of the Psalter. What is more than abundantly clear is that all Psalters are liturgical collections, Massoretic and non-Massoretic; that is not the point. The real question is whether the Qumran Psalter as we now have it is a variant form of that liturgical collection which came to be called Massoretic or is it an aberration from it, perhaps the earliest Jewish prayer book? Does it reflect on its past or anticipate its future?

III

The clue may lie just as much in how stable the first two-thirds of the Qumran Psalter appear to us, as in how unstable the last third (or slightly more) appears. The only really significant non-Massoretic features in the first half or so of the Qumran Psalter appear in two manuscripts from Cave 4, 4QPs[a] and 4QPs[q]. Both of them appear to omit Psalm 32, and so far there is no explanation for the omissions. 4QPs[a] places Psalm 71 after Psalm 38, but this has been explained quite well by Monsignor Patrick W. Skehan as simply exhibiting the similarity which exists between Psalms 38 and 70; that particular scribe, on finishing copying Psalm 38, would have erred in thinking he had just copied Psalm 70 and thus went on to Psalm 71, then later reverted to the received order. All the other variations in order of psalms at Qumran, even in Cave 11, appear in the last third of the Psalter, and all the non-Massoretic psalms in the Qumran Psalter show up in the same last third.

So far this observation is only a clue, but, as difficult as reviewing the "assured results" of scholarship may be, it requires that we think in ways in which we had not thought about the stages of stabilization of the Psalter.[16] The fluidity in the Qumran Psalter,

83–94, after trying to collect the necessary data about all pre-Massoretic psalms in *CBQ* 27 (1965), 114–23 (now outdated). After all, the siglum includes always the preface 11Q; to have used 11QapPs, or some such designation would have prejudiced from the start the necessary discussions concerning canon. Even now, one must say, regret should be expressed rather against hastily conceived hypotheses than against patience. Concerning the Column 27 prose section, see the tentative suggestions by W. H. Brownlee in *RQ* 20 (1966), 569–74.

[16] Reviewing the various attempts to date the MT collection of 150 in Begrich, Schmidt, etc., one is struck by how uncertain the "assured results" are. The observation that I Macc. 7:17 appears to quote a phrase from Ps. 79:2–3 is simply no longer impressive in discussions of the date of the

aside from the two cases just noted, is in the last two Psalter books, IV and V, Psalms 90 and following.[17] It has often been pointed out that it is this section of the MT Psalter which contains most of the highly liturgical psalms, whereas the early part of the Psalter contains mostly prayers for individuals. And this, too, may be a clue to the solutions we seek. We have for so long constructed theories about the canonization or stabilization of the Psalter on the idea of smaller collections being drawn together that we are reluctant to consider any of the smaller collections as fluid beyond a certain date. Books I to III contain three large collections, the "Psalms of David" (Pss. 3–41), the "Elohim" collection (42–83) and the so-called "guilds" collection (84–89). But in the first group Psalms 10 and 33 do not bear the name David; in the second the divine name Yahweh appears forty-three times; and even in the tiny "guilds" grouping a "Psalm of David" appears (Ps. 84). Over against a hypothetical Psalter of rigidly conceived groupings these Massoretic "aberrations" would have the same psychological effect on us that the Qumran Psalter has had.

We like to think that Books IV and V are composed of four smaller collections: "Psalms 90–104, in which the individual psalms have no special features, but which is distinguished by the fact that the majority of the songs of 'Accession to the throne' are gathered together here. This collection is concluded with Psalms 105–107." Psalms 108–110, would appear to be "poems ascribed to David, concluding with Psalms 111–118." Psalms 120–134 include "the Songs of Ascents, concluded with Psalms 135–136." And finally, Psalms 138–145 would also appear to be "psalms ascribed to David, concluded with Psalms 146–150." All of these observations are taken directly from Eissfeldt.[18] In the light now of the Qumran Psalter we simply must admit that the supposed "early collections" in the last third of the Psalter are more a product of the imagination of the rationalist mind than of realities in antiquity. Only the Songs of Ascents remains attractive as a grouping, but the decision as to

MT–150 collection, nor the mention in the prologue of Ben Sira of "the other books." B. J. Roberts has the right of it when he says, ". . . The departure from (MT) in the order of Pss., the presence of apocryphal Psalms and of pure Qumran compositions in the same scroll needs to be explained, and the old question of canonicity to be reopened" (*JTS* 18 [1967], 185).

[17] See the full catalogue and index in Sanders, *The Dead Sea Psalms Scroll*, pp. 143–49; the early effort in *CBQ* 27 (1965), 114–23, is now outdated and misleading.

[18] Eissfeldt, Otto, *The Old Testament: An Introduction*, tr. by Peter R. Ackroyd from the 3d German ed. (New York: Harper, 1965), pp. 449–50.

whether songs of similar titles had always been grouped together must be made in the light of the fragile nature of all such groupings which have heretofore appealed to our modern minds. One might as easily suggest that such songs were pulled together artificially at a comparatively late date, as that they were so neatly arranged early in the Second Temple period and then pulled apart for later, overriding liturgical reasons by the Qumran sect (which reasons are not at all evident or even suggested in the supposed "rearrangement" of the Qumran Psalter).

Observations concerning such groupings, however, are somewhat more convincing for Books I to III than for Books IV and V— precisely the portion of the Psalter which at Qumran is most at variance with the Massoretic Psalter both in order and content. Where all such observations may lead is extremely difficult to say. Avi Hurvitz, of the Hebrew University in Jerusalem, will soon publish a treatise based on new methods of linguistic analysis of the Psalms in which he concludes that the ten Massoretic psalms whose language clearly reflects the post-exilic period are all in the last third of the Psalter.[19] It will be interesting to see if his results corroborate our observations about Books IV and V and the suggestion that "the last third of the Qumran Psalter indicates a still open-ended Psalter in the first century."[20] It is precisely to the first century (at least) that we must trace the various figures concerning how many psalms the Psalter contained: 150, 151, 155, 200, 3600, or 4050![21] If the stabilization of Books I to III occurred earlier than the crystallization of Books IV and V, then the fluidity demanded by the desire to be faithful to the Davidic corpus or heritage had to be expressed in the later portions of the Psalter and threatened the earlier portions less and less as the desire and need for stabilization became greater. It must be remembered that the Psalter cannot be viewed in the same way other biblical books are viewed in the question of canonization. Each psalm is an independent entity and has its own existence in a way narratives, oracles, and even proverbs do not have within the books where they are located. The Psalter was more closely allied to the daily life of worship and piety of Israel and Judaism than any other

[19] Hurvitz, *The Identification of Post-exilic Psalms by Means of Linguistic Criteria* to be published in Hebrew by the Magnes Press, Jerusalem. Herewith my gratitude to Dr. Hurvitz for this information in personal correspondence.
[20] Sanders, *The Dead Sea Psalms Scroll*, p. 158.
[21] *Ibid.*, p. 157.

biblical book. And a sect that owed its existence and identity to dissension from the establishment in Jerusalem would be more likely to maintain the fluidity than not.

Tentatively, one might suggest the hypothesis that the Qumran group arrested the process of stabilization as it was in the period before they left Jerusalem to seek their own identity and in the then fluid third portion of the Psalter came to accept as "Davidic" what were actually Hasidic and proto-Essene (their own identity) poems, which were at least biblical in style (in contrast to the style of the Qumran sectarian hymns) and could on the face of it meet the basic standards of canonical literature. The Jerusalem group, by contrast, would have tended to arrest the process of fluidity in the interests of stabilizing their own position and sponsoring the status quo. The more eschatological group would have had little interest in encouraging stabilization. Those who look constantly to the heavens for the in-breaking drama of righteousness and vindication have little interest in five-year, or longer, programs and plans! The Psalter is also distinct, in this regard, because it bore the authority of the name David, comparable in the late Second Temple period to the authority of the name Moses. "The difference was perhaps somewhat the difference between the kinds of authority and loyalty which the names Moses and David elicited in the period in question: the one was the authority of Law, the other the authority of hope; the one represented God's theophany in the past, the other his theophany of the future, a future which in the Qumran period was believed imminent. David's name both stabilized Psalter collections and prohibited a universally invariable canon of Psalms. The tragedy of the destruction of the Second Temple in the failure of the First Jewish Revolt put an end to the fluidity of the Psalter, just as it eventually brought about a stabilization of the Hagiographa, the codification of Oral Law, the unification of Rabbinic Judaism, the writing of the Gospels, the eventual gathering and canonization of the New Testament, and the ultimate parting of the ways of Judaism and Christianity, the only two sects from Early Judaism to survive the tragedy."[22] For the Essenes, the open-ended Psalter was the more archaic Psalter, the preservation of an earlier stage of the stabilization process; just as their cultic calendar was for them the more archaic and authentic calendar.

[22] *Ibid.*, p. 158.

Until the Temple Scroll is published and its relation to the Qumran Psalter is established, further discussion would be but premature. One may sincerely hope that the Temple Scroll, which Yadin describes as believed at Qumran "to be a part of the Holy Scriptures *sensu stricto*" (p. 142) will provide the conclusive clues to the canonical status at Qumran of the Qumran Psalter. Perhaps it will also offer suggestive clues to the direction our thinking should now take on the general question of the Old Testament canon which is being now reopened in numerous ways.[23]

IV

Besides the two major Psalter manuscripts from Cave 11 there are so far two others which also contain non-Massoretic psalms. The one is from Cave 11 as well and is designated at present by the siglum 11QPsAp[a], meaning "apocryphal psalms from Qumran Cave 11." Actually, all that is so far published of it is Psalm 91, but the editor reports that at least one of the non-Massoretic psalms in the scroll bears the "Psalm of David" title familiar to all Psalter traditions. He also reports that, like the non-Massoretic psalms in the other Cave 11 Psalters, the psalms in 11QPsAp[a] are "biblical" in style rather than of the hymnic style at Qumran familiar from the sectarian Thanksgiving Hymns. And he quite rightly suggests that the manuscript attests a more ancient stage of Psalter tradition than that of the Massoretic Psalter.[24] It is for this reason that I have proposed resignaling this particular manuscript 11QPs[e]. It is very difficult at this point to see why it must not be considered in the same light as the other Psalms texts from Cave 11.

There are a number of very interesting variants in the Cave 11 Psalm 91 which do not appear either in the received text of Psalms or in the Cave 4 text where Psalm 91 also shows up in 4QPs[b].[25] Since it has never to my knowledge been rendered into English, I shall append a translation here. Where it differs from the Massoretic psalm, I have indicated the variants in italics.

[23] Cf., for example, W. H. Brownlee, *RB* 73 (1966), 178–85; B. J. Roberts, "The Old Testament Canon: A Suggestion," *BJRL* 46 (1963–64), 164–78; and the various studies of A. C. Sundberg, Jr., especially those in *CBQ* 30 (1968) 143–55 and *Studia Evangelica* 4 (1968) 452–61.
[24] van der Ploeg, *RB* 72 (1965), 210–17.
[25] P. W. Skehan, *CBQ* 26 (1964), 313–22.

11Q Ps 91

He who dwells in the shelter of the Most High,
    who abides in the shadow of the Almighty
is he who says to the Lord, "My refuge and my fortress
        is my God,
    my confidence in whom I trust."
For he will deliver you from the snare of the fowler,
    from the deadly pestilence;
he will cover you with his pinions,
        and under his wings will you *dwell in his grace* . . . ,
    his truth your shield and buckler. *Selah.*
You need fear neither the fright of night
    nor arrows in flight by day,
neither scourge of destitution at noon,
    nor plague that stalks the gloom.
Let a thousand fall at your side,
    ten thousand on your right hand,
    but you it cannot *touch.*
You will need but look with your own eyes
    and see the *fate* of the wicked.
Because you have *invoked* the Lord *your* refuge,
    and made the Most High your delight,
you will *behold* no evil,
    no scourge *will touch* your tent.
But he will charge his angels for you
    to guard you in all your ways.
They will carry you in their hands
    lest your foot stub a stone.
On the adder and the asp shall you tread,
    both young lion and serpent trample under foot.

The rest of the text, verses 14 to 16, is unfortunately mutilated, but we can be grateful that most of the psalm is fairly well preserved. While there is less of it preserved, the Cave 4 text of Psalm 91 is identical with the Massoretic as over against our Cave 11 copy. What strikes one about the Cave 11 Psalm 91 is that it relates to the Massoretic text of Psalm 91 exactly as psalms in 11QPs[a] relate to their corresponding Massoretic psalms. That is, the variants exhibit no pattern or tendency, and while a few appear to be errors, many of the variant readings commend themselves rather strongly. And if Professor van der Ploeg is right that this text attests a more ancient stage of Psalter transmission than the Massoretic text, *argumentum a fortiori* 11QPs[a].

The fourth Qumran Psalter manuscript which includes non-Massoretic psalms was found not in our Cave 11 of surprises, but in Cave 4. It was not until the Cave 11 Psalms Scroll was published that Father Jean Starcky identified the pertinent materials and took account of the fact that he was dealing also with a manuscript containing both Massoretic and non-Massoretic psalms. It is a text which apparently was continuous on one sheet of leather running from Psalms 106 to 109, though only portions of Psalms 107 and 109 are preserved in it. But beginning, apparently, on the same column where Psalm 109 ends, and continuing through column 10, are three non-Massoretic psalms, the first of which is the "Apostrophe to Zion" of column 22 of 11QPs[a]. One must say "apparently" because unfortunately one cannot be absolutely certain, but Father Starcky seems confident that the fragment on which the "Apostrophe to Zion" begins is to be placed so as to form a lower part of the original full column 7. This reidentification was made in the summer of 1965, and it is not unreasonable to suppose that further such discoveries of non-Massoretic Psalter texts may be made when all the Cave 4 materials have been published (they are to fill some nine quarto-size volumes!).

An English translation of the "Apostrophe to Zion" has been published on the basis of the Cave 11 Psalms Scroll, and then a revision taking account of the variants between the Caves 4 and 11 copies.[26] There is, hence, no need to offer the "Apostrophe to Zion" here. But, to my knowledge, no translation has yet appeared in English of the two psalms which follow it in 4QPs[f]. The second of the three may be titled Eschatological Hymn and the third, Apostrophe to Judah.[27]

---

[26] Sanders, *DJD*, IV 85–89, and Sanders, *The Dead Sea Psalms Scroll*, pp. 123–127.

[27] Translated from the text of 4QPs[f] in J. Starcky, *RB* 73 (1966), 356–57 (Plate XIII).

4Q Eschatological Hymn

. . .
Let the (congregation) praise the name of the Lord . . .
For he is coming to judge every deed,
to destroy the wicked from the earth
so that sons of iniquity will be no more.

The heavens (will bless with) their dew
and no destruction will enter their borders.
The earth will yield its fruit in its season
and its produce will never be wanting.
Fruit trees (will offer their figs)
and springs will never fail.
Let the poor have their food
and those who fear the Lord be satisfied . . .

4Q Apostrophe to Judah

. . .
Let then the heavens and the earth give praise together,
let all the stars of evening sing praises!
Rejoice, O Judah, in your joy,
rejoice your joy and exult your exultation!
Celebrate your festivals, fulfill your vows
for no longer is Belial in your midst.
Lift up your hand, strengthen your right hand,
behold your enemies go perishing
and all workers of evil go scattering.
But thou, O Lord, thou art for ever,
thy glory for e'er and aye.
Hallelujah!

The Old Testament
at Qumran

DAVID NOEL FREEDMAN

As to the central place of the Hebrew Bible in the life and thought of the Qumran community there can be no question. The initial manuscript discoveries made it clear that the original owners were pious Jews who earnestly subscribed to the divine precepts laid down in the sacred Scriptures and considered themselves to be loyal adherents to, as well as rightful heirs of, the great traditions of Israel. The vast documentary troves subsequently uncovered, along with excavations at the Dead Sea, have only strengthened the first impression. Approximately one-quarter of all the scroll materials found in the caves of Qumran are copies of Old Testament books.

Not only do these manuscripts constitute the core of the Qumran library—they exerted a pervasive influence on the rest of the extant literature. Thus in addition to the biblical books, there are a number of midrashic[1] works, adaptations, imitations, and elaborations of biblical materials (e.g. various speeches of Moses in imitation of the Deuteronomic sermons). Even more important, perhaps, are the numerous commentaries on the different books of the Bible. These demonstrate beyond cavil the authority of the Hebrew Bible in the community, and show also how the community interpreted and applied the ancient truths to the contemporary situation and its problems. The rest of the sectarian literature, with rare exceptions, conscientiously quotes, paraphrases, or alludes to scriptural passages in a conscious effort to link the current modes of faith and practice, worship and service, with the authoritative patterns of the past.

However, this elaborate devotion to and acknowledged depend-

[1] See Glossary (Ed.).

ence on the Scriptures was not just a nostalgic return to the past, to recreate the Israel of Moses in the wilderness, which would have been futile in any case. The Qumran community, in spite of its deliberate archaizing and its isolation, was as much a part and product of the Hellenistic-Roman world to which it belonged chronologically as of the earlier period to which it belonged by conviction and emotional commitment. While the roots and origins as well as many important features of the Qumran society may be traced to the tradition and practice of ancient Israel as recorded or reconstructed in Scripture, many other features arose out of contemporary conditions and needs and reflect the dynamics of a historically functioning society. In short, what we find is a devoutly religious community modeled deliberately on the ancient Mosaic society of the wilderness wanderings, but no less consciously adapted to the conditions and circumstances of a much later day. Within the archaic framework of law and custom provided by the Hebrew scriptures, many elements drawn from the Persian and Hellenistic worlds of discourse have been incorporated, blending old and new into a structure at once continuous with the past and compatible with the present.

In assessing the role of the Old Testament in the faith of Qumran, we must examine the relationship between the archaic framework and the later features. We note first that the Old Testament has been used selectively, with certain factors emphasized to the neglect of others, and next, that these elements have been further adapted through a creative exegesis which opens the way to the inclusion or addition of non-biblical elements. The final synthesis is clearly biblical in essence, format, and general appearance; just as clearly there is something quite different in its thrust and focus. To the extent that such a community could thrive in a hostile environment, a two-sided development of this kind was inevitable. Its success could be measured by its firmness of purpose and principle on the one hand (to be faithful to its traditions), and its adaptability and flexibility to contemporary pressures and circumstances on the other.

The Hebrew Bible in its present form is largely the product of the literary activity (both original and editorial) of the exilic and immediately following periods. It is not surprising therefore that the Qumran community should exhibit in its basic structure the principal concerns of the early post-exilic Jewish Commonwealth.

Thus for a society deprived of political independence and the institutions which normally embody and express statehood, an inner structure of great strength, tough discipline, and highest religious sanction was indispensable. The image of Israel in the wilderness under Moses became the primary model for both Judah in the days of Ezra and Qumran in the days of the Righteous Teacher. Each community inevitably made its own local adjustment, but it is characteristic of Qumran that its organizational pattern was more like that of the ancient wilderness community (it was even located in such an area), and its discipline more rigid as befits a society totally engaged in spiritual war.

Similarly the prophets of the exilic period, especially Ezekiel and II Isaiah, played a large role in the reconstruction of the post-exilic Jewish community. Their influence is also pervasive in the Qumran society and its literature. Just as this prophetic literature inspired the return from exile and offered a plan for the rebuilding of city and temple, so the same motifs figured prominently in the departure of the Qumran sectaries and their settlement in the wilderness. Return and restoration were their watchwords as well.

If, as we believe, the Psalter was the hymn book of the Second Temple, it served the Qumran community as well as post-exilic Judaism. The Psalter not only informed the piety of Qumran but offered a model which was widely imitated in the hymnody of the sect. All of the basic elements of biblical religion as these were understood and implemented in post-exilic Judaism were present in the Qumran community. They attempted to reconstitute the true community of God. To that end they committed themselves to obedience to the divine law as detailed in the Mosaic code; they interpreted their own history in the theological terms and dimensions of the prophetic literature and understood their experience to be the working out of moral principles in time and place; finally their piety was expressed in corporate and private worship, the great public festivals, and the innumerable personal occasions of prayer: praise and thanksgiving, contrition and repentance, supplication and dedication. In its basic beliefs and practices Qumran was thoroughly Jewish: biblical in principle, post-exilic in orientation and action.

At the same time there are numerous aspects of the life and literature of Qumran which stamp them unmistakably as emerging from the late Hellenistic age in Palestine, and reflecting the special circumstances and crises of Judaism in that era. Since many of these features appear in the distinctive Jewish religious literature of the Greco-Roman period (from approximately 165 B.C.E. to 135 C.E.) which we call "apocalyptic," we may use the term to designate the trend and tone of this major branch of Judaism.

It is to be noted that the main content of these documents is derived from the classic literature of the Old Testament, but the material is organized in patterns characteristic of a later age. The Book of Daniel is one of the earliest exemplars of this type of literature, and while it is a biblical book, it may with justice be characterized as late Jewish apocalyptic, or paradoxically as inter-testamental (dating in its present form from 165 B.C.E.). The book draws heavily upon the biblical tradition. The setting is the Babylonian Exile, and Daniel himself is a pious Jewish seer who achieves prominence at the court of a foreign king; he and his career are modeled loosely on the figure of Joseph, who was the archetypal dream interpreter. But in the case of Daniel, this skill is pressed into forecasting the end of days, not just future historical events. The special interest of the author is the conclusion of history, not simply the anticipation of the future. The chronological scheme is based upon Jeremiah's seventy-year prediction concerning the duration of the Exile (or the empire of Nebuchadnezzar), but is transmuted by a mathematical device into a projection of world history as it moves inexorably toward its denouement. Once again a fairly straightforward, historical anticipation has been transformed into an eschatological pronouncement in response to the urgent question: When will the end come?

It was equally the conviction of the historians and prophets of the classic Old Testament period on the one hand and Daniel on the other that the course of history was in the hands of God and that the faithful could be confident about its conclusion because of the overwhelming power of Yahweh, the God of hosts. But in Daniel the scheme is more rigidly deterministic than in the earlier writers, with the end decided from the beginning and the role of man as a free and responsible moral agent correspondingly reduced. We can recognize such tendencies in characteristic exilic compositions like Ezekiel and the priestly corpus of the Pentateuch, but in Daniel they are even more pronounced. The chief concern in Daniel is the revelation of the mystery of the end-time, to find out precisely what will happen and when; but there is no thought

36. *Legend to Chart of Scripts*

Line 1. The Elegant Script of Papyrus II, dating from 352/1 B.C.E. (seventh year of Artaxerxes III). The siglum 8 designates forms taken from the contemporary papyrus 8 dated March 4, 354 B.C.E.

Lines 2 and 3. Script of Papyrus I of ed-Dâliyeh, dated March 19, 335 B.C.E. The siglum 6 marks letter forms taken from the roughly contemporary papyrus 6 (ca. 340 B.C.E.).

Bullae from the Dâliyeh Papyri

37. Seal No. 4. The Persian hero dressed in tiara and Persian garb holds an ox-horned, winged lion with his left hand, a drawn scimitar in his right hand. The scene is a popular one, found among the seals of Persepolis and on Sidonian coinage.

38. Seal No. 14. The youth Jason, leader of the Argonauts, wearing *chlamys* with a wand or lance in his left hand and the *aphlaston* (stern ornament) of his ship Argos.

39. Seal No. 25. Two scorpion men with scorpion tails, lion forequarters, bird feet, and human heads crowned with royal Persian tiaras; twisted line decoration.

40. Tel 'Arad: The citadel mount during the first season's excavation.

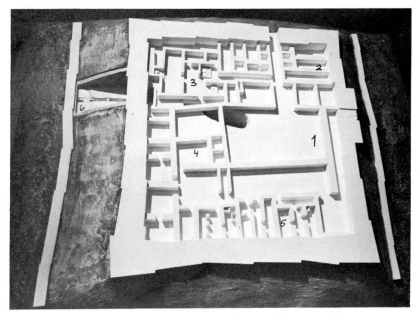

41. Model of the royal Israelite citadel of the eighth century (Stratum 8) made by the Israel Museum for the Arad Exhibition: 1. Courtyard; 2. Store; 3. Temple; 4. Industrial area; 5. Living quarters; 6. Water tunnel.

42. Strata 10-6 wall; below, the postern gate above the water tunnel.

43. Part of the "Arad Bowl."

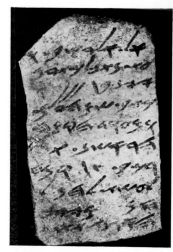

45. Three Hebrew seals (bottom row) and their impressions with the inscription: *l'lyšb bn 'šyhw*—"belonging to Eliashib son of Eshyahu."

44. One of the Eliashib ostraca.

46-47. Ostracon from an inferior of Eliashib, mentioning "the house of Yahweh."

48. The Holy of Holies of the temple.

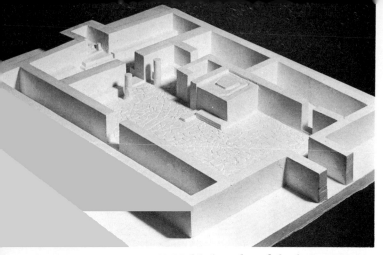

49. Model of temple made by the Israel Museum.

50. Altar of burnt offerings.

51. Bronze figurine of a lion found near the altar.

52. Fragments of a clay
    incense burner.

53. Hebrew ostracon found in one of
    the rooms of the temple with the
    inscription: *pšḥr*—Pashḥur.

54. Similar ostracon reading
    mrmwt—Meremoth.

55. Seal with general plan of the citadel.
The temple is marked by a round bulge.

56. The Temple Scroll as it was found.

57. A portion of the text describing the phases of
mobilization of the army of Israel.

of influencing or changing the fixed decisions, or affecting the pre-determined course of action.

The role of angels as interpreters and agents of the divine will, as guardians and guides of the faithful, is well known in the Old Testament, and there is a marked emphasis on their special activity as revealers in the post-exilic Book of Zechariah. This pattern has been further elaborated in Daniel and comparable literature of the later period.

The representative death and resurrection of the Servant of Yahweh is an important feature of II Isaiah's teaching; in developed form it emerges as the closing and climactic theme of Daniel, but with a distinctive eschatological orientation.

Daniel's view of history is essentially that of the earlier books of the Bible, especially the prophets. The kingdoms of this world are subject to Yahweh's authority. He orders the affairs of nations according to his purpose, granting universal suzerainty first to one great power and then another. Even Israel must submit to the rule of aliens for the allotted time. In the end, however, God will shatter the pagan powers and establish the kingdom of his people. In the later prophets, especially Ezekiel and II Isaiah, the historical restoration of Israel is fitted into a universal eschatological resolution. In Daniel there is a further development: the course of the latter days (from Daniel's time to the end) is plotted according to a fixed scheme, and kingdom follows kingdom in a predetermined plan which culminates in the establishment of the kingdom of God on earth. The four-kingdom theory expounded in Daniel is not to be found elsewhere in the Scriptures.

How important Daniel was in shaping the thought and doctrine of the Qumran community is difficult to say. At least they copied and preserved the work, along with other hitherto unknown traditions about Daniel. Extensive fragments of various sections of the Enoch literature have been recovered. Other apocryphal and pseudepi-graphic[2] books are also represented at Qumran, indicating strong interest in this kind of literature, which is commonly lumped under the headings: eschatology and apocalyptic.

We may characterize the dominant interest as eschatological and consider the other aspects of community faith and practice in relation to it. The basic category itself is eminently biblical. While

[2] See Glossary (Ed.).

some scholars trace eschatological features to the earliest days of Israel and find both cosmic and eschatological elements in the monarchy, for example, there can be little doubt that the later prophets, especially in the period of the Exile, manifest an eschatological concern of major proportions. Qumran stands fully in this tradition with added stress on the imminence of the eschaton and greater attention to the details of its realization. Among the many features which characterize the eschatological stance of the Qumran community we may mention the following:

Beliefs

(a) Determinism and dualism: while the antecedents of these doctrines are to be found in the biblical tradition, they are much more pronounced in the Qumran literature than anywhere in the Old Testament. The historic struggle between Israel and its enemies has been transferred to the cosmic realm, while the ethical conflict between the righteous and the wicked has been absolutized. At Qumran the hosts of angels and men are permanently divided into two lots, of good and evil, light and darkness. There is eternal warfare between the opposing forces until the final victory of the good. While Qumran theology is profoundly dualistic and interprets the present world crisis in terms of this fundamental conflict, it is even more basically monotheistic. Thus it analyzes the cosmic struggle as the result of a divine decision; the inevitable result, the triumph of light over darkness, is likewise foreordained. The rigid determinism of apocalyptic works generally is characteristic of Qumran and finds echoes in much of the New Testament literature. The rabbis on the other hand, while acknowledging the omnipotence and supremacy of God, nevertheless attempted to preserve for man an area of self-determination and the free exercise of his will. It must be conceded that the Old Testament generally and inconsistently allows room for both divine sovereignty and human freedom.

(b) Closely linked with the general theme of dualism is the inevitable final conflict between the children of light and those of darkness. The ultimate outcome is never in doubt, since God has predetermined the end and both the substance and manner of the final triumph. This picture of eschatological conflict is ultimately derived from the pattern of holy war in the Old Testament. It may be noted that the military organization and preparations for battle set forth in the Qumran War Scroll are based on the arrangements recorded in the Book of Numbers: in both we have the sacred community described as a holy army, the encampment of God, ready to do battle for his sake and in his name. The eschatological features are derived largely from prophetic accounts of the final warfare between God and the pagan armies in behalf of his people. Especially important is the tradition in Ezekiel which identifies the eschatological foe as Gog of Magog, and links the annihilation of his forces with the commencement of the new age of fulfillment.

(c) Other Qumran documents speak of a new or heavenly Jerusalem with its newly built Temple. Here again the influence of Ezekiel (Chaps. 40–48) is noteworthy. It is too early to discuss the so-called Temple Scroll, but it is clear that the new city and temple figured prominently in Qumran expectations. It should be both stimulating and fruitful to compare the Qumran picture with that of the New Testament Apocalypse, which is likewise dependent upon the imagery of Ezekiel.

(d) Messianism was a prominent feature of the eschatology of Qumran. While the expectation differed in detail from the views attributed commonly to Jews of the first century whether in the New Testament, Josephus, or early rabbinic literature, it conforms closely to traditional Old Testament patterns. Thus in accordance with the Law and the Prophets, three eschatological figures were expected: the eschatological prophet, i.e. the prophet like Moses, who would announce the inauguration of God's rule on earth and identify and designate both the high priest of the line of Zadok and the king of the house of David.

(e) Mention should be made too of the Qumran theory of inspiration, which served to link the community with the ancient tradition, and also to make the Scriptures directly applicable to the circumstances and present realities of their existence. The Righteous Teacher who apparently founded the community in the wilderness was the authoritative guide for the membership. He was empowered by the spirit of God to interpret the ancient and mysterious words of Scripture and expound their true eschatological meaning. Thus he alone could explain that Habakkuk's protestations and predictions about the Chaldeans were in truth secret divine warnings about the Kittites (i.e. Romans) in these last days. Similarly Nahum's paean of victory against Assyria was actually a series of dire predictions about the rulers of Jerusalem and Judah in Hasmonean times, but only the inspired interpreter could reveal this truth to the faithful. In point of fact, the central concern of the Qumran community was this mystery of the end-time. It acknowledged that the secret had been revealed by God to the Righteous Teacher, who in turn had expounded the true meaning of the Scriptures in the light of this revelation.

Practice

The organization and operation of the Qumran community were designed to achieve in fact the beliefs and expectations expressed in their writings. Thus the daily life of the community was intended to be an acted parable of the kingdom.

(a) We have already mentioned the emphasis on obedience to the law of Moses, which for the people of Qumran, was the pattern of the kingdom of God, as interpreted and applied by the inspired leader. Such meticulous observance was the rule of the kingdom and would also ensure and hasten its coming. Thus at Qumran the people had a foretaste of the life of the kingdom, which through their faithful obedience was already in being.

(b) The proleptic character of the community is further emphasized in the rituals enjoined upon the membership. These, including the elaborate rite of initiation into the covenant community and the numerous special festivals, are transparently anticipations of the way of the eschatological kingdom. So immersed in the eschaton were the people of Qumran that it is often difficult to determine whether particular practices were currently undertaken in anticipation of the coming of the kingdom or whether they were intended for use only after the establishment of the kingdom. Suffice it to say that the ritual served to actualize the future in the present, and at the same time to prepare the participants to play their proper role in the reality to come. Since the urgency of the present crisis and the immediate necessity of the new order were an essential part of the ritual, it served both as an appeal to and demand upon the deity to hasten the long-delayed consummation.

(c) The asceticism of Qumran, especially its celibacy, was another aspect of its eschatology. We cannot rule out entirely sociological and psychological factors, or parallel developments in various pagan societies, but the dominant element was the conviction that in the new order men would be like the angels in heaven who neither marry nor give in marriage. The ultimate source of this remarkable proscription is doubtless the rule of Israelite holy war requiring chastity of those engaged in the Lord's battles. Originally part of the general pattern of ritual purity, and applicable for the duration of a single campaign, this injunction became at Qumran a rule of life for those permanently enlisted in the army of God. In the current cosmic eschatological struggle there would be no discharge short of death, and therefore the regulations governing holy war would be in force permanently.

Thus in the whole range of its faith and life, the Qumran community affirmed a consistent eschatology. The end was at hand; in fact it had already begun and those who were enrolled in the lot of the prince of lights must be prepared to live and die in faithful adherence to the holy community and its divinely appointed ordinances. Those who endured the present evil age, would participate fully in the joys of the coming great one.

The Qumran community bears an important relationship both to the post-exilic Jewish community and to the Hebrew Bible which it acknowledged as its supreme written standard. However, the Qumran community was not simply continuous with post-exilic Judaism, nor was it modeled directly upon the pattern of the Old Testament. The relationship is more complex, and external factors played a significant role in the formation of the new society which emerged at Qumran. Certainly the continuing crisis in which Judaism found itself in the Greco-Roman period provided both the setting for and creative impact upon the Qumran community; although it deliberately isolated itself from the outside world, it could not finally escape the influence of that world and its all-pervading culture.

The Hebrew Bible provided the foundational elements: the common tradition to which all Jews, including the Essenes, subscribed and by which they were bound. Then there was the ideal pattern of the Mosaic Age, as reconstructed by exilic writers, but nonetheless normative for the Qumran community. It was not simply nostalgia for the past that led the Righteous Teacher and his followers to re-constitute the ancient society in the wilderness, but anguish about the present, and urgent hopes for the future. The second main ingredient was the eschatological expectations of the prophets. When linked with the older traditions of the formative period in Israel's history, these expectations produced a basic blueprint for contemporary action in anticipation of the new age. On this biblical structure were welded doctrines and practices of the Hellenistic age, ultimately derived from Persian, Greek, and other pagan sources, and shaped by the crucial experiences of the Jewish community during this period.

The Dead Sea Scrolls
and the New Testament

FLOYD V. FILSON

For the study of New Testament background the discovery of the Dead Sea Scrolls is the most significant manuscript find ever made, and its importance is by no means limited to New Testament study. The scrolls, which date from the intertestamental and New Testament period, reveal the life of a sect contemporary with the New Testament history. The circumstances of discovery preclude fraud; the scrolls are certainly authentic, and they are early; almost all of them date between 150 B.C.E. and C.E. 68. None is later.[1]

In trying, however, to assess the significance of the scrolls, we face certain difficulties.

Difficulties in Study of the Scrolls

Not all of the scrolls have been published. Probably most of the most exciting and instructive ones are now available for general study, but concerning most of the perhaps five hundred manuscripts of which at least small fragments have been preserved we still know very little. The international team of scholars responsible for preparing the remaining fragments for publication has proceeded carefully and, some would say, much too slowly.

In the meantime we occasionally hear statements, especially from members of the international team, which suggest that we will see momentous changes in our picture of New Testament origins when still unpublished material is made public. In one case a member made sweeping statements which other members of the study team

[1] For readable accounts of their discovery and significance see John C. Trever, *The Untold Story of Qumran* (Revell, 1965), and Yigael Yadin, *The Message of the Scrolls* (New York: Grosset & Dunlap, 1962).

publicly disavowed. Such public dispute over unpublished material is confusing and emphasizes the importance of publishing the remaining material as soon as possible.

It is not clear whether the Qumran sect itself produced all of the non-biblical scrolls discovered or took over some from related groups holding similar views.

Since the manuscripts discovered are fragmentary, many words are incomplete and some letters too faint to read with certainty, so the translation is often uncertain and conjectural.

A few much publicized passages, said to change our previous understanding of New Testament background, rest on conjectural readings, uncertain text, or debated rendering of rare words, and so we must proceed with caution.

It is important for the interested minister or layman to read a translation of the scrolls, remembering the limitations just noted. Easily accessible are G. Vermes, *The Dead Sea Scrolls in English* (Harmondsworth: Penguin Books, 1962) and Theodor H. Gaster, *The Dead Sea Scriptures in English Translation,* rev. ed. (New York: Doubleday Anchor, 1964); both are reasonably priced paperbacks.

Let us now discuss the Qumran Sect and note how far its characteristics have New Testament parallels.

Characteristics of the Qumran Sect

It was a Jewish sect whose members were earnestly penitent for their sins and dedicated to finding and doing the will of God as set forth in Scripture. The New Testament message had a similar accent.

It was a writing sect. Because the Pharisees emphasized the oral tradition which interpreted and applied the Law, we have tended to think that first century Jews did not write down their teaching. This Qumran sect not only copied books of Scripture and other Jewish writings, but also wrote commentaries on books or portions of Scripture, and composed other works to guide their common life and express their faith in hymns. These writings show wide use of Hebrew rather than Aramaic. The early Church soon wrote letters and Gospels, literary forms not used at Qumran.

It was a studying and teaching sect. The outstanding figure in the history of the sect was the Teacher of Righteousness (or, Right

Teacher) whose interpretation of the Law was authoritative. The members of the sect were dedicated to intensive study of the Law of God, under guidance of competent leaders. Jesus was a teacher, but not in so systematic a way, and other titles, including "prophet," were more widely used of him.

It was a sect which interpreted the Scripture as speaking of the time in which the sect was living and writing. This *pesher*[2] method assumed that the prophets of earlier days wrote of the events through which the sect was living. Jesus and his followers used the same hermeneutic.

It was a withdrawal sect. The group regarded the Jerusalem priesthood and other Jewish leaders as corrupt and unclean. To avoid contamination they withdrew from participation in official Jewish worship and life. Jesus and the Apostles went to the temple and synagogues, and, while they criticized Jewish leaders, they did not withdraw from the common life or shun the common people.

It was a wilderness sect. The Qumran sectarians interpreted Isaiah 40:3 to mean that they must go into the wilderness to prepare for participation in the right order which God would soon establish. In the New Testament Isaiah 40:3 was understood to refer to John the Baptist's preaching in the wilderness.

It was a "sectarian" sect; it lived apart from other Jews and insisted that the religion of Israel must be practiced precisely as the sect understood and practiced it. This did not mean individualism; every member was under the control and discipline of the sect through its recognized leaders. Jesus and his followers made no such radical separation from Jewish common life and worship.

It was an esoteric sect. There were aspects of its teaching that were disclosed only to those who had entered the sect and bound themselves to secrecy by an oath. The sect laid stress on knowledge, but its important teaching was a secret knowledge, a mystery, which God made known to the Teacher of Righteousness and which was handed on in the sect's life. Jesus did not withhold knowledge (I cannot believe that he used parables to conceal God's truth), and when Paul spoke of God's mystery, he meant the universal gospel once hid but now openly known and preached to all.

It was an intolerant sect. Its members were to love their own members, but to hate all "the children of darkness," a term which

[2] See Glossary (Ed.).

seems to include not only Gentiles but also Jewish believers who did not share the views of the Qumran sect. Jesus and the Apostles preached judgment, but the gospel was for all Jews—and soon was seen to be for all men.

It was a priest-led sect. The Teacher of Righteousness was a priest; priests were to be present in study groups and on governing boards of the sect and were to have a role in the forty-year war of the end-time. The priestly Messiah of Aaron was to outrank the lay Messiah of Israel, that is, the Davidic Messiah. The New Testament has no such priestly accent. John the Baptist was of priestly descent, but it was his prophetic message that counted. Jesus was not a priest, nor were the Twelve. Hebrews knows no Aaronic priest in the Church; Jesus is the high priest in the heavenly sanctuary (Heb. 9:24).

It was a ritualistic sect, conscious of the need of ceremonial purity for its members. What one should do, how one should do it, and how one's worship and life could be kept clean and pure were matters of great concern. There is no comparable concern for ritual in the New Testament.

It was temporarily a temple-shunning sect. It considered the Jerusalem priesthood unworthy and unclean, so it would not participate in the temple worship and sacrifices, but it expected, once God's perfect order had been established at the end of the age, to share once more the temple worship. Jesus "cleansed" the temple and anticipated its destruction (Mark 11:15–17; 13:2), but he did not stay away from it.

It was a calendar-conscious sect. Qumran was convinced that the calendar followed by the wicked priests at Jerusalem was not the divinely prescribed one. It favored a basically solar calendar. It seems to have observed the Day of Atonement, for example, on a different day from that observed by the Jerusalem priesthood. No such concern for a particular calendar or for calendar revision characterizes the New Testament.

It was a legalistic sect, determined to define specifically what its members should do. It had a real place for faith, but unlike Paul, who thought that faith replaced the works of the Law, the sect thought that once forgiven and dedicated to do God's will, their salvation depended on their careful observance of the rightly interpreted Law. This legal concern finds no comparable parallel in the New Testament.

It was a sect conscious of eschatology. The end of the age was near. That end did not come as soon as had been expected, but the delay was not expected to be long, and the members must be ready for the final War and the coming of the end-time. This conviction that the end was at hand was shared by John the Baptist and Jesus, and in the preaching of Jesus and the early Church it advanced to a strong statement that the end-time had already broken into this world order in the preaching and work of Jesus (cf. Matt. 12:28).

It was a sect with a dualistic world-view and a deterministic outlook, but not a complete dualism and determinism, for the dualism was God's creation and would be overcome at the end, and the determinism never took away man's responsibility; while human choice might seem excluded by certain passages in the scrolls, the scrolls never let that viewpoint crowd out the sense of human responsibility. The New Testament has a marked degree of parallelism to these views, the similarity being considerable, for example, in the Gospel and Epistles of John, in the light-darkness conflict.

It was a militant sect, not only in its outspoken opposition to those Jews who rejected its view but also in its expectation that the sect would play a prominent role in the great War that would occur at the end of the age. Its life was preparation for participation in the final decisive War. The final victory of God's cause in the New Testament is the work of God himself and his heavenly hosts; it is not conceived as a triumph partly due to human military prowess.

It was a sect dedicated to unity in community, expressed not only in a closely organized life under authoritative leaders but also in community of property. There are indications that in certain cases members were allowed to possess some property, but the scrolls suggest that new members gave up their property when they entered the sect. They shared in purpose, study, worship, daily life, and property. It is not clear how marriage was arranged, where the sect permitted it, but the dominant tendency seems to have been to share goods.

There is something of a parallel to this community of property in the New Testament—not so much in the common purse which Judas is said to have carried for Jesus and the Twelve (John 13:29) as in the testimony of Acts 2:44; 4:32 that the believers "had everything in common." This was more a temporary sharing of resources by a harassed group than a functioning economy, and there is no evidence that it long continued. However, the concern for needy comrades and the voluntary sharing of available resources resembled the community of goods of the Qumran sect more than it conforms to modern capitalist procedures.

The Sect an Answer to Syncretistic Pressures

What was the setting of these Qumran sectarians? Were they simply the Essenes of whom Philo, Josephus, and Pliny wrote? Or were there, as I suspect, a number of related Essene-type withdrawal sects? The main thing is to recognize the syncretistic threat to which the sect offered one answer. Through its history Israel had been tempted by polytheistic and syncretistic pressures. These became acute in the attempts of the Seleucid empire to get the Jews to join in Hellenistic polytheistic cultural assimilation. The Maccabees fought and largely won religious freedom for the Jews.

How to preserve this freedom, yet live without yielding to the continuing assimilative setting was a problem. A Zealot-type answer was to fight to the limit for political freedom for God's people. The Pharisees accepted foreign rule and concentrated on the study and observance of the Mosaic Law; Jesus showed a similar acceptance of foreign rule. The Sadducee leaders cooperated with the foreign rulers and joined to a considerable degree in cultural assimilation. The Qumran Essene-type withdrawal sect reacted against the Sadducees and opposed the trend to cultural assimilation. The ministry of Jesus and the emergence of the Church must be studied in the broad setting of this widespread syncretistic ferment, which the Herodians and Romans promoted. Something of the Essene reaction against it entered into the New Testament attitude to the world, but without the pronounced withdrawal tendency found at Qumran. The Church was not an Essene sect.

It has been claimed that the Qumran sect is best understood as part of the Zealot group within Judaism. One can see how this view arises. This Qumran sect was intensely zealous for their teaching as given to them by the true Teacher, and the revolutionary and militant note in the Qumran scrolls gives some support to the idea that the Qumran sect was an important part of the Zealots. But while the Qumran sectarians were preparing for participation in the great final war with the children of darkness, they were not, as far as the scrolls indicate, active in civil disturbance and guerrilla warfare such as the Zealots carried on.

But what specifically was the distinctive stance, teaching, life, and purpose of the New Testament as compared with that seen in the scrolls? Four preliminary remarks may be helpful.

New Testament Dependence on the Scrolls?

If there is direct dependence between the scrolls and the New Testament, the latter will be dependent on the scrolls, which antedate most of the New Testament books and present views essentially formed before the Christian gospel emerged.

The New Testament nowhere quotes directly from the sectarian works represented in the scrolls.

There are many details of wording or thought or practice in which the scrolls and the New Testament are parallel. This does not indicate in every case, or even in most cases, that the New Testament is dependent on the scrolls. Where something found in both the scrolls and the New Testament is found also in Pharisaic or rabbinic teaching, we cannot prove that the New Testament borrowed from the scrolls, except that something found elsewhere but especially prominent or characteristic in both the scrolls and the New Testament may suggest some special kinship between these two sources.

The point I find most neglected in comparisons of the scrolls and the New Testament is the secret character of the essential Qumran teaching. Most comparisons seem to imply that the Qumran writers wrote for general readers and the widest possible public influence. The reverse is the case. They had teaching which they delivered to full-fledged members of their group, but they did not disclose this to every visitor (if they received visitors); indeed, they were bound not to disclose it. The idea that the teaching of the Qumran sect was known generally to disciples involved in the rise and early development of Christianity is an unwarranted assumption. Are we to believe that John the Baptist, Jesus, the author of the Gospel of John, Paul, and the author of Hebrews had all joined the sect and later left it without that fact being recorded? Did the New Testament writers have access to the Qumran writings? This is most unlikely. There was a secrecy obligation for Qumran initiates. It is highly improbable that many Qumran initiates left the sect, became Christians, and so fed Qumran ideas into Christian teaching. Such a picture would not be convincing.

Agreements and Differences

There are many parallels in thought and wording between the scrolls and the New Testament. Both have a vivid sense of the holiness, Lordship, and power of God the Creator and Judge of all men. In both he is the active God of history, and the future rests in his hands. In both God demands the whole man and is never content with token obedience. Both groups are convinced that they are living in the eschatological end-time, and God will act as judge of all men when the end of history comes. To both the imminence of God's judgment is an urgent reason for repentance by sinful men. The guide of men in this situation is the Scripture, interpreted to show that the prophets were speaking of the present day. For the Qumran sect the authoritative interpreter is the Teacher of Righteousness or True Teacher of God's will as set forth in the Law of Moses; for the New Testament Church and writers Jesus' less legalistic interpretation of Scripture is normative. There is in both groups a dualistic note, more strongly stated in the scrolls than in the New Testament but present in both; and in both the rule of all by the one God prevents a consistent ultimate dualism. A strong sense of community marks both groups, with a stronger concern for community of goods in the Qumran sect. And the ideas and expressions shared by the scrolls and the New Testament indicate that both of these renewal sects concerned with eschatology had roots in the apocalyptic and renewal-dedicated Judaism of the time.

The differences between the two groups center in and develop from the two pioneer leaders, the Teacher of Righteousness and Jesus of Nazareth. We have described the Qumran teaching and indicated briefly how Jesus and the New Testament differ from it. We must now focus on the New Testament and sum up its message, and in so doing state any differences from the scrolls. The basic and comprehensive difference is in Jesus and his meaning for the gospel and the Church.

Prominent New Testament Aspects

The Incarnation involves a uniqueness of person and a link with the Father which is without parallel in the Teacher of Righteousness.

The absence of any consciousness of sin in Jesus, and the Church's confession of Jesus' sinlessness, are in striking contrast to the repeated confession of complete unworthiness and sinfulness by the author of the Thanksgiving Hymns which, it is usually thought, the Teacher of Righteousness wrote.

Jesus did not withdraw from society to center on his own self-discipline. He went to the people, especially the common people. He did not marry, and at times he withdrew temporarily for prayer or to teach his disciples, but the dominant note of his life was an outgoing ministry to his people wherever he could find them.

Jesus preached the coming of the Kingdom of God, a phrase not current in the Qumran sect. From the beginning of his ministry or at least from the time of his first healings he saw in those healings the actual beginnings of the Kingdom (Matt. 12:28). The day of salvation had come; it was a present though not a complete reality. The Qumran writings expected the end soon, and thought of the present as the end-time, but they did not match Jesus' note of realized eschatology.

The healing ministry of Jesus had no parallel, as far as we know, in the work of the Teacher of Righteousness.

Jesus thought of himself as sent to carry out a Messianic ministry, and the Church from its first days identified him as the expected Messiah. The Qumran sect expected a Messiah of Aaron and a Messiah of Israel, but the Teacher of Righteousness did not think he was a Messiah; he looked for Messiahs to come later.

A note of joy marked the ministry of Jesus, muted though it was by rejection and opposition, and the Apostolic Church had a spirit of joy prompted especially by the sense of the gift of the Holy Spirit. The Qumran sect seems marked rather by a deep sense of conscientious earnestness and dedication to the will of God found in Scripture and explained by the Teacher of Righteousness.

While Jesus carried on his ministry within the limits of Judaism, an implicit note of universality marked his message and attitude. He was indifferent to ceremonial and ritualistic features of the Old Testament; precisely the features which made for separation of Jews from Gentiles were the features he played down. Even the Jewish Christian Gospel of Matthew saw clearly that the scope of Jesus' ministry and purpose went beyond the bounds of Israel (Matt. 28:19). The Apostolic Church soon grasped this outlook, and even James the brother of Jesus granted that Gentiles had a place in the Church (Acts 21:25), though at times he did not agree with Paul as to how Jewish Christians should live in relation to Judaism and the Gentile Christians. This universal note had no parallel in the Qumran sect, which was confined to loyal members recruited in Israel.

It is recorded in the Gospels as well as in the rest of the New Testament that Jesus came to suffer and thereby to save sinners. His resurrection and exaltation to Lordship over his believers were also central features of his saving work. An attempt has been made to show from the scrolls that the Teacher of Righteousness had been martyred, had later appeared alive to his followers, and so had anticipated the gospel story of the death and resurrection of Jesus. It is highly doubtful whether the scrolls report the martyr death of the Teacher of Righteousness. But if they do, the Qumran sect had no doctrine of salvation by the martyrdom of its Teacher, and no parallel to the resurrection and Lordship of Jesus.

Both the New Testament and the Qumran sect make much of the new covenant; for both the promise of Jeremiah 31:31–34 had been fulfilled. But in the New Testament it was really a new covenant, different from and better than the old covenant Israel made with God through Moses. For the Qumran sect the new covenant was actually a renewal of the old covenant, which the sect now promised earnestly to observe by faithfully keeping the Mosaic Law.

An outstanding feature of the New Testament is its open preaching and teaching of the gospel. There is no secrecy that keeps teaching a mystery within the sect, as at Qumran. Rather, the New Testament preachers from John the Baptist and Jesus on into the Apostolic Age proclaimed their message openly and with evangelistic zeal urged their hearers to accept the gospel and be saved. When Paul speaks of a mystery of the gospel he means the once-hidden divine purpose to save all men in Christ; it is a mystery once hidden but now revealed and openly announced (Eph. 3:3–9; Col. 1:26–27). This open, aggressive, evangelistic note is not found in the Qumran sect. The gnosis or knowledge of the New Testament is not a secret way to salvation, as in some later Gnosticism. The Qumran sect holds more background for that later Gnostic position than does the New Testament.

From all that has been said it is clear that the New Testament does not offer a new legalism, in which salvation depends on the keeping of the Law. Paul was correct; Christ is the end of the Law as a way of earning salvation (Rom. 10:4). Even the Teacher of Righteousness, if he actually wrote the Thanksgiving Hymns found at Qumran, frankly and repeatedly testifies that he and other men cannot live by the Law; they are deep sinners. But at Qumran that does not lead to an acceptance of a new way; it leads to earnest, renewed effort to keep the Law, a struggle which the Hymns as well as Paul honestly confess is not a possible way to fulfill God's will.

The New Testament presents a gospel and ethic of love. It does not have a place for hating the sons of darkness, nor does it seek to organize believers for the coming final war of God's forces with the forces of evil. Love to God and neighbor, love of enemies, living by the sacrificial way of the Cross—this is the way for Christian believers. This is quite different from the scrolls' command to "hate all the sons of darkness."

Jesus and the New Testament authors have no concern for the ceremonial and ritual aspects of the Mosaic Law. They not only reject the oral tradition by which the Pharisees tried honestly to achieve faithful observance of the Law; they were indifferent to and finally broke with the highly developed ceremonial system of worship. This finds clear expression when Jesus goes to and eats with tax collectors and sinners. This attitude was necessarily anathema to the Qumran sect, which was striving to fulfill faithfully all the precepts of the Law, including the ceremonial regulations.

A fact which most Christians find it hard to see and accept is that Jesus gave no place to clericalism. He saw a place for the Temple in his day as "a house of prayer for all the nations" (Mark 11:17), but he foresaw its destruction with the city of Jerusalem. He saw a place for the priest in his day. But he set up no organization; he established no priesthood; he laid down no cult rules or ceremonies. The Church rarely sees and never long remembers the freedom of Jesus and the early Church on this point. But the freedom is there, in marked contrast to the priest-led ritualistic structure of the Qumran community.

We find in Jesus and the Apostles no anxious concern for correct calendar scheduling of the feasts and high points of worship of the

Christian observance. The Qumran sect was jealous for the observance of special days according to the right calendar. No such concern marks the life of Jesus and the early Church. Jesus went to the synagogue on the Sabbath; he went to Jerusalem for the Passover and, if we believe the Gospel of John, for other festivals. Paul acted similarly. But not a word suggests that to them there was a problem as to the correct calendar location of such festivals.

Conclusion

It is difficult to give a balanced and fair picture of the Qumran sect. Its scrolls are highly instructive, though tantalizing due to their incompleteness. They attest the presence of an earnest and dedicated group of Jewish sectarians determined to learn and to do the will of God while preparing for the near end of the age. With the general movement of which they were a part the Christian movement shared expressions and ways of thinking. The continued study of the scrolls should contribute to the better understanding of New Testament background and origins. But there is nothing in the contents of the scrolls or in a careful comparison of them with the New Testament which warrants hasty statements that the Christian gospel was taken over from the Qumran sect or is basically dependent on that sect for its message and way of life. To assert this would exaggerate greatly the importance of the scrolls and minimize unduly the originality and creative significance of Jesus and the New Testament leaders and writers.

The Temple Scroll

YIGAEL YADIN

I have the great pleasure to announce the unrolling of another of the famous Dead Sea scrolls, which came into our hands in the midst of the recent Six-Day War, one day after the battle of Jerusalem was over. I cannot at this stage disclose the way this scroll came into our hands, lest I endanger the chances of acquiring further scrolls. The story, when it can be told, will seem like a tale from the Arabian Nights.

My knowledge of the recent history of the scroll goes back to the early sixties. It can be said that, prior to June 1967, it was kept in most unsuitable conditions. There is good reason to believe that this contributed in no small measure to its deterioration, in addition to the damage it suffered in the last two thousand years, during which it was hidden in one of the Qumran caves. I am happy to say, however, that its prompt unrolling and the treatment it has received against further decay has saved for the scientific world considerable parts of one of the most important ancient scrolls ever to be discovered.

Unrolling

Let me start by describing the state of the scroll when it came into our hands and how it was unrolled. The scroll was tightly rolled, although numerous pieces were peeled off and detached and were in various stages of decomposition (see Fig. 56). The upper part was a completely mutilated brown-black stump; part of it looked like melted chocolate, a typical condition of scrolls exposed to too much humidity. The lower part, however, seemed intact, with many rolled layers; the diameter of the rolled scroll was about two inches. I was fortunate in having the services of Mr. J. Shenhav (known as "Dodo" in Israeli archaeological circles), who was the chief technical restorer at the excavations of Hazor and Masada. With skill and devotion he worked for several months until he unrolled the entire scroll. The different phases of his work were photographed in black-and-white and in color, so as to ensure full documentation in case something should go wrong in the process.

The scroll was opened in the usual manner, by exposing it for some time to 75% relative humidity under constant vigilance, thus softening the hard parchment. In many cases, layers of the scroll stuck firmly to one another; in these cases we followed with success the method prescribed by Plenderleith: ". . . The problem was to relax the membranes to a point where they could be manipulated without at the same time making the black material so sticky as to prevent this. It was necessary, therefore, to have some method of arresting the softening action of water at the crucial point. The process eventually adopted was to expose the scroll fragments to 100% R.H. for a few minutes, and then transfer them to a refrigerator for a like period. The degree of freezing was sufficient to congeal the surface of the black material while leaving the membranes sufficiently limp to be manipulated by section-lifter without danger to the script."[1] It was fascinating to watch Dodo, like an expert plastic surgeon, discern and dissect the layers. However, even this process did not yield good results in several cases, and since there was danger that further work might destroy a whole fragment, we left them as they were. We subjected these undetachable fragments to infrared, ultraviolet and X-ray photography, sometimes against the light, and thus received sufficient indication of their contents. One other interesting point: as the scroll has been tightly rolled since antiquity, the effect of humidity has meant that in several columns part of the ink peeled off from the surface and stuck, in negative, to the back of the layer above. We simply photographed the backs of the columns involved and then printed them in reverse, thus recovering the lost parts of the text.

The more we advanced to the inner part of the scroll (its end), the better was the condition of the parchment, but even here we had to face some disappointments. The parchment of the various sheets (which is among the thinnest known to me in the Dead Sea scrolls, less than one-tenth of a millimeter) was differently treated in antiquity. Some sheets, even deep inside, were more damaged than others nearer the outside.

[1] *DJD*, I (Oxford University Press, 1955), 40.

The scroll as preserved is the longest known—8.6 meters or over 28 feet, as compared with the 7.3 meters of the complete Isaiah scroll, hitherto the longest. Its end is practically intact, since there is a blank sheet at the very end. The beginning is missing, but probably not much was lost. I was able to establish a continuous sequence of the fragments and the main preserved roll; altogether parts of sixty-six columns are preserved.

The Date

The scroll was copied by a skilled scribe of Qumran. His style, which is the common so-called Herodian, indicates that the latest possible date for its composition was the second part of the first century B.C.E. or the beginning of the first century C.E. Indeed, there are good reasons for placing the date of composition at the end of the second century B.C.E.

The Contents

In addition to its unusual length, the scroll is unique in its content, which concerns four groups of subjects: (1) a large collection of *Halakhoth* (religious rules) on various subjects, among them ritual cleanness, in which the Pentateuch is often quoted with many interesting additions, deletions, and variants; (2) enumeration of the sacrifices and offerings according to the festivals; (3) a detailed prescription for the building of the Temple; (4) the statutes of the king and the army. It is hard to decide, for reasons which will be explained below, what to call this unique scroll. Temporarily, since nearly half its length deals with the temple, I have called it the Temple Scroll.

One of the strangest aspects of the scroll is that its author believed, or wanted his readers to believe, that it was a divine decree given by God to Moses, i.e. a Torah. This is manifested in many ways. The rules are given by God in the first person singular; even in his lengthy quotations of the Pentateuch, the author methodically changes third person singulars to first person singulars. For example, Numbers 30:2 ff., "When a man vows a vow to the Lord . . ." is rendered "When a man vows a vow to me." This is the style also of the many additional commandments, unknown from any version.

That the scribe of the scroll took its text to be a part of the Holy Scriptures *sensu stricto* is also obvious from the fact that the Tetragrammaton—YHWH—is always written in the same script as the scroll itself, as was the practice of the Qumran scribes when copying biblical texts. As is well known, in non-biblical texts Qumran scribes were very careful to write the Tetragrammaton in the Palaeo-Hebrew script. This is the practice in the *pesharim* (commentaries)[2] and even in the famous Cave 11 Psalm scroll. Furthermore, the scribes avoided as much as possible the use of the Tetragrammaton in non-biblical texts, either by indicating it by dots or by using the name GOD or the like. Even in these cases, they sometimes wrote GOD in the Palaeo-Hebrew script. In our scroll, the Tetragrammaton is always written in full and in the same script as the text.

The author of the scroll groups together many rules which in the Pentateuch are dispersed. The main interest in this part of the scroll lies precisely in the many additional rules which are not mentioned in the Pentateuch at all. In many cases, these are clearly sectarian and of a polemic nature. In some cases the subject matter is also dealt with in the Mishnah[3]; here the interest is in those cases in which our scroll decrees a ruling contradicting the one decreed by the sages of "normative Judaism." In most cases of this kind, our scroll is more extreme in matters pertaining to rules of cleanness and uncleanness. An interesting example deals with a pregnant woman with a dead embryo. Our scroll decrees, "If a woman is pregnant (literally, "full") and her young died in her womb, all the days that it remains inside her she is unclean like a tomb." This rule is clearly polemic, as we see if we compare it to the Mishnah, tractate *Hullin* (Animals Killed for Food) 4:3, "If the young of a woman died in its mother's womb, . . . the mother remains clean until the child comes forth." Many passages deal with rules of cleanness concerning a dead man's house; here again, the rules are much more strict than parallel injunctions in the Mishnah.

The scroll has a special chapter on the rules of burial and cemeteries. "Thou shalt not follow the customs of the Gentiles who bury their dead everywhere, even in their houses; thou shalt allot special places in the land in which thou shalt bury the dead; these places thou shalt fix between four cities." Here the author concerns himself

[2] See Glossary (Ed.).
[3] *Ibid.*

with the "economy" of cemeteries, lest the land be defiled. There are many more such rules, but enough has been said to indicate the nature of the scroll on this subject.

The Festivals and the Qumran Calendar

There is ample proof paleographically and on the grounds of spelling peculiarities and the like that the scribe of the scroll was a member of the Qumran community; indeed, there seems to be evidence to show that the author himself must have been a member of the Essene sect, or at least of the same apocalyptic circles which adhered to the special Qumran calendar, the Book of Jubilees, etc.

A considerable part of the scroll is given to prescribing detailed rules concerning the celebration of the various festivals (such as the Feast of Tabernacles, Passover, and Day of Atonement) and their sacrifices, meal-offerings and other ritual practices. In addition to the normal "Festival of Weeks" (Shavuoth—Pentecost) in which the bread of the first fruits was offered, the scroll decrees the celebration of two similar festivals, that of the New Wine and that of the New Oil, to be celebrated fifty and one hundred days respectively after the Festival of Weeks. New Oil is known to have been practiced by the Qumran community[4] and it fell on the twenty-second day of the sixth month. On the basis of our scroll, it can now be proved that this festival could fall on that day (after counting fifty plus fifty plus fifty days) only if one followed the Qumran calendar and festival reckoning. The Essene year consisted of twelve months, each of thirty days, with one extra day at the end of every three months, or 364 days. Further, the first day of the first month always fell on a Wednesday.

Now, one of the basic rifts between the Jewish sects concerns the date of celebrating the two festivals "the raising of the Omer[5]" and the Festival of Weeks. To clarify this, let me quote Professor J. Talmon: "[The dates of] these two holidays are not fixed in the Pentateuch by month and day. The second, the Festival of Weeks, is dependent on the first, since it is to be celebrated fifty days after it (*Lev. xxiii,* 15–16); and the first, 'the raising of the Omer,' depends on Passover and on the interpretation of the words 'on the

[4] See the hitherto unpublished text mentioned by J. T. Milik in *VTS,* IV (Leiden: Brill, 1957), 25.
[5] See Glossary (Ed.).

morrow after the Sabbath' (*ib*. 11) . . . The Sect began the counting of the Omer on the 26.I (see D. Barthélemey in *Revue Biblique,* 59, 1952, 200–201). This means that, like the Sadducees, Boethusians, and Samaritans, they interpreted the expression 'on the morrow after the Sabbath' as referring to the first day of the week and not to the day following after the first of the Passover (Mish. *Menahoth,* x.3). But contrary to the Sadducees and Samaritans, they started counting on the first Sunday after the festival of Unleavened Bread and not on the first Sunday falling in the middle of the festival."[6]

Thus according to our scroll and to previously known data, the festivals of the Essene sect fell on the following days: Raising of the Omer (beginning of the counting), Sunday, 26.I; Festival of Weeks (New Bread)—Pentecost, Sunday, 15.III; New Wine, Sunday, 3.V; New Oil, Sunday, 22.VI. The new evidence derived from the scroll concerning the three "first fruit" festivals, each to be celebrated after counting fifty days, will throw interesting new light on the structure and principles of the festivals practiced in the ancient Near East.

The Temple

Judged from many aspects, and definitely from the amount of space given to its description, the most important subject of the scroll is the temple. As a matter of fact, this is not really a description of the temple, but rather the commandment to build it and instructions how to set about doing that, following the manner and style of Exodus 35 ff., which deals with the tabernacle. Our scroll differs from all hitherto known ancient sources concerning the First, Second and Herod's Temples (I Kings, Chronicles, Ezekiel, the Letter of Aristeas, Josephus, and the Mishnah). It appears that our author endeavored to supply the missing Torah concerning the temple which is alluded to in I Chronicles 28:11 ff., "Then David gave to Solomon his son the pattern of the porch (of the temple) and of the houses thereof, and of the treasures thereof. . . . 'All this [said David] have I been made to understand in writing from the hand of the Lord.'" This missing Torah must have tantalized the ancients, and it is quite likely that efforts were made to supply it. Indeed (as I am reminded by Professor S. Lieberman), there is

---

[6] *Aspects of the Dead Sea Scrolls,* eds. Ch. Rabin and Y. Yadin, *Scripta Hierosolymitana,* IV (Jerusalem: The Magnes Press, 1958), 174.

a very curious reference to such a scroll in the Palestinian Talmud
(*Sanhedrin* 29a) which was ascribed to Ahitophel, who was divinely
inspired when he delivered it.

The scroll's temple is not, strictly speaking, the eschatological,
"ready-made," God-built temple which is the subject among other
things of the Qumran *pesharim* ("that is the house which He will
make thee in the end of the days").[7] In fact, a badly preserved part
of our scroll that requires much further study seems to refer to the
scroll's temple as the one to be built until the day "that I shall
create myself my temple." It is the author's prescription for the man-
made temple as ordained by God and commanded in God's words:
"Thou shalt make a second court . . . ," etc. At the same time,
it can be assumed that the sect believed that the future God-built
temple would take the same plan. Since the plan of the temple,
particularly its courts and ancillary buildings, does not tally in many
details with that of Herod's temple as known to us, it is quite obvious
that those who adhered to it could not regard Herod's temple as
the one built truly according to God's injunctions. However, this
aspect and the relation to the "New Jerusalem" literature of Qumran,
which is basically different in style, requires much further study. It
is in this section of the scroll particularly (although not solely) that
the terminology used by our author betrays the period of its writing.
Where the author could not find in the Bible the required term to
describe a technicality, he had to resort to terminology current in
his own times. In many cases he used words which are to be found
only in the Mishnah and/or the Qumran literature. He uses the word
ris, "stadium," to denote distances. In one case he mentions a distance of thirty *ris,* the very distance mentioned in the Mishnah (e.g.
Baba Kamha 7, 7m). Terms found only in the Mishnah or Qumran
include *roved,* "tread of a stair"; *kiyyur,* "entablature (architectural
term)"; *ḥil,* "the area separating the holy from the unholy"; *attaroth,*
"wall crenelation"; *mesibbah,* "spiral staircase"; and many more.
The author inadvertently used late words elsewhere in the scroll;
the word to denote pregnant woman mentioned above is "a full
woman," a designation to be found mainly in Talmudic literature.
Thus the linguistic *Sitz im Leben* of the scroll is quite fixed, being the
latter part of the Second Temple period (second and first centuries
B.C.E.).

The main interest of the temple section lies of course in the de-

[7] Cf. articles by D. Flusser and Y. Yadin in *IEJ* 9 (1959), 95 ff.

tailed prescriptions and measurements of the courts, the technical sacrificial machinery, and the procedure to be followed in the temple during the various festivals. We have a grandiose description of the celebration of the Feast of Tabernacles (Succoth) with details, including exact measurements, of the booths to be erected for the chiefs of the tribes of Israel in the temple's courts, on the roofs of the side chambers. This differs from previously known sources. The basic concept of the temple's courts is that there should be *three* courts, each an exact square, one inside another: an outer, a middle, and an inner court. Following my lecture on the scroll to the members of the American Schools of Oriental Research in Jerusalem, Mrs. William Power (the Powers are residents of the School) drew my attention to the design on the scroll wrappings from Qumran Cave 1, which represents three rectangles, one inside the other. Mrs. Crowfoot in her discussion of this design suggests "that the rectangles represent the ground plan of some religious building . . . but our figure does not really agree with this [the Tabernacle] or with the description of the Temple, or Ezekiel's Temple."[8] The possibility that this pattern represents the three courts mentioned in our scroll should be further studied, although it can be said right away that there is a basic difference between the two, since our scroll speaks of square courts.

The "round" measurements of these courts are 250, 500, and 1600 cubits for each side of the inner, middle and outer courts respectively. An interesting feature is that both the middle and the outer courts had twelve gates named after the twelve tribes of Israel. One should compare with this the descriptions in Ezekiel and Revelation of the twelve gates of the tribes of Israel of *Jerusalem,* not of the temple courts. The exact measurements of the courts, the gates, and the distances between them are of much interest, as is also the allocation of the various chambers to the tribes of Israel and to the priests and Levites. These show ingenuity in using all the data known to the author concerning the tabernacle, the First Temple, and Ezekiel's temple. He formed out of them, with many additions, a plan reflecting the temple's *mishmaroth,* "priestly courses," according to the Qumranic calendar as attested also in the "War of the Sons of Light with the Sons of Darkness."

Considerable space in the section on the temple is given over to the

[8] *DJD,* I, 25.

rules of cleanness and uncleanness to be observed in the city itself. These apply, for instance, to sexual intercourse, to lepers and the maimed, and to the nature of the vessels in which offerings should be brought to the temple. One prescription deals with the building of public toilets about 1500 yards northwest of the temple. The exact location particularly suits the topography of Jerusalem; west would not be chosen because of prevailing westerly winds, while due south and north would be precluded for topographic reasons, and east would mean placing these conveniences on the holy Mount of Olives with its extensions, where they would be on higher ground than the temple and visible. The scroll prescribes, after instructing on the exact architectural details, that the toilets should be built so as not to be visible.

The Statutes of the Kings

Although it begins with a direct quotation from Deuteronomy 17:14 ff. (Deuteronomy is heavily quoted in our scroll), the fourth and last section proceeds immediately to the two subjects of chief interest to the author, the king's bodyguard and the mobilization plans to be adopted by the king when the "land of Israel" is faced with the threat of a war of extermination (see Fig. 57). On the first subject God prescribes, according to our author, that the king's bodyguard comprise 12,000 soldiers, 1,000 per tribe. These soldiers must be without blemish, "men of truth, God-fearing, hating unjust gain." While some of the expressions and principles are borrowed from Exodus 17, our interest is in the additions, which reflect the political situation of the middle and late Hasmonean periods. The main purpose of this guard is to protect the king and his wives "day and night," lest he fall "into the hands of the Gentiles." This fear of danger from the Gentiles is paramount in this section. In another place, the scroll prescribes death for anyone who betrays the people of Israel and passes information to the enemy.

The most interesting part refers to the mobilization phases. When the king is aware of a danger from an enemy who wants "to take everything which belongs to Israel" he should mobilize a tenth of the nation's force. If the enemy force be large, one-fifth of the king's force is to be called up. Should the enemy come "with his king and chariotry and great multitude," a third of the force should be mobilized; two-thirds should remain in the land to protect its frontiers and cities lest "an enemy band penetrate into the country." If, however, "the battle be strong," the king must mobilize half the total fighting strength and "the other half will remain in the cities" to defend them. (Having read these rules immediately after the Six-Day War, I could not help remarking the parallel to actual phases of mobilization preceding the conflict. This is a strictly personal and subjective reaction; the real importance of this section is that it reflects the true political and historical problems facing ancient Israel at the time the scroll was written.) These rules, by the way, are basically different from those in the "War of the Sons of Light with the Sons of Darkness," which deals exclusively with the offensive eschatological war. Here the subject is defensive war against an attacking enemy.

In this description of the contents of this unique scroll I have only touched on very little of the contents of its sixty-six columns. Because many columns are damaged (particularly in the first half), much more time will be required before final publication becomes possible. I do hope to be able to publish in the not too distant future a detailed preliminary publication, which will enable all scholars to react, criticize, and contribute to the study of this important document, provisionally named the Temple Scroll.

Biblical Archaeology Today*

G. ERNEST WRIGHT

Archaeology in the biblical world covers virtually every ancient period. While in my judgment it is not an independent discipline, nor can it be carried on as such without dire harm to itself, it is nevertheless a primary research arm of the historian of human culture and of human events. Its importance to present-day life and culture may be quickly noted by the assertion that one of the most remarkable achievements of modern scholarship is not only our exceedingly precocious science, but also and especially the vast extension of man's knowledge of himself and of his past during the last one hundred years. Our whole perspective has been changed; our minds will never again be the same; we now know it to be axiomatic that nothing can be understood unless we know something of its history. This, in the words of the German philosopher Friedrich Meinecke, constitutes "the greatest spiritual revolution which western thought has undergone."

With all this in mind what does archaeology mean when the word "biblical" is placed before it? On this there has not been full agreement, at least in emphasis, though interest in the subject is greater than ever. One of the publishing sensations of the Western world in recent times is a book by a German journalist which captured the attention of countless thousands of people. That is Werner Keller's *The Bible as History: A Confirmation of the Book of Books* (translated from the German by William Neil; New York: Morrow, 1956). The original German title is even more eloquent: *Und die Bibel hat doch recht;* that is, after the critics have done their worst, the Bible is right after all! A comforting thought. I have met many educated people, including prominent scholars, who firmly be-

* Written May, 1965, with very minor revision May, 1969 (Author).

lieve and openly assert that Palestinian archaeology was conceived, reared, and even now nourished by those who possess a biblical bias, who approach excavation with something to prove, who have preconceptions which are hypotheses to be sustained, no matter the evidence. In the United States appeals to foundations for money must go to great lengths to avoid the term "Bible." Many people are suspicious enough when excavations are to take place in Israel or in Jordan, "the land of the Bible."

It is a simple matter of fact, however, that money from pious, conservative, or fundamentalist sources has never played a very important role in archaeology. The major excavations have been sponsored by sources dominated by a broad humanistic interest, as is clear from such names as the University of Pennsylvania (Beth-shan, more recently Gibeon, and now Tell es-Sa'idiyeh), Yale University (Jerash), Harvard University (Samaria, more recently at Shechem with the Drew-McCormick expedition, and most recently with Hebrew Union College at Gezer), the University of Chicago (Megiddo), the American Schools of Oriental Research, the University of London, the French Archaeological Mission, Hebrew University, etc.

Much more interesting is the history of the theme, "archaeology proves the Bible." In the great fundamentalist-modernist controversy, which so shook the religious life of western Protestantism at the turn of the century, archaeology played almost no role at all. In another place, I have tried to point out that it is the writing and speeches of William Foxwell Albright during and following his excavations at Tel Beit Mirsim (Debir) that must bear major responsibility for the introduction of the theme, which others then exploited with less erudition. Yet Albright had no idea of presenting a case like that of Werner Keller. He was attacking a certain reconstruction of the history of Israel by the school of literary criticism with which the name of Julius Wellhausen is so prominently associated. This view had held on in America for a generation after viewpoints in Europe had been basically revised because of the work of various scholars, most notably Hermann Gunkel.[1]

The well-known cases of Ai and Jericho can serve as familiar examples of how archaeology makes impossible any overly simple and

[1] See my remarks in "Is Glueck's Aim to Prove that the Bible is True?" *The Biblical Archaeologist Reader, I,* (New York: Doubleday Anchor, 1961), 14–21 (reprinted from *BA* 22 [1959], 101–8).

uncomplicated biblicism such as that of Werner Keller. To be sure, the tradition of Israel's capture of Ai is very easily explained, as Albright first showed us. The story of the destruction of Bethel was soon transferred to the great third millennium ruin (Hebrew *'ay*) nearby.[2] But no such simple solution is available for Jericho. Whether there was more than a village there in the thirteenth century B.C. is very doubtful, and almost no evidence of that has been found. As far as I know, no one has seriously challenged the dating by Albright, Kenyon, and myself of the small amount of Late Bronze pottery, found by Garstang, to the fourteenth century.[3]

It is indeed true that archaeology has revolutionized our attitude toward biblical historical traditions. A previous generation of scholars was inclined to make skepticism, an important element in historical method, an almost primary ingredient in the conclusions drawn from use of the method. Today most of us take a far more positive line, and are inclined to give a tradition the benefit of the doubt unless there is evidence to the contrary; this is a basic and all-important scholarly shift in viewpoint, and archaeology is its cause. There is all the more reason, therefore, to see in the Joshua tradition about Jericho a great puzzle. There is nothing but negative archaeological evidence, and the origin of the tradition and the history of its transmission cannot now be discovered.

It is more common to think of biblical archaeology as work done when excavation has ceased. It is gleaning every fact that can be of help in understanding what we read in the Bible, whether narrative, law, or poetry. Often when the general configuration of a subject is clear, there is a reciprocal movement between discovery and biblical text, to the mutual enrichment of both. The aim of it all is to read the Bible in the setting of its time, its people and its land, to reconstruct its history, to study its literature and religion comparatively. Only thus can we know the real Israel of old, as we attempt to peer at her through the mists of tradition that, over the centuries, have come to surround her like a cloud.

[2] W. F. Albright, "Archaeology and the Date of the Hebrew Conquest of Palestine," *BASOR* 58 (1935), 10–18.

[3] See Albright, *ibid.,* and "The Israelite Conquest of Canaan in the Light of Archaeology," *BASOR* 74 (1939), 11 ff.; G. Ernest Wright, "Two Misunderstood Items in the Exodus-Conquest Cycle," *BASOR,* 86 (1942), 32–35; Kathleen M. Kenyon, *Digging Up Jericho* (London: Benn, 1957; New York: Praeger, 1958), 256–65; *Archaeology and the Holy Land* (New York: Praeger, and London: Benn, 1960), 207–12.

This great effort to read the Bible as the literature of a particular historical time and place has borne remarkable fruit. We are enabled to read it today as a new, fresh and exciting literature. We are able furthermore to say more precisely what Israel was because we have adequate comparative material to say what she was not. This is a tremendous achievement of modern scholarship. No other people has been able to do such a thing with its sacred literature. And no other sacred literature lends itself so successfully to this type of research. The results are a monument to modern Jewish and Christian scholars alike.

The Archaeological Revolution in Old Testament Studies

In our discussion I shall use archaeology as including both epigraphic and non-epigraphic discoveries. As a result I should like to say a few words about each of the following: the history of the biblical text, Hebrew grammar and lexicography, the history of Israel, comparative literature, and comparative religion. At first glance the inclusion of all these disciplines within the area of biblical archaeology is surprising. Yet the Moses of our subject today, almost its very creator, is William Foxwell Albright. And this is precisely the all-inclusive view which he has espoused. Few, if any, among us can hope to attain Albright's range of tools and interests. Yet he should stand before us as a model of how the discipline should be carried on, even though several of us together can scarcely make one of him. We must fight this modern tendency of overspecialization, of extreme narrowing of interest and of training. Our students can do far better than many of us think. Some of them can be first-class linguists and exegetes, as well as archaeologists, but not if, by overspecialization we fail to give them a chance. I personally, for example, am not a linguist, but I count it merit to myself that I am safely surrounded by excellent practitioners of the art, and all of us work happily on the same students in the *same* department! This is the way Albright arranged things in the Oriental Seminary at Johns Hopkins University; it is the way we have attempted to follow at Harvard. It is not the way of things at the University of Chicago; and I can at least hope that it will be the direction of the future at Hebrew University in Jerusalem, though at the moment studies there are rapidly developing in the opposite direction. That same direction is generally taken also in England and on the Continent.

One member of our Harvard department, Frank M. Cross, has played a major part in the reformulation of the discipline of textual criticism.[4] As late as a decade ago the textual criticism of the Bible had virtually ceased to be a productive subject. We all realized that our forebears had gone much too far in arbitrary emendations, often on the basis of the Greek. The only critical Hebrew text that western scholarship has produced is Kittel's *Biblia Hebraica*.[5] Yet as Harry M. Orlinsky along with others has so eloquently shown, the text-critical work in this Bible leaves much to be desired, especially in its handling of the Greek versions.[6] As a result of the discovery of the new biblical manuscripts at Qumran, Nahal Hever, and Masada, we now have a wealth of new evidence. Only four years ago, no less a scholar than G. R. Driver of Oxford wrote in the London *Times,* (August 19, 1962) that the Dead Sea scrolls "have been of much less value than was expected when first discovered." Yet Cross among others has shown precisely the opposite to be the case, and that it is to the area of textual criticism that we must look. He believes that the great variety of text materials now point to three basic traditions or recensions, all in existence not only before the building of the Herodian Temple, but before the Greek translation of the third and second centuries B.C. He interprets them as Palestinian, Egyptian, and Babylonian, the last being the one which rabbinical authorities finally picked as the Massoretic Text about 100 B.C. instead of attempting to construct a conflate or mixed text. The views of Cross will be much debated for some time. Yet there can be no doubt that he has shown us how archaeological discovery has made the textual criticism of the Bible a very live and worth-while subject again, one in which there is a far greater possibility for the development of precision in method than existed before the last decade.

No less dramatic are the great advances which archaeology has

---

[4] See F. M. Cross, "The History of the Biblical Text in the Light of the Discoveries in the Judaean Desert," *HTR* 57 (1964), 181–99; and "The Contribution of the Discoveries at Qumran to the Study of the Biblical Text," *IEJ* 16 (1966), 81–95, No. 3.

[5] G. Kittel, *Biblia Hebraica* (3d ed., Stuttgart: Privilegierte Württenbergische Bibelanstalt, 1937).

[6] H. M. Orlinsky, "The Textual Criticism of the Old Testament," in *BANE*, pp. 140–69.

made possible in Hebrew grammar and lexicography. Nearly all our basic text and reference handbooks are now out of date since they rest mainly on the research and viewpoints of the turn of the century. At that time the attempt was made to understand biblical Hebrew on the basis of such materials as were available: that is, classical Arabic, with a bit of help from Accadian, Aramaic, and post-biblical Hebrew. Today, an almost wholly new discipline is in existence and developing rapidly in the hands of a comparatively small number of first-class scholars. The new field to which I allude is Northwest Semitic. In its background is Amorite, mostly known from large numbers of personal names. Then of course, there is Ugaritic,[7] followed by the rapidly increasing information concerning Canaanite, Hebrew, and Aramaic inscriptions and dialects. Here is where the great advances in Hebrew lexicography and in the history of the Hebrew language have been made during the past three decades.[8] Even yet, however, we do not have a basic Hebrew scholarly dictionary or reference grammar written on the basis of the new information and new perspectives. The latest major scholarly Hebrew lexicon is that of the Swiss scholar L. Köhler, but it is barely an advance on its great predecessors, the German Gesenius-Bühl and the English-American Brown-Driver-Briggs. All needs to be done afresh as a result of the archaeological activity since the First World War. The study of the Hebrew language in this historical perspective is a quite new thing. It is unfortunate that there are comparatively few places where this new field, made possible by archaeology, is being exploited.

I need say little about the history of Israel, for here the new perspectives and the rapidly accumulating mass of archaeological detail are far better known.[9] Here the scholarly achievement is most obvious; even the Patriarchal period is beginning to emerge from the mists of a distant past into a known setting of Near Eastern

[7] As recently as 1960 the French excavators of Ugarit found a whole new archive in that rich site which produced thirty boxes of additional tablets, divided between Babylonian and Canaanite alphabetic texts.

[8] W. J. Moran, S.J., "The Hebrew Language in its Northwest Semitic Background," in *BANE,* pp. 59–84.

[9] Cf. W. F. Albright, *From the Stone Age to Christianity: Monotheism and the Historical Process,* 1st ed. (Johns Hopkins Press, 1940; New York: Doubleday Anchor ed., 1957); *Archaeology and the Religion of Israel,* 1st ed. (Johns Hopkins Press, 1942); John Bright, *A History of Israel* (Philadelphia: Westminster, 1959); G. Ernest Wright, *Biblical Archaeology,* rev. ed. (London: Duckworth, 1962; Philadelphia: Westminster, 1963).

history. Yet this setting is debated and not all are agreed as to its time or nature. In fact, the most astonishing thing to be said about the field of biblical history is that in spite of the vast mass of new evidence which archaeology has provided, there is no starting point that can be agreed upon by the various groups of scholars, no method of extracting history from tradition that forms a consensus. In the words of George E. Mendenhall in the Albright *Festschrift,* "the 'fluidity' in this field . . . may with perhaps less courtesy but more accuracy be called chaos."[10]

Perhaps this is an exaggeration, especially for the period beginning with the tenth century B.C. and the reign of David. Here the problems are not as acute as they are for earlier periods. Hence the word "chaos" is best used to describe attempts to write the history of Israel before the time of David. One need only contrast the histories by W. F. Albright and John Bright with the very different works by Martin Noth and Yehezkel Kaufmann to make the point.[11] More archaeological discovery will help, but one cannot predict when, if ever, a larger measure of agreement will be reached.

Work in comparative literature, that is, in comparing Hebrew literature with contemporary documents from other parts of the ancient Near East, has been most productive. Yet it is possible to exaggerate and to lose perspective at this point. The fact of the matter is that biblical literature as a whole has no parallel whatsoever in the literature of any nation. The productive parallels that scholars have been exploring lie solely within legal, poetic, and wisdom portions of the Bible.

With regard to law, despite assertions to the contrary, I would venture to predict that Albrecht Alt's distinction between legal types will stand, that is, the distinction between the ancient Near Eastern common law as Israel adapted it and the more typically covenant law in which Israel's divine Lord addressed his people directly and individually, "Thou shalt." The second type is Israel's creation, deriving from her distinctive religious perspectives, and giving fresh meaning and setting to the common law. Those who suppose that this covenant law can be compared to declaratory formulae in the Hammurabic Code, or to interdictions in funerary inscriptions, have

---

[10] George E. Mendenhall, "Biblical History in Transition," in *BANE*, pp. 27–58.
[11] Albright, *From the Stone Age to Christianity;* Bright, *A History of Israel;* Martin Noth, *The History of Israel,* tr. by Stanley Godman, (New York: Harper, 1958); Yehezkel Kaufmann, *The Biblical Account of the Conquest of Palestine* (1953).

not, in my judgment, really understood the issues from the standpoint of form criticism.[12]

Another major discovery within the realm of law which I venture to predict will stand the test of time is George E. Mendenhall's pioneer work on the formal background of the Mosaic covenant.[13] This background, he has shown, is not to be found in the covenants of Bedouin society, as Johannes Pedersen had supposed. Instead it is to be found in the realm of international law, specifically in the suzerainty treaties of the Late Bronze Age found among the Hittite archives. This discovery has meant a number of things, of which I can mention only one. For the first time, we can gain a clearer perception of the way Deity was conceived in Israel and of the reason why certain types of language were permissible when used of him and others were not. The God of Israel was not the head of a pantheon which represented the primary powers of the natural world. He was first and foremost a suzerain, not a king among kings but the Emperor, the "King of kings and Lord of lords" who had no equal. Consequently, the Hebrew term, *melek,* rarely used of God before the time of David, was not strictly applicable to him because it had received its primary political definition from the rival Bronze Age dynasts of Syro-Palestinian city-states. The suzerainty of Israel's God concerned the whole world, and the focus of attention was not on the life of nature but on the administration of a vast empire. The language was thus closely geared to history and historical perspectives.

With regard to Hebrew poetry, I will again mention the im-

[12] Cf. T. J. Meek, *Hebrew Origins* (New York: Harper Torchbooks, 1960), p. 72; Stanley Gevirtz, "West Semitic Curses and the Problem of the Origin of Hebrew Law," *VT* 11 (1961), 137–58. The really comparable material will derive from legal sections of the suzerain-vassal treaties in which the suzerain declares his will to the vassal: cf. J. Harvey, "Le 'Rîb-Pattern' réquisitoire prophétique sur la rupture de l'alliance," *Biblica* 43 (1962), 172–96.

[13] Several years ago Mendenhall began work on the Hebrew term, *nāqām,* usually translated "vengeance"; he possesses at least one unpublished paper and monograph on the subject; his one published piece on the term is "God of Vengeance, Shine Forth!" *Wittenberg Bulletin,* 45, No. 12 (Dec. 1948), 37–42. This led him to a study of ancient Near Eastern law generally and of the Hittite treaties in particular: see his *Law and Covenant in Israel and the Ancient Near East,* originally published in the May and September issues of *The Biblical Archaeologist* in 1954; then issued as a monograph by the Biblical Colloquium in Pittsburgh, 1955. Meanwhile Klaus Baltzer of Heidelberg had been working independently on the same theme: see his *Das Bundesformular* (1960).

portance of Ugaritic literature. Working from fresh perspectives provided therein and from the fresh disciplines of Northwest Semitic and textual criticism, Albright has been able to chart in rough outline the development of Israel's poetry by types and stages between the thirteenth and tenth centuries, and to put the dating of the earliest biblical poetry on a much more objective basis than has hitherto been possible.[14] Many obscure passages in the earlier Psalms can now be understood, and new discoveries here are being made constantly.[15]

Finally, it is only during the last three decades that the discipline of comparative religion in the ancient Near East has become possible. The problem has not been a dearth of material. Indeed, archaeologists add more and more each year. Instead, comparative religion can begin only when the linguists and philologians can provide us documents whose meaning is fairly clear, and when historians are able to chart at least the main outlines of the history of a given religion. To mention only two of the pioneering works in this area, Albright's *From the Stone Age to Christianity* (Johns Hopkins Press and Doubleday Anchor) did not appear until 1940, because, as he said, it was only then that the wide-ranging historical syntheses necessary for such a work had become possible. Equally pioneering is the work of Henri Frankfort, Thorkild Jacobsen, and John Wilson in *The Intellectual Adventure of Ancient Man,* which first appeared in 1946 and was soon reprinted by Penguin Books under the title, *Before Philosophy.* I gratefully acknowledge that my own monographs and articles on the religion of Israel rest on the base which the work of these men provided.[16] Frankfort's few pages on Israel

[14] See W. F. Albright, "The Oracles of Balaam," *JBL* 63 (1944), 207–33; "The Psalm of Habakkuk," in *Studies in Old Testament Prophecy,* ed. H. H. Rowley (New York: Scribner, 1950), 1–18; "A Catalogue of Early Hebrew Lyric Poems (Psalm 68)," *HUCA* 23 (1950–51), 1–39; Frank M. Cross, Jr. and David Noel Freedman, "The Blessing of Moses," *JBL* 67 (1948), 191–210; "A Royal Song of Thanksgiving: II Samuel 22=Psalm 18," *JBL* 72 (1953), 15–34; "The Song of Miriam," *JNES* 14 (1955), 237–50; Frank M. Cross, "Notes on a Canaanite Psalm in the Old Testament (Ps. 29)," *BASOR* 117 (1950), 19–21; David Noel Freedman, "Archaic Forms of Early Hebrew Poetry," *ZAW* 72 (1960), 101–7.

[15] Note especially the extensive use of Ugaritic by Marvin Pope and Mitchell Dahood in their respective volumes of *Job* (1965) and *Psalms 1, 1–50* (1966) and *II, 51–100* (1968) in The Anchor Bible.

[16] For example in *The Old Testament Against Its Environment* (Chicago: Regnery, 1950) and *God Who Acts: Biblical Theology as Recital* (Chicago: Regnery, 1952); cf. Jay Wilcoxen who independently noted this influence in an article on the writer in *Criterion,* 2, No. 3 (Summer 1963), 25–31.

at the end of *The Intellectual Adventure . . .* , and his brief treatment of Israelite kingship at the conclusion of his great work on
Kingship and the Gods (University of Chicago, 1948) are in my
judgment far more penetrating than any on the subject by biblical
scholars of his generation. He was able to write as he did because he
had a clear picture of contemporary religious life and practice with
which Israel's could be compared and contrasted.

One characteristic of biblical Israel which has received a great deal
of discussion, especially during the last two decades, is the historical
consciousness which gave her a sense of urgency about preserving
her historical traditions. This is a unique phenomenon among the
religions of the world. It led to a particular form of self-understanding
and manner of expression and interpretation. Certain actual, datable
happenings among a particular people were related and rehearsed
as the special activity of the God who otherwise to that world was
an unknown God. Purpose was set within time so that the past was
remembered and recited as crucially important for action and commitment in the present. Biblical man thus spoke of ultimate Reality
as being revealed in the forms of history. Instead of a language
composed of universals—timeless, true in all circumstances, after the
manner of the great Greek thinkers, Israel was concerned with events.
Instead of the language of myth that was current among her neighbors, Israel, no less than the Greeks, in her own way, demythologized
nature. Israel saw nature as the servant of history and interpreted
the Purpose that was working itself out through history.

This perspective gave rise to a particular mode of thinking and
expression which intellectuals of previous generations were often inclined to dismiss as a primitivism of a primitive people. Today, I
have been surprised at the number of serious thinkers who, in the
changed view of the nature of physical reality and of the nature
of space, no longer dismiss this language of historical event as inap-
propriate to the interpretation of the ultimately Real. Elsewhere I
have had occasion to express the matter as follows:

> An event is expressed by means of a subject conjugating a verb.
> Neither the subject nor the verb will be analyzed as an entity in
> itself; it is the former realizing itself through the latter, giving to
> the latter its tense, its time. Thus an event is an attribute of an
> active subject which reveals itself only to the degree that infer-
> ences can be properly deduced from what it does. Since in the
> Bible . . . [the supernal mystery of all things is metaphorically

referred to as the sovereign Lord], there is no attempt to penetrate what this mystery is in himself. There is only the testimony of what he has done, together with the body of "inferences" or assumptions as to what may be deduced from the events. . . .[17]

This event-centered mode of religious thinking and speaking cannot be systematized, for it includes the confessional recital of past events together with the deductions drawn from them by a worshiping community as a means of renewal in various historical situations. This, I have maintained, is the primary nature and substance of the descriptive discipline, biblical theology.

By way of illustration let me refer briefly to the Creation story as used in Babylon and in Israel. In Babylon it was rehearsed as a myth which presented the timeless, cosmic pattern to which all life must adjust and continually readjust. Central to the cultic life was the dramatic reenactment of this primordial event each year in order that the world of nature might remain in balance, safe for the year ahead. Mircea Eliade of the University of Chicago in his book on this subject calls this *The Myth of the Eternal Return* (tr. by Willard R. Trask from the French, New York: Pantheon, 1955). Human life is cyclical in movement and must always keep returning to its moment of origin.

By contrast, biblical man told the story as no timeless primordial event. For him it was the first great event in history, the beginning of time and life, of man's service to divine sovereignty. Yet the Creation never took central place in liturgy. Instead the historical events that brought into being a new nation were central. These were rehearsed; they were the content of memory for present renewal. Yet matters did not end there, for the perspective looked beyond the present to a future that would resolve present evil. Human life is called to responsible vocation which the evil of any present can never annul. In the midst of history's horror, there is new life born, new opportunity, new possibility. Secularized versions of this perspective lie at the very foundation of Western society and so sharply distinguish that culture from all others, wherein this sense of the meaningfulness of history was never an integral part of the tradition.

[17] See the writer's "The Theological Study of the Bible," in *Interpreter's One Volume Commentary on the Bible* (forthcoming), and "Reflexions Concerning Old Testament Theology," *Studia Biblica et Semitica* (Th. C. Vriezen *Festschrift;* 1966), p. 383. For elaboration see his forthcoming volume, *The Old Testament and Theology* (1969).

Perhaps what I have said in this paper does not sound like archaeology. Yet to me all of it falls within the scope of *biblical* archaeology. The study of the results of excavation continually opens new fields for work, and reopens facets of old fields. It is difficult indeed to keep up, yet the proper study of the Bible can neglect none of it.

Archaeology, History, and Theology

Palestinian archaeology is pursued by those in this country who for the most part are teachers of Bible in theological seminaries for the training of clergy and in religion departments of our colleges and universities. This holding together of Bible and archaeology is part of the interest and influence of W. F. Albright in this country. That is, archaeology is not an independent discipline; it is a contributory one and it suffers when it is not so understood. Only a few people can make a living from archaeology; they must generally do something else while they work in the discipline as a research interest. It is natural and proper that biblical scholars who in order to comprehend and to exegete the Bible must take responsibility for the history of Palestine, should also be concerned with the archaeology of Palestine and of the ancient world generally. Indeed, when the study of the Bible and of archaeology is conducted with standards of high scholarship, both subjects are immeasurably enriched. The desire to hold the two disciplines together, however, is characteristic of the biblical scholarship of this country, of Israel and in Roman Catholic biblical circles, where the influence of Albright has been greatest.

Biblical scholars with an interest in archaeology who work in theological schools, however, often find themselves on the defensive before their theological colleagues because of this interest. I would suggest that this should not be so. It is indeed most peculiar that in the Judaeo-Christian tradition with its emphasis on history one is able to say: "Among Christian scholars you can almost predict the degree of interest in archaeology and history by the degree of their interest in theology!" I do not mean that everyone should be an archaeologist and historian. But history and archaeology are of basic importance, furnishing primary data that must be one focus of the theologian's concern.

The theological mode in the classic type of Christian theology, however, has drawn the discipline into different channels. In medieval days and in post-Reformation orthodoxy, the mainstream of theology proceeded along the Greek pattern, in which the vocabulary is composed of abstract universals whose meaning and coherence are elaborated primarily by logic. This derives from an era when the universe was conceived as primarily a rational *structure*. What is essentially important in such a universe is its unchanging structure which possesses the power to arrange every particular within the whole. One's search is for universals which are always valid, and which must be discussed by means of noun plus copula plus another noun or adjective. (Contrast the biblical mentality which is concerned with the changing, the personal, the events which typically will express significance by means of a subject conjugating a verb, giving to the verb its tense and time.) Man participates in the unchanging structure by reason and he finds it possible to elaborate systems of thought in which every particular can be arranged by a variety of givens, axioms, deductions. In this worldview a systematic theology as the rational content of faith is possible. Logic is the primary clue to reality, and a correct system can be seen as truth, as the adequate restatement of revelation.

Theological battles were once so terribly fierce because our fathers believed it really possible to state in rational terms what revelation is. Consequently, slight variations of phrasing that today we would consider unimportant, could be for them all important. The first theological seminary for the training of clergy was established in Andover, Massachusetts, in 1808, by those who warmly held to the old Puritan theology and who believed that Harvard was hopelessly liberal and openly and consciously persisted in that "evil." In order to protect the school the founders devised a creed to which all professors had to subscribe, not just once, but every five years. And the creed was considered final; it was a part of the constitution of the school, so that the institution and its creed would hold forever or fall together—and fall they did! This was because the creed was believed completely "supported by the infallible Revelation which God constantly makes of Himself in His works of creation, providence, and redemption."[18] Such a view was only possible in a particular type of world to which the rationality of structure was basic. The liberals in Boston and Cambridge believed that they were bibli-

[18] See Leonard Wood, *History of Andover Theological Seminary* (1885), p. 257.

cal and their opponents were not.[19] Yet their worldview was sufficiently comparable as to make possible the Transcendentalist revolt
in their midst, a revolt which insisted that intuition and feeling were
better guides to truth than the excessive rationality of logic.

Today the world in which such a theological mode was possible
has disappeared. To be sure, science finds its regularities and "laws"
based on normal expectancy. Yet in the world of human affairs
logic is not king. Consequently, the classic philosophy is gone, and
systematic theology is in trouble because it cannot find its system.

Karl Barth's *Church Dogmatics* (tr. from the German, 4 vols.,
London: Allenson, 1936–61) is a theology of the Word of God,
but it has been criticized as still dominated by the seventeenth-
century mode wherein the Bible as the revelation of the Word per-
mits the elaboration of a complete system of thought which involves
many volumes because nothing can be excluded and every possible
rival to it must be critically considered. My colleague Richard R.
Niebuhr has put the matter this way: In Barth's theology of the
Word, "Christian faith, as participation in the Word of God, does
not issue preeminently in the love of God, as it did for St. Augustine,
nor in trust in God, as it did for Luther and Calvin, nor in the
glorification of God, as it did for Jonathan Edwards. . . . The effect
of this procedure is to make Christianity into a faith that is basically
a body of knowledge. . . . Thus at one and the same time Barthian-
ism endeavors to lift Christianity above human history (by making
it discontinuous with history) and is constantly fighting rearguard
battles and skirmishes with human religious assertions about God
(as in philosophy and liberal theology), because it has clothed itself
in the same human language that philosophy and religion employ
and it looks exactly like them."[20] Yet contemporary biblical research
and the present world in which we live have rendered this type of
rationality, considered as the proper depiction of revelation, increasingly rare, if it is not the last of its kind.

Because of the very nature of the Christian religion as derived
from its biblical heritage Christian scholars today *must be* vitally

[19] Hence the early curriculum of Harvard Divinity School centered in biblical criticism: see *Three Prophets of Religious Liberalism: Channing, Emerson,
Parker,* intro. by C. Conrad Wright (Boston: Beacon Press, 1961), 13–17;
also the same author's chapter in *The Harvard Divinity School,* ed. George
H. Williams, (Boston: Beacon Press, 1954), 27. Cf. G. Ernest Wright,
"History in Theological Education," *HDSB* 27, No. 1 (Oct. 1962), 1–16.
[20] Richard R. Niebuhr, "Religion and the Finality of Christianity," *HDSB*
27, No. 4 (June 1963), 25–30, especially p. 28.

concerned with history. The biblical scholar and church historian are required to attempt the self-transcendence necessary to discover the factual data in a series of events within an era not our own. They must do this as objectively as possible, using all the tools of historiography. This our era requires of us. By all the logical processes of the historian the student must collect data from every available source; he must assess their significance and relation to one another; he must test his witnesses and attempt to penetrate the history of particular traditions within a possible variety of settings. Yet as regards the meaning, significance and value of all this critical collecting and combinatory activity, his "scientific" tools cannot help him, for they are neutral. Ultimate meaning comes only from a coherent organism of meaning: that is, from religion and from the reflective or theological activity within it. Hence historian and theologian are involved in the same ultimate end. Yet the question arises as to the appropriate method for the articulation of the Christian faith.

The basic content of the Bible as it is understood today cannot be properly stated by the mode of classical theology. A century and a half of historical research has so altered our perspectives that current theology—that is, the attempt to state the biblical case meaningfully in our time—finds itself floundering and uncertain. The first thing to be said about man today is not that he possesses certain faculties of reason and nature that are unchanging in all situations, so that it can be said that human nature never changes. Instead, what is to be said is that man is man in the whole complex of his relationships and commitments, that man is first and foremost a historical and time-full being, and that human nature does indeed change, and has repeatedly changed, though, of course, within a biological structure that defines *Homo sapiens*.[21]

The first thing to be said about the God of the Bible concerns his historical actions. These have created a new people and have placed acknowledgment of sovereignty and vocation as the meaning and content of their life. There is no other realm of knowledge available to us whereby this God is to be known except the historical. Hence the first thing to be said about God is the "historicity" and time-full character of the knowledge we have of him. And the first

[21] Cf. Gordon D. Kaufman, "The *imago dei* as Man's Historicity," *Journal of Religion*, 36 (1956), 157–68. See also the same author's *Relativism, Knowledge and Faith* (University of Chicago Press, 1960), especially Chap. 4 and Appendix I.

thing to be said about the Bible as the testimony to this new Reality and the fountain of the religious movements that have emerged from it, is not that its revelation can be characterized as a *torah* (law), or a rational reality of primary importance solely to the mind, or an otherworldly mythology encased within an outmoded geography of the universe. Instead, the historical character of the Bible, its revelatory events, strike deep within the human soul at the springs of human action, and bring about a restructuring of the self within a new historical community.

The current movement of biblical theology, in Germany especially, has emphasized the event-character of the Bible, so that such words as *kerygma* (a Greek word for "proclamation" as distinct from ethical teaching) and *Heilsgeschichte* (a German term for the biblical story of God's saving activity) have become standard fare in theological circles. Yet strange things happen in the work of the New Testament scholar Rudolf Bultmann, for example, and of his Old Testament counterparts. The theological confession of God's activity is so wrenched apart from history as to leave it almost completely a cultic myth, divorced radically from the concrete reality, the significance of which the confession claims to be expounding. Any interest in the facts which concern the archaeologist is dismissed as foolish historicism, or a mere factuality in which a person should not be interested without feeling embarrassed about it. *Heilsgeschichte* in the Old Testament becomes a series of confessions within the cultic life which present an open future, but their fulfillment is so new and complete as to render them of no further value except as they hold in themselves some prefiguration of the new existence revealed in the fulfillment.[22] In other words, the "history of salvation" becomes non-historical, and resort is made to a type of existentialism in order to make it relevant.

Existentialism here attempts to draw the main categories for theology from the central concerns of existence: namely, existence or non-existence, life or death, and all the anxiety which the threat

[22] For a more elaborate treatment of Bultmann's position from this writer's standpoint, see the paper, "History and Reality: The Fundamental Importance of Israel's 'Historical' Symbols for the Christian Faith," in *The Old Testament and the Christian Faith,* ed. Bernhard W. Anderson (New York: Harper, 1963), Chap. 10. For a critique of Gerhard von Rad's *Theologie des Alten Testamente,* see Walther Eichrodt's incisive remarks in his *Theology of the Old Testament,* tr. by J. A. Baker from the German 6th ed. (Philadelphia: Westminster, 1961), 512–20.

of non-being holds before us. This is an ultimate concern, but it is non-historical for it sets the center of religious attention at the bounds of life, not at its center. Thus these concerns are kept away from the forefront of biblical faith. It is not the tree of life, but the tree of the knowledge of good and evil which is the center of the interpretive story in Genesis 3. Just so in the New Testament, life after death is God's prerogative and life in Christ is the central concern. In short, this type of biblical theology uses history to get rid of history, and thus actually to evade the central issue of both the Bible and human existence. It is small wonder, then, that systematic theology of the older style having become problematic, numbers of younger theologians are attracted by the Bultmann program, though they may attempt minor adjustments in the position without significantly altering it.[23]

Yet I must still affirm the position that history cannot be evaded. The question of man's existential concern can never be solved apart from the context of society, history, and the struggle of civilization to be civilized. The sovereignty of God in the biblical context is encountered precisely in this wide human context. The struggle to understand our past is a crucial question for both historian and theologian. And it is in this frame of reference that a biblical scholar may defend the archaeological endeavor in all its particularity and facticity to his theological colleagues, and beyond them to all those who are concerned with our spiritual background and with its context in time and space.

[23] Cf. for example, Carl Michalson, *The Hinge of History: An Existential Approach to the Christian Faith* (New York: Scribner, 1959); and Schubert M. Ogden, *Christ Without Myth* (New York: Harper, 1961).

A Qumran Bibliography

EDWARD F. CAMPBELL, JR.
AND ROBERT G. BOLING

From Edmund Wilson's *The Scrolls from the Dead Sea* (first published in slightly abridged form in *The New Yorker* magazine in May 1955) to Archbishop Athanasius Yeshue Samuel's *Treasure of Qumran: My Story of the Dead Sea Scrolls* (Philadelphia: Westminster, 1966), a veritable library of popular writing has appeared on the Qumran finds. One respects Wilson for his literary facility and the excitement he engendered, and the Archbishop for the depth of his own pilgrimage of piety, but one must make a selection among English language writings on the discoveries that will emphasize the more responsible, cogent, and thorough publications. We propose here a listing of the key books one can profitably turn to now, two decades after the fateful "day of the goat."

Five sumptuous volumes of *Discoveries in the Judaean Desert* (Oxford University Press, 1955, 1961, 1962, 1965, 1968) are the starting point for confronting the texts themselves. The first volume contains texts from Cave 1, the second those of the caves in the Wadi Murabbaʻat, the third those from Caves 2, 3, and 5–10, the fourth the Psalms Scroll from Cave 11, and the fifth a group of twenty-nine fragmentary texts, mostly of biblical commentary (*pesher*), from Cave 4. Other manuscripts from Cave 1, including two of Isaiah, the Manual of Discipline, the War Scroll, the Habakkuk Commentary, the Genesis Apocryphon, and the Thanksgiving Psalms, have been published under various auspices, all listed in Dr. Boling's article on pp. 81–88.

But for a full listing of the places where one can see photographs of all the manuscripts and fragments published so far, the easiest recourse is to an excellent catalogue prepared by J. A. Sanders in the December 1967 issue of *The Journal of Biblical Literature,* under the title "Palestine Manuscripts, 1947–1967" (pp. 431–40).

We should mention here especially, by the way, the more popular edition of the Cave 11 Psalm manuscript which Dr. Sanders brought out in 1967, published by Cornell University Press. Called *The Dead Sea Psalms Scroll,* it contains a bonus not in the *editio princeps,* namely the so-called fragment E which came into the hands of Professor Yigael Yadin some years ago and proves to be a part of the Psalms manuscript. This is only the latest episode in the often amusing, sometimes alarming saga of the peregrinations of the Scrolls.

English translations of the sectarian literature from Qumran are available. The most fluent and paraphrastic is that of Theodor H. Gaster, *The Dead Sea Scriptures in English Translation,* which has appeared in two editions from Doubleday Anchor (New York, 1956 and 1964). The second edition contains more texts and employs brackets to indicate places where the translator has supplied proposed readings to fill gaps in the text. In 1962 the translations of Geza Vermes came out in a Pelican paperback from Penguin Books, entitled *The Dead Sea Scrolls in English.* Vermes has less flair for poetry than Gaster, but his renderings are competent. Millar Burrows provided translations in his two big volumes, *The Dead Sea Scrolls* and *More Light on the Dead Sea Scrolls* (New York: Viking, 1955 and 1958), which are still worth referring to. Now that more texts are being published, those from Cave 11 especially (see Professor Sanders' article on pp. 101–16), a new complete edition of the texts will soon be called for.

As a general introduction to the whole field of Qumran studies, by far the most competent and valuable continues to be *The Ancient Library of Qumran* by Frank M. Cross. First published in 1958, it was brought out in a revised edition in 1961 by Doubleday Anchor. Dr. Cross has produced in one volume both a handbook and a standard reference work. A host of other publications of a general introductory nature might be cited (see Professor Filson's recommendations in his article on pp. 127–38), each with its own angle of vision. A very fine, brief presentation is *Scrolls from the Wilderness of the Dead Sea,* the catalogue of the exhibition of the Scrolls which toured America, Canada, and England in 1965.

Three studies of the Qumran community should be mentioned. The first is *The Dead Sea Community: Its Origin and Teachings* by Kurt Schubert (New York: Harper, 1959). These are lectures given by a Roman Catholic to a Zionist organization, translated by a

Lutheran clergyman. The book is especially effective in portraying the emergence of the Jewish sects in the intertestamental period, and the relation of the Qumran community to these sects on the one hand and to the rise of Christianity and Rabbinic Judaism on the other hand. Helmer Ringgren has written a Fortress Press paperback (Philadelphia, 1963) entitled *The Faith of Qumran: Theology of the Dead Sea Scrolls,* which is a translation of a 1961 Swedish work. Ringgren's work is informed by his sensitivity to issues in Comparative Religions, and presents a description of Qumran theology under standard theological rubrics ("God," "Dualism," "Man," etc.). The third study is a thorough and careful commentary on one of the Qumran sectarian documents, the Manual of Discipline. It is *The Rule of Qumran and Its Meaning* by A. R. C. Leaney (Philadelphia: Westminster, The New Testament Library, 1966).

Several of the volumes already mentioned include discussions of the Scrolls in relation to the New Testament. Directly on that topic is a collection of pioneering articles by excellent New Testament scholars, most of which appeared in various journals from 1952 to 1955. The collection appeared under the editorship of Krister Stendahl as *The Scrolls and the New Testament* (New York: Harper, 1957). Here one sees the revolutionary effect of the Scrolls upon New Testament studies in those first important years after the contents and terminology of the texts began to be known. Another collection of a similar kind and similar quality is *Paul and Qumran* (London: Geoffrey Chapman, 1968). Edited by Jerome Murphy-O'Connor, it contains nine essays originally published elsewhere between 1958 and 1965; it represents a further stage of the enterprise portrayed by the Stendahl volume. A volume primarily devoted to pointing out the influence of Qumran Judaism upon Christianity, and to identifying the channels for such influence, is *The Scrolls and Christian Origins,* by Matthew Black (New York: Scribner, 1961). The content of this book was first given in a series of lectures at Union Seminary in New York in 1956, and some of its hypotheses are vulnerable, but it does underscore the relation of Qumran to the early Church.

In the last few years several volumes have shown the mature effect of Qumran studies upon specific areas in the intertestamental and New Testament fields. D. S. Russell has written a thorough study of Jewish apocalypticism, *The Method and Message of Jewish*

Apocalyptic (Philadelphia: Westminster, The Old Testament Library, 1964).

Another volume of this kind is a very good little study guide on the intertestamental period prepared for the Westminster Guides to the Bible by Lawrence E. Toombs. Its title is *The Threshold of Christianity* (Philadelphia: Westminster, 1960). Dr. Toombs succeeds in portraying the period in a vital and interesting way, and once again Qumran plays its responsible part. We mention here as well a superb New Testament commentary upon which Qumran has had a profound effect, that prepared by Father Raymond E. Brown in *The Gospel According to John,* Vol. 29 in The Anchor Bible (New York: Doubleday, 1963–). Father Brown has been highly instrumental in creating a new understanding of the Fourth Gospel in the light of Qumran. Only the first twelve chapters of John are treated in this first volume, with a second volume to appear within a year or so, to be followed in turn by a third volume, on John's Epistles. The massive industry displayed makes this book perhaps the most valuable new commentary to appear in the years since the Scrolls came to light.

When one realizes that the discoveries at Qumran are not yet fully published, and that these discoveries were only the first of a whole series of manuscript finds that have subsequently come to light, he senses what a period of ferment lies ahead. Evidence is now available or is being readied for publication that will throw new light on the whole period from Alexander the Great to Bar Kokhba, and the effect will be immense. It is an exhilarating prospect.

Glossary

ACHAEMENID—Royal Iranian dynasty during the period of the Old Persian Empire (sixth–fourth centuries B.C.E.).

AHITOPHEL—a member of David's court, who became counselor for the rebel Absalom, and afterward committed suicide.

AKKO—important seacoast city in Palestine north of Haifa, modern Acre.

AMORITE—from Babylonian *Amurrium,* "Westerner," semi-nomadic people, speaking Northwest Semitic dialects in Mesopotamia and Syria; dated in the early second millennium B.C.E.

ANACOLUTHON—lack of grammatical sequence; passing on to a new construction before the original has been completed.

ARAD—one of the major cities of the Negev (Negeb) in the Early Bronze Age; important for Iron Age Judah; site of first excavation of an Israelite sanctuary certainly dedicated to Yahweh.

ARISTEAS, LETTER OF—a Jewish letter written in Greek in which the composition of the Septuagint is described.

ASHDOD—one of the five principal towns of the Philistine pentapolis, twenty miles south of Jaffa (ancient Joppa).

ASHKELON—coastal city of the Philistine pentapolis, south of Ashdod.

B.C.E., C.E.—before the common or Christian Era; the common or Christian Era (equivalent to B.C. and A.D. respectively).

BEN SIRA—Deuterocanonical or Apocryphal book of the Bible, otherwise known as Wisdom of Jesus Ben Sira (Son of Sirach); commonly called Ecclesiasticus.

BOETHUSIANS—a particular Jewish group or sect related to the Sadducees.

BULLA—a seal impression on clay or other material.

CARITATIVE—a shortened or diminutive form, applied to proper names.

CASEMATE WALL—characteristic Israelite city fortification; a double wall partitioned into casemates or blind rooms which were used for storage or filled with earth and stones to strengthen the wall.

CHRISTOLOGICAL—Christ-centered, with the person and work of Christ as focal point, as, "a Christological view of history."

CROCE, Benedetto C. (1866–1952), neo-Hegelian philosopher of Italy, who tried to correlate history and philosophy.

CRYPTOGRAM—a document in cipher or code.

CUBIT—a unit of measure based on the length from elbow to tip of the middle finger; the Egyptian cubit had two standards, the common, which was about 18 inches long, and the royal, about 3 inches longer.

CUNEIFORM—wedge-shaped signs impressed on clay tablets with a stylus or carved on stone; used for Sumerian, Akkadian, Ugaritic, etc.

DAGON, TEMPLE OF—Dagon was a Canaanite god of vegetation; several temples dedicated to this god are known: one is mentioned in the Bible at Ashdod, another was excavated in Syria at Ras Shamra (Ugarit).

DAMASCUS DOCUMENT—also called Zadokite fragments; doctrinal exposition and rule of community life, discovered first in the famous Cairo Genizah; numerous fragments of earlier copies of it have been found recently at Qumran.

DIATESSARON—the edition of the four gospels in a continuous narrative prepared by Tatian in the second century, C.E.

EMILIANI CORRELATION—a time scale, developed by Cesare Emiliani of the University of Miami, for dating the Ice Ages by means of correlating geological evidence of ice advance and recession with ancient ocean temperatures.

EPIGRAPHY—the science of writing concerned with the analysis, classification, dating and interpretation of scripts and inscriptions.

ERECH, SUMERIAN EMPIRE OF—Erech (modern Warka, 160 miles south of Baghdad), one of the largest and most important cities of Sumer in the fourth and third millennia B.C.E.

ESCHATON—the end of time, the consummation of the world, the last days.

ESSENES—a Jewish community, successors to the Hasidim mentioned in the Book of Daniel. The Essenes flourished from about 150 B.C.E. until about 70 C.E.; their main settlement was at Qumran where the famous Dead Sea scrolls were discovered.

EUSEBIUS, CHRONICON OF—a historical work in two books by Eusebius (260–340 C.E.), bishop of Caesarea, summarizing the history of the world, including dates.

EXILIC PERIOD—that period in the history of Israel from the time of the Babylonian exile, 597 B.C.E. (or 587, the second deportation), to the edict of Cyrus, 538, allowing the Jews to return to Jerusalem.

'EN FESHKHA—a spring near Qumran, part of an irrigated area.

GENTILIC—an adjective or noun derived from the name of a tribe or nation.

HABAKKUK—one of the minor prophets, who lived in the last days of Josiah and the reign of Jehoiakim, on the eve of the Babylonian invasion.

HAGIOGRAPHA—"holy writings"; a Greek name for the third division of the Hebrew Bible, a miscellaneous collection of books, including Job, Psalms, Proverbs, etc.

HAPLOGRAPHY—the omission in writing or copying of one of two or more adjacent and similar or identical letters, syllables, words or lines.

HASMONEANS—name of the Maccabean rulers; it is often restricted to 135–63 B.C.E., after the death of Simon, the last surviving brother of Judas Maccabeus.

HEKAL—in Sumero-Akkadian the word means "palace" (*ekallu*), and in Phoenician and Hebrew it is used for "palace" of a god; the Temple in Jerusalem is referred to as a *hekal*.

HERMENEUTIC—principle of interpretation applied to the Bible or other authoritative literature.

HERODIAN STYLE—a type of massive, squared stone, like those of the Wailing Wall in Jerusalem, used in the building projects of Herod the Great.

HIPPOCAMP(US)—a mythical sea horse, with two front feet and the tail of a fish or dolphin, represented as drawing Neptune's car.

HODAYOT—the collection of thanksgiving psalms found among the Dead Sea scrolls.

IDUMEANS—designation of the Edomites in Greco-Roman times; Herod the Great was of Idumean ancestry.

INTERTESTAMENTAL—the period or the literature of the period between the Old and New Testaments, ca. from the third century B.C.E. to the first century C.E.

JACHIN AND BOAZ—twin bronze pillars on either side of the entrance to Solomon's temple.

JORDAN RIFT—the Jordan valley; a tertiary fissure in the earth's crust running from north to south between two faults, northern-most part of a line stretching to the Great African Rift that runs through Kenya.

JOSEPHUS—Jewish historian (ca. 37–100 C.E.), author of *The Jewish War Against Rome* and *The Antiquities of the Jews;* military leader in the war, later joined Vespasian as interpreter and apologist.

JUBILEES, BOOK OF—a Jewish work of the third or second century B.C.E.; an expanded version of Genesis in terms of jubilee periods, and an adaptation of the patriarchal narratives to show that the details of the law were observed even at that time.

KENITES—a semi-nomadic class of smiths, associated with the Midianites, and through them with Moses and the Israelites.

KUTIM—a minor tractate of the Talmud, composed of regulations concerning the relation of Samaritans, Jews, and Gentiles. The book concludes that when the Samaritans renounce Mt. Gerizim, return to Jerusalem, and accept the resurrection of the body, they will be accepted as Jews.

LACHISH—modern Tell ed-Duweir, halfway between Jerusalem and Gaza; ancient city, key Judean fortress from 900 to 600 B.C.E. Lachish letters of early sixth century B.C.E. are ostraca referring to military activity in the area during the Babylonian invasion and furnish an important source for the Hebrew script and language of the period.

LAPIDARY—a form of any script engraved on stone.

LUCIANIC—referring to an important recension of the Septuagint attributed to the presbyter Lucian (d. 312 C.E.), now often called "Old Palestinian."

MASADA—an almost impregnable rock fortress on the west shore of the Dead Sea, built by Herod the Great, where the Jewish zealots made their last stand before the Roman armies and perished by their own hands in 73 C.E.

MASSEBAH—a stone set in an upright position, a commemorative stele; associated with sacred sites, a menhir.

MASSORETES—Jewish grammarians of the seventh to tenth centuries C.E. who introduced into the Hebrew text a system of vowel marks and accents to facilitate reading and preserve the text.

MASSORETIC RECENSION—the official version of the consonantal text of the Hebrew Bible edited by rabbis of the first century C.E., transmitted to and preserved by the medieval Massoretes.

MAXIMS OF SHURUPPAK—from Sumerian wisdom literature, a collection of precepts of King Shuruppak addressed to his son with instructions on wise behavior. The oldest copies known date from about 2500 B.C.

MEGIDDO—a very important archaeological site in Palestine, furnishing a continuous history from the 4th millennium to the fourth century B.C.E.; major city and fortress of Canaanites and Israelites on a hill dominating the plains of Esdraelon, and at the junction of the coastal routes from Egypt and the Mediterranean with trade routes from the east and north.

MELCHIZEDEK—a Canaanite king of pre-Israelite Jerusalem, linked with Abraham in Genesis (chapter 14).

MIDRASH—a Jewish method of homiletical exegesis directed to discovering a meaning beyond the literal interpretation of scripture; allegorical illustration is often used.

MISHNAH—the codification of the oral law by the rabbis under the supervision of Judah the Prince (ca. 200 C.E.).

NAHUM—one of the minor prophets who proclaimed the imminent destruction of Nineveh (612 B.C.E.).

NUMISMATICS—study of coins, or of other tokens or objects similarly used.

OMER—A Hebrew measure, the tenth of an *ephah*.

ONOMASTICON OF AMENOPE—Egyptian word list from about the eleventh century B.C.E.

ORTHOPRAXY—body of practices accepted or recognized as correct.

OSTRACON (ostraca)—inscribed fragment(s) of pottery, cheap and abundant writing material used chiefly for letters, dockets, bills, receipts, etc.

PALEOGRAPHY—the study of ancient writing, the science of dating ancient written materials.

PATRIARCHAL PERIOD—the Biblical period described in Genesis 12–50, corresponding roughly to the period between the twentieth and the sixteenth centuries B.C.E.

PATRONYMIC—a name derived from the name of a father or ancestor.

PENTAPOLIS—a confederation or group of five towns.

PERDICCAS—Macedonian general under Alexander the Great, ruling as regent (323–321 B.C.) after Alexander's death.

PESHER—a commentary or interpretation of a biblical book, of the type called by this name in the Dead Sea scrolls, as, "the Habakkuk Pesher."

PHARISEES—a Jewish religious sect which required not only strict obedience to the law of Moses, but also emphasized the importance of the oral law.

PROLEPSIS—treating something future as already completed.

PSEUDEPIGRAPHA—those Jewish writings from about 300 B.C.E. to 200 C.E., not included in the biblical canon or apocrypha; many of these are attributed to some well-known figure of the past, such as Enoch, Moses, Solomon, Isaiah, et al.

QUMRAN—site on the west side of the Dead Sea around which most of the Dead Sea scrolls were discovered.

RECENSION—a form of early hand-written text which had become standardized, either by accumulation of copyists' errors or by systematic scribal effort to establish uniformity.

SADDUCEE—conservative Jewish sect of the priestly class which held to the written law but rejected the oral additions to the law accepted by the Pharisees, and held much more conservative theological views.

SAHIDIC—a secondary translation of the Bible into Sahidic, a dialect of Coptic spoken in Upper Egypt, made from the Septuagint; and therefore a witness to an early form of the Greek translation of the Old Testament.

SAMARIA—later Sebastiyeh, capital of the northern kingdom of Israel, founded by Omri and Ahab.

SANHEDRIN—the supreme council of the Jews, having legislative, executive and judiciary functions. It lasted from the mid-third century B.C.E., if not earlier, into Christian times.

SATRAP—governor of a province in the ancient Persian empire.

SECOND TEMPLE—the temple rebuilt on the site of the Solomonic temple by the returning exiles after the edict of Cyrus; completed 515 B.C.E. It was rebuilt by Herod the Great (from 20 B.C.E. on), and was destroyed by the Romans when they captured Jerusalem in 70 C.E.

SELEUCID KINGS—dynasty of Greek rulers in Syria vying for power with the Ptolemies of Egypt after the death of Alexander the Great.

SHAVUOTH—Hebrew Feast of Weeks; feast of the wheat harvest, celebrated seven weeks after the first reaping of grain.

SHERD, POTSHERD—a fragment of pottery; broken earthenware.

SIGLUM—a letter or other character used to denote a word.

SINAITICUS—fourth century C.E. Greek manuscript of the Bible found in the monastery of St. Catherine below Mt. Sinai. It contains the entire New Testament and a small part of the Old Testament; it is a primary witness to the texts of the Septuagint and the New Testament.

STATER—a golden coin, having the value of four drachmas.

STELE—an upright slab, bearing inscriptions or sculptured designs.

STOCHASTIC—theoretical, hypothetical.

STRATIGRAPHY—that branch of archaeology dealing with the order and relative position of the layers of material remains in mounds or tells, the abandoned sites of ancient cities.

SUCCOTH—Lit. "huts"; Hebrew feast of tabernacles, held in autumn; originally, a harvest festival, later historicized to commemorate the desert sojourn.

SYNCELLUS—Byzantine historian (ca. 800 C.E.), author of a "Chronicle," extending from creation to the time of Diocletian.

SYNCRETISM—the attempted synthesis or mixture of conflicting beliefs or practices; as, that involving Canaanite and Israelite religions during the monarchy in Israel.

TA'AMIREH BEDOUIN—a tribe of semi-nomadic Arabs living between Bethlehem and the Dead Sea. Its members were responsible for the discovery of the Dead Sea scrolls.

TARGUM—Aramaic translation or paraphrase of Scripture.

TATIAN—Gnostic author (ca. 160 C.E.) of the Diatessaron.

TETRADRACHMA, DIDRACHMA—one silver drachma was the basic Greek monetary unit; a didrachma had the value of two drachmas, a tetradrachma the value of four.

TETRAGRAMMATON—technical name for the four letters of the personal name of the God of Israel: YHWH (vocalized *Yahweh*).

THEOPHORIC—bearing a divine element; hence a theophoric name is one containing a divine name as chief component.

UZZIAH (or Azariah)—Judean king (ca. 783–742 B.C.E.), during whose long reign Judah achieved a considerable measure of political success and economic prosperity.

VESPASIAN—Roman emperor (69–79 C.E.), founder of the Flavian dynasty.

WADI DÂLIYEH—an almost inaccessible cave north of Jericho in which were found the Samaria papyri, economic documents from the fourth century B.C.E.

WADI MURABBA'AT—a site south of Wadi Qumran in the Judaean wilderness, where documents of the second Jewish revolt against Rome 132–35 C.E.) were found.

YAHWISTIC—of or pertaining to Yahweh, as in "Yahwistic poetry."

ZADOKITE—a line of priests descended from Zadok, who served as high priest in Jerusalem in the days of David and Solomon. They continued as high priests down to the middle of the second century B.C.E. when they were displaced for a period by the Hasmonean dynasty; they regained the office intermittently until the destruction of the Temple in 70 C.E.

INDEX